A LATIN LOVER IN ANCIENT ROME

A LATIN LOVER IN ANCIENT ROME

READINGS IN PROPERTIUS AND HIS GENRE

W. R. JOHNSON

The Ohio State University Press
Columbus

Copyright © 2009 by The Ohio State University.
All rights reserved.

Library of Congress Cataloging-in-Publication Data
Johnson, W. R. (Walter Ralph), 1933–
A Latin lover in ancient Rome : readings in Propertius and his genre /
W. R. Johnson.
p. cm.
Includes bibliographical references and index.
ISBN-13: 978-0-8142-0399-6 (cloth : alk. paper)
ISBN-10: 0-8142-0399-X (cloth : alk. paper)
1. Love poetry, Latin—History and criticism. 2. Elegiac poetry, Latin—
History and criticism. 3. Propertius, Sextus—Criticism and interpretation.
I. Title.
PA6059.E6J64 2009
874'.01—dc22
2008030949

This book is available in the following editions:
Cloth (ISBN 978-0-8142-0399-6)
CD-ROM (ISBN 978-0-8142-9179-5)
Paper (ISBN: 978-0-8142-5648-0)
Cover art: J. W. Waterhouse, Britain, 1849–1917,
Circe Invidiosa, 1892, London, oil on canvas 18.7 x 87.4 cm
South Autralian Government Grant 1892
Art Gallery of South Australia, Adelaide

Cover and text design by Jennifer Shoffey Forsythe
Typeset in Adobe Bembo

FOR LIZ AND MIKE AND ANNE

Whose love is given over-well,
Shall look on Helen's face in hell,
Whilst those whose love is thin and wise
May glimpse John Knox in paradise.
 —Dorothy Parker

We cannot be sure of the master-cause, so we pile cause upon cause, hoping that it may be among them.
 —Montaigne

The degree and kind of a man's sexuality reach up into the ultimate pinnacle of his spirit.
 —Nietzsche

CONTENTS

PREFACE
AND ACKNOWLEDGMENTS ⁓ XI

CHAPTER 1
THE D/EVOLUTION OF LOVE ⁓ 1

CHAPTER 2
AENEAS IN LOVE ⁓ 27

CHAPTER 3
TWO PORTRAITS OF THE LADY ⁓ 58

CHAPTER 4
PROPERTIUS AND THE POETICS OF DISGREGATION ⁓ 97

CHAPTER 5
WHATEVER HAPPENED TO LATIN LOVE ELEGY? ⁓ 124

CHAPTER 6
CODA ⁓ 146

BIBLIOGRAPHY ⁓ 149
INDEX LOCORUM ⁓ 155
GENERAL INDEX ⁓ 157

PREFACE AND ACKNOWLEDGMENTS

 IN THE CENTURY before the birth of Christ, a new fashion in thinking about love, about falling in and out of love, about making love, gradually took shape in the city of Rome. What we know about the nature and spread of that fashion, like much else that we know about those turbulent, fascinating years in which the Roman Republic was in the process of coming to pieces, is somewhat fragmentary. Nevertheless, somehow evading the wide ruin that overtook Latin literature when the Roman Empire declined and dissolved, a sizable portion of Latin love elegy remains to us. The spirit that informed this body of love poems, both those we have the fortune to possess and those we have lost, in part fueled and in part reflected the new erotic fashion in question, and it is this new perspective on the erotic that serves as the background for the readings of Propertius that I offer here.

Central to Latin love elegy, in my belief its vital core, are the poems and the poetic career of Propertius. Lacking the poems of his immediate predecessors (those of Gallus in particular), we depend for our knowledge and enjoyment of Latin love elegy on the poems of its three extant masters: Propertius, Tibullus, and Ovid. Whatever his charms and virtues—and they are many and varied—for Tibullus the thrills and spills provided by a powerfully erotic identity matter less to him than his subtle ruminations on his cultural identity (to which his girlfriends and his boyfriend function chiefly as fashionable decoration) and his "sentimental nostalgia for the beauties of nature" (Conte, 329). As for Ovid, who came at the tail-end of the elegiac project, his love poems, glittering with flawless technique and polished to a durable sheen by ruthless irony, concern themselves mostly with cataloging—as for a museum exhibit—the prime themes and tactics of love elegy and with displaying them as a sort of gaudy collection of outworn clichés. As a recent critic sums up the machinery of the *Amores:* "He turns elegiac conventions into tongue-in-cheek comedy, ditches emotion for clever puns, and his graphic, literalizing style leaves little to the imagination" (Rimell, 209). (But Ovid, by the time he was revising his collection of love elegies for their second edition, was getting to move on to fresher fields and newer pastures.)

It is, then, not without reason that when critics of Latin love elegy set about constructing a theory of its genre, very many of their illustrations of what they take to be its essential forms and themes, its defining conventions, they draw from Propertius. They do this not only because, among their three possible sources, his corpus is the largest and his improvisations the most varied in tone and mood, but also because his poems are closest to what the genre uniquely offers and what it demands: rich linguistic and rhetorical inventions and the steady obsession and bitter wit that nourish them. Theorists of the genre go mainly to Propertius to design their theories of Latin love elegy because he is its most original and most powerful exponent extant. Hence, my subtitle: this is a book about Propertius and the genre he made *his* own. (Despite his mastery, however, down the centuries he was rarely to influence other love poets very directly or even to meet with the quantity and quality of readers he deserved: Quintilian's schoolmasterly sneer, "There are readers of the sort who actually prefer Propertius" to Tibullus, Ovid, and Gallus [*Institutio Oratoria* 10.93.1], more or less adumbrates his future in European literature.[1])

Propertius is currently a contested area in the study of Latin poetry, but for the most part, he is now examined less for his own sake than for the purpose of exemplifying—one might almost say, of testing—current literary theories, particularly as they address themselves to the problem of how modern theories of gender, identity, and metaliterary processes

---

1. For Propertius' reception, see Benedikston, 117–32; Conte, 337–38; Gavinelli; Zimmermann; and, for Donne, with Pound his best successor, see Revard's admirable essay.

can be made to relate to the literature of ancient Rome. This book is a product not of critical theory but of literary criticism. This style of reading is, to be sure, not innocent of theory, but the theories that ground it are shaped and directed by a love of poetry. Its chief function is to serve the poets who make the poems.

This book, then, is intended for undergraduates and graduates in classics and for other readers of European poetry who want a sketch of the kinds of pleasure and thought that Propertius has to offer them. Specialists in Propertius or in Latin Poetry may find some of what I have to say useful to them, but, though I have at times attempted to speak to some of their concerns, they are not my primary audience.

In the footnotes, a surname followed by page numbers (or in some instances by name, date and page numbers) indicates where the reader can go for further information about the topic at hand or for an opposing opinion. (See the Bibliography.) The translations throughout, unless otherwise noted, are my own. The language of Propertius is famously crabbed and condensed, and in rendering what I take to be his meanings, what I offer, in an attempt to get at what seems to be lurking beneath a verse's literal surface, is sometimes rather free. For this reason, some readers, on occasion, may want to consult translations that provide uniformly literal versions (for example, the recent renderings of David Slavitt or Vincent Katz, but the slightly older translation by Guy Lee is generally as trustworthy as it is charming).

Some of the materials in my book have their origins in The John and Penelope Biggs Lectures, which I gave at Washington University in the spring of 2004. I wish to tender my heartiest thanks to Mr. and Mrs. Biggs, to Robert Lamberton and his colleagues in the classics faculty for a delightful week of work and play. I am also grateful for a Mellon Emeritus Grant which gave much welcome aid in the completion of this book. David Wray's timely advice and generous support made a crucial difference to me. I want to thank Ray Kania and to Jessica Seidman for their expert help in preparation of the manuscript. Finally, my cordial thanks to Eugene O'Connor for his generous encouragement and advice.

CHAPTER 1

THE D/EVOLUTION OF LOVE

> Love is a god and marriage is but a word.
> —*Arden of Feversham*

> This 'affective contagion,' this induction proceeds from others, from the language of books, from friends: no love is original. (Mass culture is a machine for showing desire: here is what must interest you, it says, as if it guessed that men are incapable of finding what to desire by themselves.)
> —Barthes, *A Lover's Discourse*, 136–37

SOME EIGHTY YEARS ago a book called *The Legacy of Rome,* edited by Cyril Bailey, was published by Oxford University Press. It contains fourteen essays whose topics range from the origins of empire to agriculture; from law, architecture, and engineering to literature, religion, and philosophy—to every aspect of the culture and civilization of ancient Rome that had, century after century, exercised a pronounced influence on Western thought and life. The topic that concerns us here, however—how the idea of love came to be altered in ancient Rome in the last years of the Republic—finds only in this volume what I take to be a strongly judgmental silence. The closest Love comes to inclusion among Rome's legacies to later ages occurs when Hugh Last, while commenting on the status and character of women in the late Republic, remarks that the Greek ideal of womanhood (wife as "silent servant" and "far too inferior to share" her husband's life) was disastrously imported into Rome:

> When this ideal was brought to Rome, where such effacement of the women was impossible, the result was that they clung to the care-free life

of the house that was not a home sanctioned by Greek tradition, without surrendering the claim to equality with their husbands justified by Rome. So there arose a race of unlovely woman who bulk large in the history of the early empire—all unattractive, some repulsive for their attainments as intriguers, poisoners, adulteresses, and even worse—the destroyers of the Roman home, who taught every one with whom they came into contact to live for themselves alone. In the sordid picture which the age presents the only feature of encouragement is the promise of extinction which their selfishness contains. Already by the end of the Republic race-suicide had shown itself to be a threat full of danger, and social legislation aimed at an increase in the birth-rate was at once among the most important and least successful of the undertakings of Augustus. (231–32)

In emphasizing this important yet futile undertaking (the Augustan sex and marriage laws), Last appears to be in the grip of a grim foreboding mixed with a poignant nostalgia (the year is 1923, and he seems to have a powerful presentiment that Miss Tallulah Bankhead and her *Fallen Angels* will presently be invading a Britain no longer protected by Victoria's ghostly benevolence). Last's anxiety here matters less than the silence with which he attempts to mask it. Why can't he bring himself to say something about the body of poetry that accompanies the derangement of 'family values' and 'female duties' he complains of? Why ignore, why try to erase, the existence of a fashion for extravagant passion in ancient Rome, one that briefly yet memorably challenged the conventions which had shaped Rome's ideology of 'docile bodies'—that venerable cluster of moral prescriptions and proscriptions, of taboos and superstitions—and which Augustus and his advisers labored to revive and enlarge? In attempting to compensate for Last's silence here, I am hardly claiming that Rome's reformulation of erotic experience was its greatest contribution to Western civilization, but I do think it was an important one, and one whose nature is as often misunderstood as its importance is underestimated.

CAESAR ENTERS GAUL, CATULLUS EXITS VERONA

Let me begin the story of Rome's devolution/evolution of Love *in medias res*. In 58 BCE, Julius Caesar headed off to Gaul to pacify its natives and in the bargain train that crack army with whose help he would extinguish those of his fellow oligarchs who resented and feared his astonishing talents, the ones that would eventually and briefly make him the dictator of Rome and its empire. At exactly the same time, back home in Rome, the poets Catullus and Calvus and some of their friends were experimenting with new styles of feeling and form that, to the dismay of Cicero and *his* friends, were beginning to revolutionize the contents, the styles, and the boundaries of Latin poetry.[1] These two activities, in conjunction with the mentalities they gave rise to, disconnected though they might seem, were both symptoms of a slow and often imperceptible process of transformation in which the political systems and social patterns of the Roman people were altered for the worse or for the better, devolved or evolved, depending on who you were and what perspective you happened to have. Our chief interest here is the poets and their poems, but to understand them we need to consider the changed and changing society in which and for which they wrote their poems. And it is the career and achievements of Julius Caesar that best define the transformation of that society.

Caesar was, to put it with blunt economy, a megalomaniac with enormous talents in warfare, politics, and public relations. (For a different version of Caesar, sympathetic, plausible, and engaging, see Parenti.) Like some of his other gifted contemporaries, and like his immediate predecessors (Marius and Sulla, for instance), Caesar felt himself painfully constrained, he found his ambitions cruelly thwarted, by the decrepit, crumbling mechanisms of government that he was called upon to serve. One doubts that, when Caesar galloped off to Gaul, he knew that nine years later, on his return, he would be crossing the Rubicon with those loyal, victorious, indomitable troops in order to put his finishing touches to the destruction of what little was left of the Roman Republic and thereby make himself master of the known world. But he did know, as he headed off to Gaul and the legions there, that, merely to survive in the style of survival he was becoming accustomed to, he would need to get much more power (that is to say, brute force and money and popular support) than any of his rivals could get and keep. He probably guessed, moreover, that eventually he would have to fight his enemies to the death. He probably did not know—he had yet to meet Cleopatra—that he would end his career and life trying to become something like a

---

1. For recent perspectives on this generation of poets, the Neoterics, see Knox, 129–37; Johnson 2007.

king, but he did know—by that time perhaps only Cicero did not—that the Republic was on its last legs. The elaborate system of checks and balances that had worked for a pugnacious and hungry city-state, that had sustained it throughout the centuries in which its boundaries and appetites increased, all those cunning mechanisms devised piecemeal by citizen-farmer-soldiers, could no longer cope with the complex malfunctioning that, increasingly, incompatible goods and unintended consequences combined to inflict on it.

By the time Caesar went to Gaul, indeed, long before he arrived there, Roman politicians and the Roman people whom they served and made use of, no longer understood themselves or their city, could no longer figure out the disconnection between what they were doing (in and with the world, in and with their lives) and what they were supposed to be doing, what their inherited values required them to do and not to do. For brevity's sake, let me reduce the complex elements of this intractable phenomenon by recalling the old song from the last century's World War I: "How You Gonna Keep 'Em Down on the Farm After They've Seen Paree."[2] Increasingly, Romans who returned from their victorious wars, generals and common soldiers alike, came back to their cities and their families, still Romans to be sure, but no longer exactly the men who had marched off to protect family and country, to enlarge the common good, and, in the process, to win for themselves some share of profit and glory. They had eaten, these returning veterans, new kinds of food, they had drunk different vintages, and they had kissed new women and new boys. They also came back with more money than they'd left with and with a sharper sense of their importance in the scheme of things, having seen for themselves how big a world it was and having begun to guess how crucial was their role in mastering it. These were Rome's soldiers, of course, but they also were or could become the soldiers of the generals who commanded them (a Marius, a Sulla, a Pompey, a Caesar). They were and they remained Romans, but they were also becoming men of that new and wider world that their weapons and their courage had helped to create; they didn't stop being Romans, but their loyalties, like their worldviews and their identities, were becoming divided. From the end of the First Punic War down to the assassination of Julius Caesar and beyond even that, the world

---

2. For ancient observations on this shift in manners and morals, see Livy 39.6.8; Polybius 31.25.4; Aulus Gellius 4.14. For good modern descriptions of it, see Balsdon, 32–37; Lyne 1980, 8–10.

these soldier-citizens fought and lived in grew ever more complex than the worlds their ancestors had inhabited. Increasingly, imperceptibly, often bewilderingly, as regards its manners and morals no less than its boundaries, the nature of the expanding city-state that these Romans fought for and voted in, kept being transformed. The world of course is always changing, but some changes are more massive than others, and for imperial cities, which are the natural repository for new wealth, new customs, new fads, new ideas, the changes tend to be as huge as they are frequent.[3]

Catullus, Calvus, and their friends were part of this pattern of change just in the years that it was gathering momentum for its final collisions and implosions. This generation of poets was not unfamiliar with the ordinary masculine repertoire of the Roman citizen-soldier (Calvus, for one, would achieve some distinction both as orator and as soldier), but their activities (that is, how they spent their days and nights) and their identities (that is, who they thought they were, how they wished to appear to be) were hardly limited to and by no means governed by that repertoire. For one thing, nearly half a century of civil wars had left the mechanics of the Roman masculine identity in some disrepair. Even if they had wanted to behave like and to be normal Roman citizen-soldiers (we are talking here, obviously, of upper-class young men with good prospects for traditional careers as officers and officials), these poets, with their good educations and independent means, were well aware that opportunities for putting their feet on the ladder had dwindled considerably, had become as few and far between as they were perilous (you did not, naturally, want to find yourselves on the fatally wrong team when a civil war began). Then, as their luck would have it, these poetic Roman males discovered for themselves new subjects of utterance and new styles of shaping and ornamenting those subjects. They became attracted to, and would soon be fascinated by, a new style of identity, that of a strange figure, a lover, a charming erotic monster, a creature whose passions dismantle what he wants and who he is and then help to fashion, force him to fashion, from himself, for himself, a new identity, a new me.[4]

The Catullan generation became infatuated with the figure of the erotic madman, with the obsessed, abject, un-Roman lover, because he,

---

3. For useful speculations about the origins of the new eroticism, see Clarke, 59–61, 83–85.

4. For a fascinating formulation of the nature of erotic selfhood, see Gregory.

or rather it, provided them and their audiences with ideal forms for their new contents, their new feelings. What made the crazy lover so suitable for the Catullan generation (and so repulsive to some of their immediate elders, the generation of Cicero) was his utter lack of the qualities that best define the Roman citizen-soldier: he does not want to follow in the footsteps of the paterfamilias, he does not (as Propertius would blithely and famously admit; 2.7.13–14) want to father a new crop of Roman citizen-soldiers; he does not want to serve in the military or make speeches in the forum or increase the wealth of his clan or run for public office or even support the candidacies of those who choose to run for public office; he does not want to relax from the exertions of performing his civic duties, balancing business with leisure, *negotium* with *otium*. What he wants, instead, is a life of total leisure, one he can squander on what—only—matters to him now and forever more: being in love with HER. This person, this poetic figure, this poetically rhetorical figure, is the ideal writerly mold for what this generation has to say about who they are and who they are not. They are, yes, Romans, but they are not the kind of Romans, Roman males, that their fathers and grandfathers were, they are a new (confused, ambiguous, ironic) kind of anti-Roman Roman; they belong to a losing, becoming-lost generation. This lover's pathological idleness, his utter self-absorption and glazed-eyed derelictions, perfectly accord with a new awareness of "the world we have lost" and of "the world that has lost us." The public world has no use for us, no place for us. We will make our own world, out of outrageous poetry and outrageous erotic adventure. That is the main reason the Catullan generation found this ridiculous (and gorgeous) creature so attractive, so apt to their new needs and new purposes.

But where did the creature come from? Catullus and his friends may have costumed him appropriately (given him a suitable makeover, so to speak), but they did not invent him out of nothing. Poems are made of words (as Mallarmé told Degas after perusing the painter's sonnets); that is to say, they are made in part from other poets' poems, and there had existed, in literature, distraught and even insane lovers long before the generation of Catullus made such a lover their own and gave him what would be, for a long time, until the Arabs and the Provençals and Petrarch got hold of him, his final form—until, that is, Heine and Baudelaire gave him his modern makeover. But poems are also made out of life, or at least out of what human beings, and not just poets, think and say about the lives they lead. Life does indeed imitate art, but art also imitates life, and it is out of this messy and inescapable cross-pollination of art and life that both poems and styles of living (and loving) are generated.

LOVE'S FOUNDING FATHERS

No need to play here the game of Chicken-Or-Egg-First. Instead I offer two converging lines of descent of the Erotic Madman in his Roman incarnation. The first from art, the second from life. Just twenty years before the birth of Catullus, there was elected to the consulship (102 BCE) an aristocrat whose achievements in warfare and politics were matched by his literary gifts and his mastery of the language, literature, and philosophy of Greece. Q. Lutatius Catulus, who had in his entourage two Greek poets of some distinction (Archias and Antipater of Sidon), seems to have taken a liking to the epigrams of Callimachus and perhaps to the great and recently published anthology of erotic epigrams, the *Garland of Meleager*. All that remains of Catulus' verse are two charming epigrams in the Alexandrian manner that our good luck caused first Cicero (*De natura deorum* 1.79) and then Gellius (19.9.10) to quote and so preserve. Here are the verses Gellius saved for us:

> aufugit mi animus; credo, ut solet, ad Theotimum
>   devenit. sic est; perfugium illud habet.
> quid si non interdixem ne illunc fugitivum
>   mitteret ad se intro, sed magis eiceret?
> ibimus quaesitum. verum, ne ipsi teneamur,
>   formido. quid ago? da, Venus, consilium.

> That no-good slave, my soul, vile runaway,
> Has fled for refuge—where? To Theotimus,
> Of course. It's not as if I'd not decreed
> He must not give the creature shelter, no—
> I told him: Send the bastard back! Yet now,
> Yet now—I guess I must myself go claim it,
> My slave, my soul. But if I do, I fear
> I will myself be snared. Ah, Venus, now
> If ever give your servant aid and counsel.

And here is the poem that Cicero preserved for us:

> constiteram exorientem Auroram forte salutans
>   cum subito a laeva Roscius exoritur,
> pace mihi liceat, caelestes, dicere vestra,
>   mortalis visus pulchrior esse deo.

> I rose from bed and saw the rising sun
> With prayers of joy, but suddenly, no less
> Propitiously, my Roscius then arose.
> Permit me, Heaven, to speak my impious truth:
> More lovely glowed the mortal than the god.

It is also Gellius who happens to quote, in the same passage, three more erotic epigrams, glittering fragments of early Roman Alexandrianism, two of them, by Valerius Aedituus, the other by Porcius Licinius, neither of whom are otherwise known to us. Here is Aedituus:

> dicere cum conor curam tibi, Pamphila, cordis,
>   quid mi abs te quaeram, verba labris abeunt,
> per pectus manat subito <subido> mihi sudor;
>   sic tacitus, subidus, dum pudeo, pereo.

> When I, Pamphilia, struggle to express
> To you my heart's unease or tell you what
> I'm asking, begging, of you, my tongue thickens,
> All at once my chest with sweat is moist,
> Mute as a stone, crazed as a bitch in heat,
> Amazed, ashamed, I perish where I stand.

(The free translation of the final two verses is perhaps justified in part, given a text troubled with its dubious repetition of the rare word, *subidus*.) Here is the second poem by Valerius Aedituus:

> quid faculam praefers, Phileros, qua est nil opus nobis?
>   ibimus sic, lucet pectore flamma satis.
> istanc aut potis est vis saeva extinguere venti
>   aut imber caelo concitus praecipitans;
> at contra hunc ignem Veneris, nisi si Venus ipsa,
>   nullast quae possit vis alia opprimere.

> Why bother with your torch, Phileros? See—
> We need no torch to light us on our way

Through darkness, for my heart is filled with fire.
That light you hold aloft a gust of wind
Could snuff or a sudden shower from heaven douse.
But this, the stubborn blaze that Venus kindles,
Her power alone, no power but hers, can quench.

And here is Licinius:

> custodes ovium teneraeque propaginis, agnum,
>   quaeritis ignem? ite huc; totus hic ignis homost.
> si digito attigero, incendam silvam simul omnem,
>   omne pecus; flammast omnia quae video.

> You who guard your gentle lambs, you search,
> It seems, for embers for your fires. Stop here:
> For I who stand before you, I am fire,
> And should I touch my finger to this tree
> All this forest, all your flock, would blaze—
> Everything I gaze on bursts in flame!

It won't do, of course, to make much of a mere five poems, but it's not stretching things too far to suggest that this less than a handful of amorous warblings indicates an audience (however small as yet) for subtle, elegant fashionings of erotic experience.[5] These brief poems are not, so far as we can tell, representations of the Latin poets' own "memories of emotion"; rather, they clearly mark a moment of literary transfusion, one in which what the Roman poets borrow from Greek form and feeling they offer to their Roman readers as a new pattern for what is likely to be to them a new or at least somewhat unfamiliar way of feeling about sexual desire. Though many of his readers will not know as much Greek as Catulus or possess his knowledge of Alexandrian epigram, they will have heard Greek singers perform both Greek golden oldies (Anacreon, for instance) and new hits. Much of the erotic themes and vocabularies of Greek love songs, their clichés, their erotic signs, words, and pictures that Barthes has christened the "Image-Repertoire" will have been familiar to them. What was new—and perhaps a bit unsettling—was to hear these sentiments in Latin, in the Latin they speak on the street and in their homes, in the language that their Roman identities are rooted

---

5. For these poets, see Bardon; Wheeler, 69–70. The most recent, now definitive, comments are those by Courtney, 70–78.

in. Suddenly, when these poems were read (and remember, they were mostly read aloud and in groups, with friends), the Roman male, any Roman male who heard them, may well have had a fleeting glimpse of another self, not just of the self that lets itself be diverted by Greek song in an evening of recreation after a day in the forum or on the parade ground, but an unfamiliar self, a divided Roman self, one that finds itself exposed to a different erotic register; one that requires of it a delicacy and a tenderness and perhaps a sort of surrender that are alien to everything that it, that he, the Roman male, has been taught to be and worked hard to become. One can only barely imagine what one of Catulus' first auditors (think of the least cultivated among them) may have thought or felt when he heard, in the Latin language, a Roman male (like himself) express his powerful desire (not merely lustful, indeed romantic) for a youth (who may or may not be a slave), or his awed admiration of (and, apparently, his yearning to possess) the masculine beauty of an adult Roman male, the actor Roscius.[6]

The same-sex sexuality of these poems is not without consequence for our topic, but, in the long run, it matters less than the shameless abjection, the intensity and exaltation that mark the voices of these speakers. Though it adds to the frisson, forget for the moment that it is a Roman general who is here adapting Greek themes and tones in Latin verse. At point here is this: the speakers of these poems are Latin males, and they are saying things that Hellenistic Greeks, echoing archaic Greeks, say without compunction, almost by rote; namely, I abandon what control I have over myself and the world. I am powerless in the hands of Eros; I whine my prayers to the divine spirit of lust to come to my aid, I am consumed by the beauty of the creature I see before me. I have become enslaved by a mere mortal, by one who is in fact my inferior. Greeks could say those things. Romans hadn't, couldn't, shouldn't. But in these poems, a Roman male speaking in his native Latin tongue, a Roman male, master of many slaves, one of the masters of the world, confesses that he has become the slave of someone who is very possibly *his* slave. Or, blaspheming, in a moment of high erotic inspiration, he shouts to the world that the beauty of his lover (a mere actor, by the way) is more divine than the sun god himself. Three decades later, after Catullus and his friends have got busy with these borrowed forms and feelings, these sentiments will not (*pace* Cicero) sound quite so surprising in Latin. But when Catulus composed these poems, what in Greek sounded utterly ordinary, in Latin sounded, at best, bizarre.

6. For a recent discussion of him, see Gruener, 19–20.

It is true that those first audiences of Catulus, Aedituus, and Licinius had encountered plenty of foolish young lovers in the theater where they had heard swarms of amorous youngsters squeal and whimper when they found themselves thwarted in the acquisition of the objects of their lust or (perhaps) their love. These comic whippersnappers, having dared to face their comic fathers' wrathful opposition to the satisfaction of their desires, managed, with the help of a cunning slave, to outwit, more often than not, their sires and so accomplish their aims. The Roman males in Catulus' first audience had laughed for years at these antics, had been entertained by this droll fantasy (in real life Roman sons were unlikely to outwit Roman fathers, and cunning slaves were likely to find themselves being brutally whipped when they showed excessive ingenuity). As likely as not, they recognized, with rueful pleasure, something of their own young voices (and vices) in the voices (and vices) of Plautus' or Terence's young lovers as they attempted to sow their wild oats before their fathers succeeded in transforming them into chips off the old block. Not a little of the speech and sentiment of the classic Roman elegiac lover does, in fact, derive from the lovers of Roman Comedy, and when that comedic form fuses with the psychological template of Alexandrian elegy, the chief poetic materials of Catullus and Calvus and their heirs are ready for them.[7]

What matters most to us here, however, in these early erotic epigrams is the transvaluation of values that occurs in this moment when an Alexandrian refinement of the erotic imagination is first seeded in alien ground, in the Latin language and in the Roman identity that the language fosters and preserves. Catulus was a soldier-citizen with the best of them, but by the time he wrote the two poems in question he had been touched by—some would say tainted with—something quite foreign to everything he had been taught to be and to honor. Something that paid too much attention to shades of feeling, to beauty that had no sense of purpose (to ornament for ornament's own sake), to the charms of, the absolute thirst for, leisure and imagination and "sensuous enjoyment of every kind" (as Cavafy, the last of the Hellenistic poets, would put it). It's hard here not to call to mind the splendid polemics of Oscar Wilde against duty, discipline, purpose, against the entire ideology of Victorian manhood and its empire; hard not to conjure up his brave and witty elaborations of the gospel of radical hedonism or what one might call an enlightened egoism. That anti-civic, aesthetic individualism is what is what is beginning to breathe its first breath when Catulus puts down his stylus.

   7. For a precise description of what was involved here, see Konstan, 141–42.

CHAPTER 1

AN AMOROUS DICTATOR

An extreme and telling example of this incipient identity is one that Pliny the Younger (5.3.5) mentions in a list of distinguished statesmen who, like him, happen to have been in the habit of writing light verse (most likely amatory in nature). The name that stands next to Catulus' in this list belongs to none other than Sulla, brilliant general, ferocious and successful dictator, and indefatigable bon vivant with a special interest in exotic erotics. His Latin nickname (Felix, Sulla the Lucky) got the Greek translation, Epaphroditus, favorite of Aphrodite, Venus' darling, lucky at cards (or, Romanly speaking, at dice), and so in life; but one wonders if there isn't here another connotation that pleased him no less: lucky in love, divinely loving and lovable. If that's the case, and even if it isn't, he certainly devoted much of his spare time (and had done so before he got or took the epithet) to carnal diversions. Even after we make generous allowance for Plutarch's puritan fascination with Sulla's sexuality and the elaborate surmises that it doubtless inspired, what's left over is enough to slightly raise an eyebrow. But try as he may to paint his subject as as a priapic freak, what glimmers just beneath of the surface of Plutarch's finished portrait of Sulla is something rather different. Whether the germs of that version come from mere gossip that Plutarch romanticizes or from bits of truth that he embroiders, what matters here is that Plutarch, though he wants to reduce Sulla's erotic behavior to sheer brute carnality, keeps discovering that Sulla, beneath his lecher's skin, is a lover at his heart's core.

From early manhood onward, Sulla was a party-animal who, says Plutarch sourly,

> used to spend his time with ballet dancers and comedians and shared their dissolute way of life; and when he had won supreme power he was always organizing parties of the most impudently outspoken characters from the stage with whom he used to drink and exchange witticisms, with the result that people thought that he was acting in a manner ill-suited to his age; and he not only cheapened the reputation of his high office [that of dictator] but actually neglected much business which required attention. (2; Warner, 67)

Well, actually, as Plutarch immediately admits, Sulla worked hard and regularly at being and remaining a dictator; but when he let loose he did so with gusto, and the fierce countenance he showed the world when on the job, being Roman dictator, quickly dissolved when he relaxed with his chums, "comedians and professional dancers" (2; Warner, 67). Plutarch, who seems really annoyed when he encounters people who are bent on trying to enjoy themselves, suggests that "because of this habit of relaxation Sulla seems to have been almost pathologically prone to sexual indulgence, being quite without restraint in his passion for pleasure." Then comes something odd:

> It was a passion which he continued to gratify even in old age. He remained attached from his early youth to an actor called Metrobius [of whom we will hear more in a minute]. Another experience of his was with Nicopolis, a woman rather easily accessible, but well off. He began by falling in love with her, but as she got used to his society and to the charm he had in his youth it ended in her falling in love with him, and making him her heir when she died. (2; Warner, 67[8])

This is an extraordinary paragraph. This ne'er-do-well lecher, vile when he was young and more vile still in his decrepitude, this bosom-buddy of actors and other gutter trash, manages both to become master of the known world (until he decides, under no compulsion to do so, to take early retirement from the job) and also, contrary to Plutarch's expectations and ours, to win and keep and reciprocate the love of two people. In his desire to resolve the complexity of his subject, the biographer finds himself having recourse to a baffling antimony: on the one hand, this strange man keeps a firm, capable hand on the rudder of government, and, on the other, he squanders his time, wealth, and energies on frivolous, nay, on decadent diversions; on the one hand, ready to bed whoever chances his way, he consorts almost automatically with the vilest of the vile; on the other, he has more than a penchant for examining sustained romantic attachment, for, in addition to Metrobius and Nicopolis, there is another love, one whose sweet and sentimental tale the biographer saves for a place near the close of his portrait of Sulla.

Toward the end of his life, on the death of his wife Metella, Sulla tries to assuage his profound grief in his usual way, "by indulging in drinking bouts and expensive parties with vulgar entertainers," but "a few months later, there was a show of gladiators ... " and "there happened to be sitting near Sulla a very beautiful woman ... ," who, "when she

---

8. Keaveney, 10–11 notices his charm and good looks but minimizes the dictator's amative virtues.

passed behind him, pulled off a piece of wool from his toga and then went on to her seat. When Sulla looked around at her in surprise, she said, 'There's no reason to be surprised, Dictator. I only want to have a little bit of your good luck for myself'" (35; Warner, 109). This woman was Valeria, recently divorced (the institution is increasingly fashionable at this time and after it, and it is very much a part of our story). "The daughter of Messalla and a sister of the orator, Hortensius," this woman's charming remark immediately stirs, we are told, the Dictator's "amatory propensities." He and the lady begin, instantly, to flirt. Plutarch insists that her behavior is wholly innocent, for she is "chaste and worthy"; as for the Dictator, he is only lusting for her, "carried away, like a boy might have been, by a good-looking face and a saucy manner—just what naturally excites the most disgraceful and shameless sort of passion."

That is one way of reading this wonderful meet-cute anecdote, but other readings might be possible. In one of them, this witty, aristocrat divorcée is a little less innocent than Plutarch seems to believe her to be (I have no notion of what her motive might have been for her clever stratagem and her clever remark—maybe she desired him, maybe she was ambitious); as for Sulla, maybe he was carried away with a quite ordinary emotion (not with the bad, sad cravings of a geriatric satyr). In any case, the interesting thing here is that Sulla didn't just whisk Valeria off and have his way with her (as the young Octavian was later to do when the mood struck him, whenever, wherever) and then toss her out into the street; instead he married her (and she bore him, after his death, a daughter, Postuma, as such daughters were commonly named). Which may just mean that Sulla 'loved' Valeria in the good old-fashioned way that the Roman paterfamilias may very often have 'loved' the woman or women he found himself, for various reasons, married to. Or maybe this last love was more ardent than the norm set for conventional conjugal affection would allow. This story, in short, may be (and may not be) a love story. Plutarch tells it because, despite himself, he is fond of love stories[9]; but he immediately untells it, because Sulla and the age that Sulla lived and loved in baffle him. Sulla is both a good Roman husband and he is also, at the same time, incarnate, the forerunner of the Mad Lover who will presently come to furnish Latin poetry with the core of its matter and manner.

Plutarch skips from the flirtation scene and what he regards as its

---

9. For interesting observations on Plutarch's handling of such material, see Walcot, 177 and *passim*.

childish salacities to Valeria as wife in the dictator's home thusly: "Nevertheless, even though he had her as a wife at home, he still kept company with women who were ballet dancers or harpists and with people from the theatre. They used to lie drinking together on couches all day long. Those who at this time were most influential with him were the following: Roscius the comedian" (who, interestingly enough, turns up also in that erotic epigram by Lutatius Catulus), "Sorex the leading ballet dancer, and Metrobius, the female impersonator." Metrobius (whom we found at the beginning of the story as one of Sulla's amours and who may have been the love of his life) "was now past his prime, but Sulla throughout everything continued to insist that he was in love with him" (36; Warner, 109–10). In another man, in another story, with a switch of genders, such constancy and devotion might be unobjectionable even without the blessings of matrimony, but in Plutarch's eyes, coupled with all the evil companions and wanton convivia, they bring down upon Sulla a dreadful and merited doom. "By living in this way he aggravated a disease which had not been serious in its early stages, and for a long time he was not aware he had ulcers in the intestines. Soon, his flesh is turned into worms that devour him" (36; Warner, 110). Plutarch admits that Sulla was, within ten days of his end, still occupying himself successfully with public affairs, but this display of civic devotion does not rescue him from Plutarch's condemnation or keep Plutarch from fashioning the contradictions of Sulla's erotic life into a cautionary tale whose central purpose is to condemn the figure of the Mad Lover which he has encountered fully embodied in the figure of Sulla, and which he is soon to meet in what is its most perfect real-life, not literary, incarnation.

LOVE'S PARADIGM IN
FLESH AND BLOOD

Sulla died in 79 BCE, three years after the birth of Marc Antony, who would turn out to be his most zealous successor, not so much in the forum as in the bedroom. I will here sketch Antony's claim to the title of the definitive Mad Roman Lover briefly since Jasper Griffin has already provided an excellent argument for that claim (32–42). Suffice it now to recall a couple of scandalous anecdotes whose veracity hardly matters, since what concerns us here is plausible gossip that gestures to what

Antony's contemporaries would be able and willing to accept as feasible not only in respect of Antony's amative reputation but also as consistent with fashionable erotic behavior. The stories come to us chiefly and most vividly by way of Cicero in his *Second Philippic*.[10] Cicero's purpose in telling them, of course, is to finish blackening his victim's character. In the first story (76–78), having been absent from Rome for a while, Antony dashes back there on both public and private business. To delude his adversaries, he hides himself in a louche bar in a suburb, drinks there steadily (*perpotavit*) until dusk, and then, his head wrapped in a cloak, goes directly to his own house, knocks on his own door, answers his own doorman's query by saying that he has a message from Marcus (*a Marco tabellarius*), and, having been ushered into the presence of Fulvia, his wife, he gives her the letter he has been clutching. He watches her, peering out from his disguise, as she reads it and begins to weep. The epistle is written *amatorie*, in the style of a love letter, amatively, maybe even elegiacally. In the letter Antony promises to dump—forever—the actress he has been famously infatuated with and promises to restore all his affections to her, his wife. *Cum mulier fleret uberius, homo misericors ferre non potuit, caput aperuit, in collum invasit.* "And when his wife began weeping uncontrollably, that tenderhearted man, he could stand it no longer. He threw off his disguise and hurled himself into her arms." Fulvia may have been fooled by Antony's cruel charade, but Cicero is not. *O hominem nequam!* he cries. "You worthless rotten bastard" (2.77). He also, for reasons we will presently learn, calls Antony a catamite and insists that this elegiac moment was in fact a subterfuge—Antony had sneaked into Rome not to save his marriage, not for the sake of love, but for the sake of money, to clinch a shady deal.

It would not astonish me to learn—if learn we could—that such a scene was in fact enacted. But if it was, I doubt very much that it transpired exactly as Cicero represents it. From what little we know of Fulvia from elsewhere, she was not so much given to tears. When Antony threw back his cloak to reveal his face, she laughed—if she wasn't already laughing before he revealed himself, before, even, she finished the letter. Antony may have succeeded in disguising his handwriting and even his voice, but he could not disguise his style—I don't mean of his prose, but of his jokes and—quite possibly—of his lovemaking. It was a flamboyant way of saying, "I'm sorry, take me back, I'll never see that woman again"—flamboyant and possibly even sincere. Fulvia will have been used

---

10. For a shrewd recent discussion, see Langlands, 305–10.

to her husband's play-acting, as she doubtless was, though they had not been married very long, to his infidelities. She herself had previously been married to Clodius (notorious brother of the notorious Clodia, alias Catullus' Lesbia) and, her second trip to the altar was with Curio, who happened to be, along with Antony, Caesar's favorite henchman, and who, moreover, figures prominently in our next anecdote. Fulvia knows how, in this moment of its history, Roman aristocratic marriage works and how it doesn't work. She doesn't much care if her husband is temporarily involved in a dalliance with a vulgar performer who achieved stardom in soft-porn sit-coms (that is what Roman mimes, Augustus' own favorite art form, essentially were). Fulvia doesn't even care if her better half is besotted permanently with Volumnia (or Cytheris, the stage name of this ravishing celebrity). We don't know why Fulvia married Antony, but it very probably was not because she had any illusions about him or about her other husbands or about any Roman male or—not to put too fine a point on it—about herself. Antony may have been sincere in his dramatic palinode, but the sincerity would have interested her less than the imagination and silly bravado that mark the escapade. Like other people, she probably found Antony amusing and charming as well as handsome and virile (but that wouldn't be why she married him). Fulvia knew, in short, how the erotic game was now being played (whereas Cicero apparently, despite his satire on it, here and in the *pro Caelio,* did not quite understand it, from the inside). But however we read the story, however we interpret it, it is elegiac in spirit, and, even if it is mere gossip that Cicero shapes and embroiders, it represents an action, a style of behavior, that mirrors or wants to be taken as mirroring 'real life.' In any case, either Antony himself or the gossip-begotten Antony that represents Antony in the story seems to have read Catullus and Calvus (life imitating art), and soon Gallus and, after him, Propertius, will be imitating him (art imitates life).

Our second anecdote is far from plausible; it belongs closest to the category of malicious slander and goes a long way toward explaining how Cicero's tongue ended up being nailed to the rostrum that had witnessed his greatest verbal triumphs. (See Appian's vivid representation, 4.20.) Long before he'd met Fulvia or Volumnia, when Antony had just turned teenager, his father went bankrupt: *Sumpsisti virilem, quam statim muliebrem togam reddidisti* (44). "You'd no sooner donned the toga of Roman manhood than you quickly changed it for the toga that we make our harlots wear." "At first you were a common streetwalker," says Cicero, "and you charged fixed fees for the services you rendered, and you did not sell yourself cheap." Luckily Curio (Fulvia's second husband you recall) snatched this shameless hustler away from the squalors of the gutter, and, almost as if he'd dressed him up in the garb of an honest Roman wife (*tamquam stolam dedisset*), he married him (*in matrimonio stabili et certo collocavit*)—and the language here recalls vividly one of Latin elegy's most favored and most subversive themes, the blessings of a permanent (illegal) union. Cicero goes on to state that no slave boy purchased to satisfy his buyer's lust was more in power of his master than was Antony when he found himself married, so to speak, to Curio.

The tale now shifts securely into the style of Roman comedy. The unspeakable lust of the crazy Son is vigorously opposed by his shamed and desperate Dad who throws the new bride out of the house and hires a guard to keep him out. To no avail. Antony is so driven by his lust and his greed (giving his all for lust and money) that he tears a hole in the roof and shimmies down a rope to the starved embraces of his rich groom. Antony can't be gotten rid of, Curio won't give him up, and Dad, of course, is now going out of his mind. In fact, this nightmare is killing him; he takes to his bed; he seems to be dying of a broken heart. But Curio, though he loves his father dearly, cannot bring himself to give up his Antony; he would endure anything, even exile, rather than let his lover go. It is all a hopeless mess. But Cicero, ever wise and patient, manages to resolve these difficulties—or rather, to cure them (*sedavi vel potius curavi*). He gets Dad to buy the whore-bride off; he gets Curio to divorce, as it were, his boyfriend, thus bowing to fatherly authority (*patrio iure et potestate*, 46) and thus refusing to waste on the wretched hoodlum the talents that belonged to his family's glory and his nation's needs. A wonder to behold—how Cicero here restores the now vanished morality of the good old days, how he reconciles father with son, putting the misguided youth back on the path that will take him to fatherhood and responsibility and away from Antony and rotten eros.

The anecdote is, as I said, utterly fabricated from traditional homophobic materials. What it reveals, aside from its author's personal animosities, are the now firm outlines of the new Roman fantasmatic, the new romantic Roman script for a new erotic ideology. On its surface, the story may read like the scenario for an unwritten Plautine comedy, with Antony perversely cast as the whore with the heart of a cash register. But in its deeper structure, under the sordid tale of the hustler and his john, we glimpse something else: wildly caricatured though they are, the degree and fidelity of Antony's passion are matched by Curio's willingness, indeed his utter need, to defy the law of the father and risk all for love. From the fusion of these two mock lovers there gleams the outline of the Mad Lover in his new Roman incarnation. But Antony's performance in this role is not complete, and will not be until he falls on his sword in Alexandria.

I have no need to rehearse here the glorious and messy jumble of fact and fiction that was to furnish Shakespeare with perhaps his greatest love story. Propertius for his own purposes, and the Augustan propaganda machine for its, would transform Antony from Roman statesman and soldier to a pathetic misfit who, falling into the cruel hands of an oriental dominatrix, woke from his stupor only to find himself a contemptible degenerate, ruined by wine and lust and blind ambition—and by the fatal charms and machination of Egypt's monstrous queen. Here the Mad Lover achieves his final perfection: this shadow of a man had come to desire that his old (patriarchal) identity be destroyed so a new one could be fashioned for him. He had wanted to die for love, to die into love, and when Octavian and his army arrived in Egypt, his wish was granted. In a transport of self-abnegation and abjection, Antony traded empire for kisses and Roman manhood for effete humiliation. Appian was not fooled by this version; he allows him a touch of fine romantic coloring and not a little sympathy as he introduces Antony into his last amour (5.8): "The moment he saw her, Antonius lost his head to her like a young man, although he was forty years old. He is reported to have been always prone to such behavior, and also in the case of Cleopatra to have been provoked by the sight of her a long time previously when she was still a girl and he was a young captain of cavalry." But Appian's sketch of the faithful, tender lover did not prevail, and only Shakespeare's imagination could rescue him from his long opprobrium.

MISSING GALLUS

It was a hard act to follow, this epiphany of the Mad Lover in his splendid and miserable self-immolation, but C. Cornelius Gallus gave it his best shot. Born thirteen years after Antony and Catullus, Gallus may be regarded as belonging to, or better personifying, what I take to be the third generation of those involved in the devolution or evolution of Roman love. First generation: Lutatius Catulus and his fellow writers of Alexandrian epigram at the beginning of the century; then, roughly twenty years later, Catullus and Calvus and Antony; then Gallus, whose heyday as Mad Lover overlaps that of Antony (who was still going strong long after first Catullus, then Calvus, had dropped by the wayside). In the person of Gallus, even more so than in the case of Calvus, two personae, the Mad Lover as Failed Roman Citizen and the Poet who imagines and represents the Mad Lover, were perfectly fused. Gallus combined the career of soldier/statesman with that of elegiac poet, he inherited Volumnia/Cytheris from Antony in real life (she became the Lycoris of his poems) and, in his collection of love poems, named the *Amores,* he seems finally to have given all but the finishing touches to what we now call the genre of Latin love elegy. Unfortunately, here as often in Roman literature, a crucial piece is missing from the puzzle. We don't have nearly enough sense of what he did with elegy and therefore of how he influenced the fourth generation of Roman elegists, that of Propertius and Tibullus or the fourth-and-a-half (call it the fifth), that of Ovid, nor do we know precisely in what way these poems centered around the woman they addressed (or praised or blamed or both).[11] This is, alas, a blank wall that brings our story of the devolution and evolution of Love to its close, until we turn to the poems of Tibullus, Propertius, and Ovid and see how they went about recording the transformation of Roman Eros in the Roman world just before the birth of Christ, how they contrived to elaborate and deepen its meanings, and, in Ovid's case, to exhaust them and witness their demise.

In order to fabricate a useful history of Roman love elegy, what we would need to know about the work of Gallus are the following: to what degree did he make his Lycoris the fixed center of his poems and of his collected volumes as a whole? How wide was the spectrum of his responses to her favor and disfavor? Did he range from bliss through anxiety to rage to grief, reveling in the full Propertian gamut? Or, as Vergil's tenth eclogue seems to hint, was the erotic subject that spoke his poems overwhelmingly tender, bemused, querulous? Did the poems show much in the way of the poet's sense of being opposed to the doctrine of docile bodies that their own erotic imperative called into question? Or were they relatively unconcerned both with the imperative and its Catullan origins and with any hint of the ideology that would eventually try to crush it? Another way of stating these questions more succinctly would be to ask, How Propertian were the poems of Gallus, how tinged were they with some of his irony and satiric bent? Was Gallus' fatal break

---

11. For the tantalizing and incomprehensible fragments (nine rugged verses) discovered on a bit of papyrus in Nubia in 1978, see Courtney's cogent discussion, 263-68.

with Augustus entirely political or did his erotic perspective, whatever its shade and depth, contribute to their disengagement?

These questions are worth asking, not because they are capable of finding any definitive answer, but because, in failing to contemplate them, we tend to imagine that we can write (diachronically) a history of this genre in its Roman form or that we can construct (synchronically) a plausible picture of this genre's system. In neither case can we. Missing Gallus—and missing Calvus, too!—our knowledge of what Roman love elegy was remains fragmentary, illusory, frustrated.[12]

LAST'S LADIES

Before I sum up my story to that point where extant elegies continue it, I need to say a little more about a couple of the ladies whom Hugh Last vilified. Lycoris was the name Gallus gave his love object in the *Amores*. Behind this name there was probably a real woman, Volumnia, a freedwoman who was mistress to an actual Roman, Volumnius, and who took the stage name of Cytheris. She, Volumnia-Cytheris-Lycoris, was the torch, so to speak, that Antony passed on to Gallus; as such, she is, so to speak, the bridge not only between one elegiac generation and another but also between elegy's actualities and its fictions, and she, this fact who is fiction and this fiction who is fact, reminds us that women and what they signify are central to Roman love elegy.[13] Her name, moreover, her names, her triple name, gestures us toward the ambiguities that shape both the genre of Roman love elegy and the milieu and moment that engendered it. As Cytheris (the Cytherian, Venus), a performer suited to and famous for the sexy characters she portrayed on stage (think of Zola's incomparable Nana), she attracted the attention of Antony. He, like Sulla before him, had a passion for theater and especially for actors and singers and dancers, those radiant creatures who manipulated the machinery of illusion that, then as now, nourished the erotic imagination, furnishing it with its imperative of liberation from convention and its promise of new identity, new modes

---

12. For the most recent attempt to fill in these blanks, see the intricate speculations of Cairns 2006, 104–45.

13. For an excellent survey of this complex figure, both as fact and as fiction, see Traina; for a subtle, judicious discussion of the the ways that reality and imagination seem to collide, or mesh, in Latin love elegy, see Hemelrijk, 175–78.

of being. Finally, as Lycoris (the wolf? the hook? lustful?, see Propertius 4.1.141), in those volumes of Gallus that suffered barbaric triage in the pious scriptoria of Christendom, she rivals Catullus' Lesbia as the founding mother of her genre, even as she adumbrates the figure that perfects elegy's erotic object, the Cynthia of Propertius.

But our interest in Cytheris does not stop there. According to the gossip that Cicero's funny sketch of Antony set in amber, the reason that Cytheris passed from the hands of Antony to those of Gallus was Fulvia's jealousy. And once we have firmly fixed in mind the polarity designed by this pair, Cytheris and Fulvia, *meretrix* and *matrona,* whore and wife, the dynamic of Latin love elegy emerges from its complexities. Fact or fiction, fiction trying to explain fact, or fact trying to explain fiction, the conflict between the hooker and the honest helpmeet over who will possess the Roman male, body, mind, and soul, captures in small the crisis in the masculine Roman identity that the poetry in question reflects, magnifies, and distorts. Like Hercules at the crossroad where Vice and Virtue branch off on their separate ways, Antony (in this pretty story) was faced with the choice between decadent hedonism and the Roman Way: Think like a Roman, not like a filthy Greek.[14]

And now, a few words about Fulvia. In the interests of brevity, I pass over Plutarch's charming conceit: how Fulvia, once she had managed to rescue Antony from the wicked entertainer, surrendered him, tamed and meekly obedient, to the tender mercies of Cleopatra (*Life of Antony,* 10.3).[15] Unlike Cato's Porcia or Augustus' Livia (at least as she appears in her photo-ops), Fulvia does seem to have loathed spinning and housekeeping. She married, in succession, you remember, Clodius, Curio, and Antony, and she joined Antony's brother Lucius in fighting the forces, led by Octavian, that were threatening the power of her husband in Italy (he was off in the East, busily defending his interests there). I doubt Fulvia spent much time reading Catullus or Calvus, and I doubt that, had she survived long enough, she would have taken much interest, despite her accidentally close connection with Volumnia-Cytheris-Lycoris, in the poems of Gallus or the materials (legends of lovers as glamorous as they were crazed and luckless) that Parthenius had assembled to help him write them.[16] But she belonged to, and very well represents, that class

14. For interesting speculations on this erotic antithesis, see Ancona's "(Un)constrained Male Desire."

15. See Baldson's sympathetic version of her, 49–50; Fischer provides an extensive, helpful discussion of Fulvia's character and significance, 7–63, 221–23.

16. For a recent and thorough discussion, see Lightfoot, 50–76.

of women who are as crucial to devolution/evolution of love as their menfolk. Because, like their menfolk, Fulvia and women like her found themselves in a process of transformation, a process that later, Augustus' sex and marriage laws were designed to call a halt to.[17] These women, some of them at any rate, also wanted new identities, ones far different than those that their mothers and grandmothers had endured.

These patrician women had, for decades, lost their fathers, uncles, brothers, sons, and husbands on countless battlefields of civil war, or seen them assassinated or murdered in proscriptions. The institutions, the system of government they were part of and contributed to, by being daughters and nieces, sisters and mothers and wives, became ever more fragile as the Republic careened toward its collapse upon itself. They were as likely to be widows or divorcées as they were to be wives. Some of them, like Fulvia, were ambitious (not just for their men) and wanted to stroll the corridors of power or to help dismantle them; some, like Clodia, wanted mostly to make use of the new forms of freedom that the absence of their menfolk had occasioned. For many of these women, adultery became a sort of entertainment, and the new love poetry that celebrated that entertainment must have been delightful, engrossing, amusing; it reflected and at the same time it helped refine a new fashion in erotic imagining, in erotic identities. If the men who managed to escape from the dangers of the Republic's death rattle could experiment with trying to remake themselves by means of new fantasmatics, of new 'Image-repertoires,' why shouldn't there be new Roman women as well as new Roman men? Erotically speaking, in life as in art, patrician women joined high-class hookers and actresses in becoming, for a few decades, the partners of Roman aristocratic males in pleasure, in illusions, in love. These lovers and their loves, like the poetry that represented them and offered them models for their loving, were, to be sure, engaged in playing a fashionable game. However, that game was, beneath its gaudy surfaces, at least for some of its players, a serious game, one that seemed to promise escape from defunct conventions into fresh selves and fresh freedoms, into a sort of erotic utopia where the self's sense of its core-self, of its individual, unique powers and liberties and creativities, was no longer subject to being squandered by the city or crushed by the Voice of the Father.

---

17. For a recent reliable account of his efforts to curb sexual behavior and promote marriage, see Langlands, 20–21, 218–24, 329–33, 362.

For a few decades, along with their men, they were the children of Antony and Cytheris, of Lesbia and Catullus, the playmates of the Mad Lover, the Grecianized Dandy, the *Sonnenkind,* the Good-time Charley, the Fond and Abject Swain. They became, these women, and Fulvia among them, his slave, his paradise, his dominatrix, his doom. Though it was mostly not very real perhaps, it was a lot of fun while it lasted. But it didn't last that long. To quote from Browning's "A Toccata of Galuppi's," "What became of soul, I wonder, when the kissing had to stop?" There isn't much soul left and the kissing is definitely coming to a stop in the poems that reflect those terminations, Ovid's *Amores,* his *Heroides,* his *Ars Amatoria.* Adultery, affairs, liaisons, all that continues, of course, after the Julian laws have been promulgated and after Ovid has gone into exile, but the peculiar, the essential, the unique moment in the Roman Love Story has come and gone.[18]

CATO VERSUS AMOR: A DIALECTIC

To recapitulate: That moment consists in the confrontation between the traditional Roman erotic ideology and a hedonistic, libertarian erotic ideology that sought to replace it; between sexual instinct viewed as procreative and sexual instinct viewed as amusement or as a form of self-fashioning, one in which the peculiar intensity that Aristotle finds in classical Greek pederasty has been transferred to the love between men and women who are not married to each other (*Nichomachean Ethics* 9.10.5, 1171a). This brief and temporary upheaval occurred along with and was abetted by other, larger upheavals that were shaking Roman society and the Roman state. When it ended, it left behind it, almost by accident, only a few rolls of poetry books, ones that would have, almost by accident, considerable impacts on other poetries, at other times, in other places, when there arose a need for refashioning the dominant erotic identity and its ideologies and when a culture of personality replaced, for a while, a culture of character.

If you could ask Cato the Elder or Cato the Younger if he loved his wife, after some quibbling over nuance and considerable debate over primary definition, he (either of them) would doubtless finally admit

---

18. For the aftermath of the Augustan legislation, see Langlands, 319–63.

that, yes, indeed, he loved her. She had brought him money and some influence; she gave him children; she attended to the running of his house and farm; she gave him her counsel when he asked for it; and she was, as Aristotle had suggested was the case, his partner, his partner in ways that his male relatives and male friends could never be. In this sense, she helped to confer on him some of his identity, and he was grateful for that, and that gratitude expressed itself in tenderness for her, in concern for her, in his profound desire for her happiness. But she was not, probably, at most times and at most levels, the center of his life. That center was an image (he could see it daily in the faces of the masks of dead ancestors hanging up on his walls), an image of the kind of man his father had taught him to become. Anything that altered that image, anything that disrupted its erotic components—anything, that is, that shifted the meaning of what we call love, would seem to him a scandal, a degeneration, a devolution.

When the rot began to set in (as Cato saw the matter), when young men began to like Greek food and Greek women and Greek poetry too much, bad things inevitably began happening to them and to the world they were being called on to conquer and govern. Cato (I'm talking now of one of Cato's grandsons, a contemporary of Lutatius Catulus), wouldn't have objected to Meleager, he might even have whiled away an evening listening to some pretty Greek (boy or girl) intone the poet's verses (about pretty boys or girls), but he wouldn't have liked hearing that some Romans were actually engaged in translating or imitating him. There was nothing wrong if a Greek warbled some analogue of "The Very Thought Of You and I Forget to Do the Little Ordinary Things That Everyone Ought To Do." But when a Roman says or sings the same or similar things in Latin, something starts to stink—it's like somebody trying to piss against the wind—because, for a Roman, love is certainly not all that matters. What matters, all that matters, is the Public Thing, everyone's Duty to do the big and little things that everyone ought to do. Hearing these new Latin poems that Catulus serves up, Cato has the queasy feeling that, to quote Emerson, "the coming age is the age of the first person singular."[19]

What distinguishes Meleager and Alexandrians from Catulus and Catullus and Gallus and Propertius is that in their world (the world of the Graeculi, the Greeklings) there can be no real conflict between

---

19. For an excellent decription of the 'hegemonic masculinity' that the new erotics contests, see McDonnell, 165–205.

passion and duty because those Greeks have no duties worth talking about (which is why they have ended up being colonized and why Romans have not); their identities are not shredded when they scream and whimper and sob because some loose woman or heartless boy has done them wrong. Their eros is not incompatible with their (unburdensome) civic duties, their selves are not split between what they desire and what (little) their society demands of them. But with Romans the case is altered. About the time that Catulus penned his adoration of Theotimus and Roscius, Rome enters a new phase, its focus and its values begin to shift. For various reasons, because some of the brightest and the best young men (and women) had too much money and too much spare time, because their fathers were busy killing each other, because of who and where they were, these Romans (accidentally) caught a glimpse of Love of an un-Roman kind, of a love that transfigures, that takes away the identity you were born with and into only to confer on you the possibility of a new and better and richer one, the priceless maddening gift from the woman or boy you love. For these Romans, men and women alike, this transformation will have seemed all but miraculous, a radical, inexplicable shift from the confinement and monotony of prescribed erotic identities to (through and beyond eroticism) possibilities of variety, beauty, imagination, liberty. Looked at from that unexpected and astonishing perspective, in its unfolding over decades and generations, this transformation most likely looked not like the ruin of love but rather as its evolution, one that promised to end always in hours of bliss and perhaps in years of happiness.

CHAPTER 2

AENEAS IN LOVE

> But for me, as an amorous subject, everything that is near, everything that disturbs is received not as a fact, but in the aspect of a sign that must be interpreted.
> —Barthes, *Discourse,* 66

> But in fact Werther is not perverse, he is in love: he creates meaning, always and everywhere out of nothing, and it is meaning that thrills him: he is in the crucible of meaning.
> —Barthes, *Discourse,* 67

 AENEAS, FOR REASONS that may seem so obvious as to require no comment, is not widely celebrated as a Latin lover, but he is deeply implicated in the network of erotic fashions that developed in the last days of Rome's republic. Therefore, before we turn to Propertius and his Cynthia, it might be worthwhile to examine how and why Aeneas fell victim to an ideology so alien to his character and to the poetic project, high epic, that his creator intended him to serve, indeed, to incarnate. To suggest that Aeneas is an elegiac lover would clearly overshoot the mark, but to entertain the idea that he was inevitably—if unsuccessfully—conscripted by the erotic ideology that flourished during the years of his production is perhaps feasible. Numerous readers, including those who support the notion that the *Aeneid* is first and foremost a celebration of the Augustan Empire, have had no difficulty—once Dido is equated with Cleopatra—in reading him as a sort of reluctant and temporary Antony. And Antony, as Cicero was among the first to notice, was nothing if not a living emblem of what would come to be seen as the elegy's erotic imperative. Before I discuss the ways in which Aeneas/Antony strikes me as a vivid representation of the elegiac ideal, I need to review some of the literary

materials from which he and his Dido were manufactured. And before I do that, in an effort to provide an alternative to the fashionable model furnished us by Lacan's reworkings of Freud, I want to look at another model, one that seems to me to shed a more compatible light on the erotics of Propertius and the genre he perfected.[1]

Not only does 'love' mean different things in different times and different places, but it can also mean different things at different times to the same person. The spectrum of its myriad connotations is baffling, and the gradations between the points that constitute its poles (for example, Christian agape vs. bestial lust) are subtle and at times barely perceptible. In his impressive, still influential study, *Love in the Western World,* Denis de Rougemont solves the problem that haunts this erotic spectrum by turning to history, where he discovers a deadly virus that arose from the fusion of Manichean beliefs and the poetry of Provence and that thereafter burgeoned into a plague which inflicted itself on European literature and European societies and which continues to damage the modern psyche and contributes hugely to the 'breakdown of marriage' (17, 275–79, 291–96). This version of passionate love (supremely incarnated by Tristan) is grounded in a radical distrust of the goodness of life; in a powerful antipathy toward monogamy and family life; in an overwhelming appetite for adultery; and, at its core, in an irresistible death wish. In a more recent study, one that eschews a historical solution, the authors of *A General Theory of Love* agree with de Rougement about the virtues of successful marriage and are especially eloquent about the dangers that currently threaten it (Lewis et al., 204–9). But they offer a fascinating description of how the erotic identity is constructed and how it functions in all humans at every time and in every place. This perspective is, to my mind, possessed of greater explanatory power than those offered by de Rougemont or by various reformulations of the Family Romance. Briefly, what this general theory accounts for is the manner in which, acting for the most part independently of its rational (neocortical) counterpart, the emotional (limbic) portion of the human brain encodes changing patterns of erotic expectation and response as it encounters new erotic stimuli, thus fabricating the individual's erotic identity (113–44). In this version of how Eros behaves, the formation and activities of obsessive, irrational Love become, as nearly as possible, intelligible and cures for it become feasible (163–82). Aeneas may end

---

1. For an incisive analysis of the "inconsistencies and fallacies" of the Lacanian oeuvre, see Evans.

by desiring such a cure, but Marc Antony and Propertius will have none of it. They inhabit the realm they share with the splendid maniac who is the voice of Tennyson's *Maud,* Albertine's compulsive ruminator, and, in recent times, the definitive expert in these matters, Humbert Humbert. The joys and calamities produced by their limbic brains meet with an unscientific yet eminently lucid analyst in Stendhal.

THE CRYSTAL BOUGH

Stendhal's *On Love* is a strange farrago of often obscure anecdotes, savage travel writing, witty anthropology, and up-close and personal meditations on sex and passion. It breathes some of the same air as Rabelais, Montaigne, and Voltaire, it gives off now and then a strong Cartesian scent, and it is drenched in a potent concoction of High Romantic mentality. It was Stendhal's favorite among all the books he authored, but it has not been successfully exported to Anglo-Saxon climes. It has no central narrative, moreover, and it is by turns lushly mystical and antiseptically clinical. It mercilessly dissects domesticated romance of the Valentine's Day variety, and, prefiguring Proust, it canonizes the blissfully, incurably crazed erotic subject who has the luck and the misfortune to fall hopelessly in love. In American culture its best analogue is perhaps the central donnée of Country and Western music (e.g., "You grabbed my heart right outta my chest / And you stomped on it up and down—/ But, Honey, I'm still your man"), the sort of song which ends with the loving madman speeding off in his pickup, rifle at the ready, to shoot his rival, his sweetheart, and probably himself. Stendhal examines every variety of erotic behavior he can think of, every style of lusting and loving he has felt, witnessed, or heard about. But what interests him most, because it all but devoured him and because it kindled and continued to fuel his authorship, is the love that demands the lover's entire waking and sleeping existence, that transforms his identity, and stains his consciousness with its own dye even as it enlarges his very being and clarifies it. This fatal commitment, this determination to risk and sacrifice one's all, is what is meant by a 'consuming passion' (it is not what St. Augustine cleverly trivializes when he condemns himself for having been "in love with love," *amare amabam, Confessions* 1.31). This grand, sometimes fatal passion is what Stendhal's maddening, exhausting, and wonderful book is mainly about, and that is why I have decided to use it as a theoretical template for my investigation of Propertius and his colleagues in erotic elegiacs.

Stendhal's essential gambit is deceptively simple. He insists that his readers face a fact that they know well but mostly choose to ignore: that the word 'love' is far more complex and far less precise than we are wont to admit. Accordingly, he takes up his scalpel and divides the word into four parts, four species of love, only one of which he deems truly worthy of the splendor that, when we are in the proper mood for it, we want the word to radiate. Stendhal's four kinds of love are as follows: 1) *l'amour-passion* (43), passionate love, exemplified by the Portuguese Nun and by Heloise (but not, note, by Abelard) as well as by a nameless gendarme and a nameless captain. (It is curious that Stendhal balances his famous females with two anonymous males, as if he could not, or was reluctant to, supply well-known masculine representatives of what, even in *that* modern, post-Werther era, usually was regarded as a primarily female condition or complaint.) The author himself, moreover, throughout his book, has no choice but to present himself as an expert in passionate love, and the book's subtext, which glimmers not very far from its surface, verifies that expertise: the author is clearly constructing his paradigm of Real Love, his analysis of its labyrinths, its illusions and its imposters, from his own encounters with his own obsession, his—but she never in the slightest became his—Méthilde Dembowski. 2) *l'amour goût* (43), which "flourished in Paris about 1769," and is found in various "memoirs and novels of the period." Lovers who are gifted or beset with this style of lovemaking enact a kind of fashionable, very public parody of what is thought of as the real thing (that is, Love): they follow an erotic script which is shaped by "the demands of etiquette, good taste and delicacy." Whereas "passionate love carries us away against our real interests," this cafe-society variety of eros never does; what matters here is good theater and a plausible, nuanced, and decorous imitation of sincere passion. 3) *l'amour-physique* (43), sheer carnality, called 'love' by the very shy or the very hypocritical. Stendhal describes it thusly: "You are out hunting, you come across a handsome peasant girl [*belle et fraîche paysanne*] who takes to her heels through the woods, and however desiccated or miserable [*sec et malheureux*] you may be, there is where your love begins when you are sixteen." Pure animal spirits, then, casual, brief, serendipitous, utterly satisfying. It hardly deserves the connotations that 'lust' in the mouth of a puritan would confer on it, but Love it isn't either. Finally, there is 4) *l'amour de vanité* (43–44), vanity love. This imposter sometimes entails some sort of carnality, "but not always."

Though Stendhal doesn't say so, vanity love sometimes resembles *l'amour goût* since often it will, apparently, also make its appearance in public places: the term trophy-beloved can perhaps capture what is at stake here: "the great majority of men, specially in France, both desire and possess a fashionable woman, much in the way that one might own a fine horse." As an example of such a 'lover' from the distaff side he cites a "pretty young woman from the Hague who was quite unable to resist the charm of anyone who happened to be a duke or a prince, but if a prince came her way while she was enamored of a duke, she fell for the prince (she was rather like an emblem of seniority in the diplomatic corps!)." This 'insipid' species of love gains a certain degree of authenticity when physical love becomes habitual and gives rise to "memories, which in turn produce something that resembles true, passionate love." When this state is reached, "the atmosphere of romantic fiction catches you by the throat, and you believe yourself love-sick and melancholy, for vanity will always pretend to be grand passion." But sometimes, through "habit or despair" vanity love turns into a "friendship of the least attractive sort, which will boast of its *stability,* and so on" (emphasis in original).

If one were to evaluate the four species of love and rank them in respect of their worth, clearly passionate love, which will dominate the rest of this book, would win hands down. It would be followed by physical love, which is as harmless as it is healthy (at least as Stendhal represents it here at the outset) and which does not claim to be or even to resemble passionate love. Somewhat below natural carnality would come mannered, fashionable love, which is artificial, insincere, trivial, and (for Stendhal and his kind) deadly boring. But it, too, has the virtue of a sort of sincerity: it is transparently disengaged from the genuine emotions that constitute passionate love, and there is probably something admirable to be found in its devotion to the disciplined enactment of its fantasies, in its strict adherence to the rules of its game. That leaves the last place to vanity love, which is a perversion of genuine love in that, in order to achieve its ambition, it does its best to be mistaken for the real thing.

True love, then, shares some attributes with these other erotic categories which dispute with it the name of love, but it distinguishes itself from them by virtue of its intensity, its durations, its total willingness, its need, to persist, to grow and thrive despite any and all rejections, despite its utter failure to achieve the consummation it craves (and in fact rejection and failure are close to being its life's blood). When

Stendhal is trying to sum up his preliminary analysis of these varieties of 'love' at the end of his first chapter, he is driven to confess that his fourfold schema is too crude even to gesture toward the myriad subspecies of eros: "one might as well admit eight or ten distinctions. There are perhaps as many ways of feeling as there are of seeing." He insists that "every variety of love mentioned henceforth is born, lives, dies or attains immortality according to the same laws" (44). This conclusion suggests that a certain equality obtains among these four species and their countless subspecies, all of which can then be subsumed under the single word, 'love.' This notion is exactly contrary to what Stendhal has been arguing as he carefully distinguishes the characteristics of his four major categories. In fact his second chapter is devoted to his famous doctrine of crystallization, an explanation of the origins and evolution of love that is truly suitable only for passionate love.

"Here is what happens in the soul," says Stendhal. The lover admires a woman and fantasizes about kissing her, his fantasies inspire him with hope that they might somehow become realities, he begins to think that this splendid creature might come to reciprocate his desire. This is the moment of the first crystallization. By which he means: In the mines at Salzburg, when a tree branch is tossed into the diggings and is recovered a few months later, it is found to have been transformed beyond recognition. Each of its twigs has been covered with glittering crystals, as if by an infinity of diamonds that shift and dazzle as the light hits them. For the lover, crystallization is a process that takes place in his mind, a process in which everything that happens to him, everything that he experiences, produces for him new evidence of his beloved's perfection.

The first crystallization clearly has no essential connection with physical love (beyond those imaginary kisses), nor will it really manifest itself in the operation of mannered love or vanity love. In these 'loves,' the 'lovers' may pretend or imagine that they have undergone something like crystallization, but they have not. In passionate love, however, the process, though it might seem to the skeptic to be an illusion, actually takes place: that is to say, the passionate lover does not pretend that his perception of the beloved (and his identity and consciousness along with it) has been transformed (like the crystal bough); he really does think of nothing else but her, wherever he goes, whatever he sees or hears. He does not fake his responses, nor does he delude himself when he discovers that his idea of the beloved is constantly enduring a sort of automatic exponential magnification (and dazzling clarification). The physical lover will have no need of this elaborate mechanism in order to achieve the quick satisfaction he has in mind. The mannered lover is too interested in how he is doing (how he looks to his cultivated fellow players) to be worried about his feelings. And the vanity lover is not going to be dazzled or transformed by the value of the current trophy-prey he has fixed his sights on. These three categories of lover are immune to the doubt and anxiety that produce in the passionate lover a second crystallization, one in which, poised on a precipice, just in sight of the promised land, he finds himself "torn between doubt and delight" and "convinces himself that his beloved could give him such pleasure as he could find nowhere else on earth" (47) Only the passionate lover is consumed by these three ideas: 1) She is perfect; 2) she loves me; 3) how can I get the strongest proof of her love? After this first crystallization is complete, a second occurs: the passionate lover becomes subject to a dreadful moment when he realizes that he may in fact be mistaken about the truth of his passion or about the worth of his beloved, and he therefore decides that the crystal bough must be smashed to pieces, all his faith in the process of crystallization having been (temporarily) lost. But once this grave danger has passed and the second phase of crystallization is complete, this (true) love will persist (forever), for the lover knows that he must win the woman's love or perish: the thought of life without her is intolerable; indeed, the very thought of such an existence is all but unthinkable. True ('*véritable*') love (so Stendhal is now willing to call it, 96) "pervades the whole consciousness and fills it with pictures, some wildly happy, some hopeless, but all sublime; the love which blinds one to everything in the world."

Thus, despite his careful mappings of the spectrum of erotic behavior, Stendhal insists that there is one variety of 'love' that surpasses all others in value, in authenticity. This kind of love (passionate, true, real) is *not,* no matter what the merchants of roses and candy would have us believe as February 14 approaches, universal, nor, apparently, is it all that common at any time, in any place (though we may firmly believe that it is because we have been trained to confuse it with one or another of the erotic behaviors that seem to resemble it).

Having invoked Stendhal's help in approaching Propertius, it pains me to admit that he would doubtless disapprove of the use I am putting him to. For him, the kind of love he prizes came to Italy and to Provence from the Arabs by way of Moorish Spain (both its theory and its practice having been transported thence by music, poetry, lyric song; for a recent corroboration of his belief, see Goody, 125–26). Any occurrence of passionate love in modern times must, for Stendhal, have its roots in that complex of sources: Arabia, Spain, Provence. Even in the nineteenth century, just as Romanticism is gathering full force, True Love was still rare, in Stendhal's view, outside Italy and Spain (for instance, in France, Germany, England, and America, the national temperaments throw up huge obstacles against its development). In ancient Greece, moreover, Homer was ignorant of it, and for Sappho eros was purely physical (though somehow rendered sublime in her poetry by a strange sort of crystallization she can't be bothered to ponder: fragments 35 and 36 in Sales' translation, 223). As for ancient Rome, Stendhal seems willing to allow something like True Love in the poetry of Vergil (he cites Dido and Corydon), and, as an afterthought, he gives the nod to Dido's primary model, the Medea of Apollonius' *Argonautica* (fragment 94 in Sales' translation, 242).

When Stendhal turns to Tibullus, Propertius and Ovid, he praises them for having "better taste than our poets" (by which he presumably has in mind what he regards as the deficiencies in form, restraint and clarity that he finds in the poetry of his Romantic contemporaries?), and he congratulates the Romans for showing "love as it could have existed among the proud citizens" of ancient Rome. He seems to feel that Augustus subverted the erotic program of these poets when he sought to reduce (*ravaler*) Roman citizens to being mere subjects of his monarchy. Such an observation seems to suggest that these elegists had some experience with True Love and Real Passion, but as Stendhal continues his description of their poetry it turns out that the objects of their eros were "unfaithful and venal coquettes" from whom "they sought only physical pleasure, and I am inclined to believe that they never had an inkling of the sublime feelings which throbbed thirteen centuries later in the heart of tender Heloise" (236).

Stendhal then goes on to provide his readers with lively, not inaccurate sketches of the elegies of the three poets in question. Like Ovid, in his elegy for Tibullus, *Amores* 3.9, he is careful to ignore Tibullus' youthful male beloved, Maranthus, and, believing that Book 3 was written by the poet who wrote Books 1 and 2 (as was the received opinion in his time), he includes Neaera among Tibullus' "inconstant" female beloveds. In summing them all up, he awards first place (reasonably, to my mind) to Propertius' Cynthia (*parait la plus aimable*) "of all these women immortalized in the verse of the three great poets" (241). Charming she may be, and talented (for like the other elegiac ladies of her kind she knows how to sing, dance, and read poetry), but what interested her most were fun, wine, and money, whereas what interested Propertius, what enslaved him to her, was sheer carnal hankerings. Like Tibullus and Ovid, he was, aside from his lovely verses, just another well-off gentleman lusting after expensive whores, and he misses by miles the real passion that Abelard (whom Stendhal fails to mention) so perfectly incarnates.

In the erotic paradigm that Stendhal finds unsatisfactory and that he is busily engaged in replacing with his paradigm of crystalline love, the Roman elegists had provided powerful support for the existence of a universal (or at least European) tradition of romantic love, one that extended from ancient Greece, through ancient Rome, through the (Latin) Middle Ages, down to modern times. By demoting the Roman exponents of such a tradition to ordinary whoremongers (with a genius for versifying), Stendhal seeks to confirm the validity of his fourfold scheme: these three famous, now notoriously lecherous poets convince us, by the counterexample they furnish, that Stendhal's category of physical love is not identical with passionate love; thus bereft of its Roman linchpin, the European erotic tradition must give way to the Arabian tradition that Stendhal champions. In his eyes that tradition is not strictly European, nor is it universal (he takes no interest in erotic models in India, China, or Japan). Moreover, to call it a tradition is misleading because, after its emigration to Moorish Spain, it shows little in the way of development or evolution. Instead, there are rare and random occurrences of passionate lovers in times and places that are conducive, or at least not hostile, to the appearance on the scene of someone like the man whose life and work and soul would be crystallized by the ravishing and indifferent Méthilde Dembowski.

In that man, erotic matter and erotic mind were in perfect balance, had somehow achieved a dialectical harmony in which each renewed and strengthened the other. This equilibrium contrasted starkly with other erotic modes in which such fortunate symbiosis was defective or absent. In mannered love erotic instinct was put in the service of an intellectual enjoyment that had little or no need of carnal consummations. An exact reversal of this equation is displayed in physical love, where qualities of mind or spirit find themselves banished along with any concern that might intrude on the body's sexual gratification. In vanity love the spirit and the flesh are involved only incidentally, that is, only in so far as they are needed to assist in the pursuit of the trophies that will slake the social climber's ambitions (no matter whether the trophy is a duchess or a ballerina, a king or an actor) or that will confirm the aristocrat's claim to being the best by his or her having the best (the loveliest chorine, the hunkiest fullback). Only in passionate love do flesh and spirit, body and soul, matter and mind, discover a union that is at once possible and ideal. Needless to say, this union does not always (or ever) produce what the world calls happiness. But the ecstasies and sorrows of true love are both sublime. They and the refulgent identities they confer have no need of mere happiness.

I have paraphrased and commented on Stendhal's paradigm at such length because its subtle demystifications (and remystifications) of Love remind us to exercise some caution when we use the (for him) sacred word that is constantly on our lips and in our ears, particularly when we are talking about something as remote (yet seemingly graspable) as Roman love elegy. It would be cumbersome perhaps to talk of lust poetry or to constantly find ourselves distinguishing poetry produced about amorous games played in high society (or the freshman quad) from poetry produced about status seekers who enlarge their egos and their reputations by seducing living status symbols. But better to nitpick than to lump all the styles of love poetry together.

In the case of the Roman love elegists, when attempting to distinguish Propertius from the other poets who wrote various kinds of love poems, I will be making use of something like the erotic spectrum designed by Stendhal. I will be arguing that in his poems something like the mechanics of crystallization can be observed. I don't mean that these poems record the poet's actual experience (though I'm not entirely sure we have any valid proofs that they in no way make use of aspects of his own erotic identity), but rather that they record, comment on, and critique the fashions in erotic behavior that I have sketched in my previous chapter.

ST. AUGUSTINE READS DIDO

Another reader, much earlier than Stendhal, also singled out Dido as an emblem of Passionate Love. Augustine was an exquisite close reader of poetic texts, and he was also a fervent and indefatigable investigator of erotic phenomena. He encountered Dido—as many of us have—in the classroom (*Confessions,* 1.13). Looking back on that encounter, he describes and passes judgment on the memories of his emotions when he engaged with her. Who can be more wretched,

Augustine asks himself, recalling the ignorant (and sinful) young reader that he had been. Who could be more miserable than a reader who bewailed the fate of Dido, she who died for the love of Aeneas, yet would shed not a tear for himself as he sat there dying for his want of loving God? Apparently this tearful lamentation took the form of a successful recitation, for even as he committed fornications against God by loving Dido too much and God not at all, his audience (teacher, fellow students) commended him with cries of *euge, euge,* bravo, bravo! Augustine does not, he continues, weep for this vile and complex sin, the shutting out of God, sorrowing for an erotic female suicide, basking like a ham actor in the adulation of his fellow sinners. Instead he weeps for Dido, who surrendered her life to Aeneas' phallic sword. But that is not the worst of this dreadful Dido business: at times when he was forbidden to read the *Aeneid* and other such books he grieved at being unable to peruse what caused him grief, that grief being his obsession with the sublime—and abysmal—erotics that mark his late adolescence and early manhood, the obsession for which Dido had presented him with a forceful, enduring. and cruelly seductive model.

In later years, when he is beginning to move toward God, Augustine will, paradoxically, shirk all his allegiance to the grand and fatal passions as they are represented by Dido (and, more obliquely, by Aeneas himself) and will instead content himself with embracing the grand renunciation of Aeneas. The nameless woman with whom he had lived for seven years (4.2) and who had borne him a son is finally sent packing (6.15). As his mother, St. Monica, sees it, his concubine is the real obstacle to the marriage she yearns for her too wayward son to contract with someone suitable, some decent Christian girl from the right background, of the proper social standing (and gifted with a decent bank account: this speculation, witty, malicious, and shrewd is that of West, 49). When Augustine first describes how this misalliance came into being, he suggests that his reason for choosing to take up with this woman was all but happenstance: she was a convenience he had stumbled on when searching for something to ease his itch. But out of the aftermath of his random lust there developed a surprising (and for St. Monica an irritating) monogamy, from which in turn was produced a son. Against all odds, he finds himself ensconced in something very like a loving wedlock with the woman who had taught him how to be a father.

St. Monica was not of the same mind. When she sends her son's common-law wife back where she came from ("she was torn from my side," *avulsa a latere meo,* 6.15; trans. Pine-Coffin, 131), Augustine confesses that this "was a blow which crushed my heart to bleeding, because I loved her dearly," *cor ubi adhaerebat, concisum et vulneratum mihi erat et trahebat sanguinem.* He does not leave her, then; rather, she, forced by her mother-in-law to leave him, goes back to Africa, alone, without her son, vowing never to give herself to another man. Augustine has no such strength of character and soon finds he cannot wait out the two years until his fiancée is ready to marry him. Not a lover of marriage but a slave to lust, he takes a new mistress, but this remedy proves useless. "The wound I had received when my mistress was wrenched away showed no sign of healing. At first the wound was sharp and searing, but then it began to fester, and though the pain was duller, there was all the less hope of a cure" (6.15).

Note here the fascinating ambiguity in Augustine's medical imagery. The wound that cannot heal by sustained application of further fornication is, on one level, his propensity to lust, but, on another, deeper level, the wound is the wound of Dido: because "I loved her dearly." The wound is lust, but it is also his banished, his murdered love. In regretting that he could not follow his beloved's virtuous vow of chastity, he says, *at ego infelix nec feminae imitator,* "unhappy I, who had not the heart to imitate a woman" (6.15; in the charming translation by William Watts, 1631). But in a peculiar way, of course, he is imitating his mistress (and Dido) even as he finds himself in the awkward situation of Aeneas (a man who is also forced to give up the woman he loves for the sake of God's plan and the city of God). To give up all for love, to yield oneself to another is (in ancient Greece and Rome) a female failing (or prerogative); the same behavior (or choice) in a man is effeminate. A real man must do the manly thing and accept, among many losses, the loss of the woman he loves (even as Aeneas did). But in his man's body, Augustine bears a never-healing wound (never, until God's love heals it), a woman's kind of love. It was Dido who taught him, as she was to teach countless others through the centuries, that love, even, especially, luckless love, is forever.

In Augustine's case (nor is his case all that rare), what began as lust ended as love. Very much of the power of Augustine's memoirs of his journey to God derives from the honesty with which he portrays the violence of his sexual needs, and not a little of that power, in turn, is furnished by that peculiar transition from horny guy to sober, loving, almost-married man. Though Augustine himself might want to deny it, he passed, unconsciously, imperceptibly, from being a feckless addict of physical love to becoming an adult male blessed by passionate monogamy (a category ignored by Stendhal, who regards it as something of an oxymoron, since in his eyes passion and marriage are incompatible goods). That was the saint's jagged progress toward earthly happiness until God and Monica rescued him from the path onto which Dido had helped divert him. But what concerns us here is that Augustine, this peculiar fusion of Dido and Aeneas, is among the earliest and best of Dido's close readers, reminding us, in unforgettable prose, of the role that Dido would play down through the ages, whenever poets and their readers set about reconfiguring the nature of passionate (reckless, lawless) love for themselves and their own times.

WHERE DIDO CAME FROM: PHAEDRA AND MEDEA

Before Dido there were countless legends (in Greek life and literature) of beautiful, passionate, faithful (and faithless) women. How did this Roman latecomer to the long catalogue of 'women in love' manage to command and keep the supreme rank Vergil obtained for her?

She was, in a very simple sense, in the right place at the right time. Vergil's epic concerns itself with the exploits of Aeneas, founding father of the Roman empire, but its core, its pervasive subtext, is the triumph of Augustus Caesar over his rivals, a victory that brought lasting peace to the world that Rome had conquered and that, in its later transformations, provided Christian Europe with some of its most essential ideologies. Vergil and his Augustus were lucky to have found one another, the one having been inspired (or coerced) by a monumental topic, the other, perhaps the luckier of the two, having been blessed with the arrival of a monumental poet. Dido and her love story found themselves, then, in a poem that bore witness to a crucial hinge of European history, and they hitched a ride with Vergil's world-historical epic, a poem destined to endure through the centuries, as heirs of Augustus, the kings and popes who patterned their reigns on his, saw to it that the guardians of language and culture kept the *Aeneid* at the center of their curricula and their endeavors. Bad example though she was as a spectacular advertisement for the glamorous subversion of erotic taboos (a fact that did not escape the notice of young Christopher Marlowe), Dido was part and parcel of the imperial manifesto. As long as rulers offered Aeneas and Augustus as their warrants for power, the ruined queen would continue to represent the dangers (and exaltations) of loves that were illicit and attractive in equal measure.

Before Vergil got hold of her, Dido was no more than a name from an obscure, all but mythical moment in the history of Carthage. Neither myth nor history provided her with any of the vitality that Vergil was to endow her with. Much of that vitality he borrowed from the Medea of Apollonius' *Argonautica;* she in turn had lifted some of her intensity and some of her conflicted self-scrutiny from the Phaedra of Euripides. Or from some of his other erotic heroines (whom Aristophanes sniggers at in his *Frogs,* 849f., 1042f.), all but a few of whom have disappeared, leaving behind them little more than their names. What we do know is that in Phaedra, grievously and fatally smitten with her stepson, Hippolytus, we encounter a woman who displays something new in Greek literature.

What was new about Phaedra? The Helen of the *Iliad* is the disenchanted victim of a passion whose destructive powers she became the instrument of, whose sinister influence she knows well and loathes. In her great scene in Book 3 (379–417), when she attempts to withstand the force of Aphrodite's will even as we see her succumbing to it, she mirrors, in her shame and confusion, the strong disapproval that her elopement with Paris has occasioned both in the city she left behind and in the city to which Paris has brought her. What she has met with is the insuperable force that Sophocles describes in his Fragment 94: Cypris, Aphrodite, mother of Eros, a power and a presence ubiquitous throughout the world of nature, an entity that appears in many disguises, has many names (Hell, immortality, insanity, unmitigated lust); she eats at the innards of anything that breathes, fish in the sea, animals on dry land, even the gods in heaven; she is truly omnipresent and omnipotent; she is beyond good and evil. That is the pitiless power that takes hold of Helen. Yet when we encounter her later in the *Odyssey,* back home in Sparta, safe and contented, her shame now all but vanished, she mentions the goddess' intrusion into her life (long ago) almost in passing, a sort of charming footnote to her story, her adventures abroad. The goddess Calypso (*Odyssey* 5.118–44) gives no evidence of being ashamed of her love for the hero whom Zeus forces her to let go of. She grieves at his going, but quickly assents to Zeus' commands, helps her lover prepare for his departure and sends him, almost serenely, on his way. But dispossessed of her will, forced to return to the bed of Paris by Aphrodite, what the *Iliad*'s Helen feels is impotence and shame; what she does not feel is guilt.

The feelings and thoughts she may have had as she left Sparta for Troy Homer leaves unrepresented. The speech or scene that would have represented Helen in that crucial moment of her existence is merely a transparent backstory in the *Iliad,* and beyond that such a speech or scene was alien to Homer's art and to his audience's interests. Helen had done a bad thing, a thing of which she was (quite properly) ashamed (bad but perfectly comprehensible: a goddess made her do it). What she had thought or felt while doing the bad thing (whatever qualms or hesitations might have flickered through her mind as Paris unfurled the sails of their loveship) was beside the point, uninteresting, irrelevant.

The scene that is missing from Homer turns up, magnified and magnificent, in Euripides' *Hippolytus.* For just over four hundred lines (121–534) Euripides not only dramatizes the grim dilemma confronting Phaedra (she has fallen in love with her stepson), but he also contrives to put us inside the workings of her mind at the same time as we are watching her as she tries to communicate with (and escape from) the world outside her (the Nurse, the Chorus). We are able to see her, then, from without and from within. This means that we can steadily understand (and feel) her conflicts from her perspective (until, as the play progresses to its catastrophe, the sufferings of Theseus and Hippolytus compel us to add their perspectives to hers). Loving her stepson (more than a stepmother should) means, if she cannot shake this passion from her, the ruin of her own life, of the lives around her, and, probably of the realm whose queen she is. Phaedra feels shame about the situation she finds herself in, to be sure, but she feels other emotions as well, and it is her complex and brave struggle to work through that mess of incompatible needs, desires, and values that makes her so suitable a pattern for Dido.

When we first encounter her, Phaedra is speaking (and singing and dancing?) a lyric poem about her desire to join her stepson as companion, to hunt out in the pure, natural, green world where, ardent devotee of the chaste goddess of the hunt, Artemis, that he is, he hunts wild beasts. This lyric delirium (she is sleepless, she refuses food) allows Phaedra to displace—or try to—her forbidden lust with chaster, healthier desires (but of course she wants to be out there, in the unspoiled, unpeopled wilderness, alone, with the object of her affections: a complex, oxymoronic sublimation that only the intricacies of lyric song can permit her to attempt). When she wakes from her delirium the Nurse and the Chorus, anxious for what seems to them a severe sickness, try to question her as to its causes. Phaedra attempts to fend off these questions, but she finally allows the Nurse to squeeze the unspeakable truth out of her. Then commences her effort to 'explain' to the Nurse and the Chorus (and herself) the causes of her sickness and to speculate on its progress and its possible remedies. But before she offers them a lengthy summary of the intellectual probings that have issued in her decision to kill herself (373–440), while still trying to evade the Nurse's interrogations, she says a curious thing. The Nurse, by now suspecting that Phaedra may be guilty of some terrible crime, asks her: "But, my child, your hands—your hands are not stained with blood?" (316). Phaedra's answer is famously ironic and somewhat obscure: "My hands are clean, but my *phren* (my heart, my mind, my reason: my bodysoul) has been polluted" (with worse than blood). This may not yet be the language of guilt (Europe would have to wait for Christians to supply it with that addition to its moral toolkit in its perfected form), but it is not the language of shame either. (Compare this moment with a similar one, *Orestes,* 396, where the hero fumbles to invent the idea of 'conscience,' *sunesis*—and with it the idea of guilt—as he tries to explain to his uncle how he feels about killing his mother.)

Phaedra has not yet done anything wrong (had she done so and it had got about, her feeling shame would be inevitable). But she still feels as if she had done the bad thing and she is fearful that she will do it. Furthermore, she does not live in Helen's world (or Sappho's where Aphrodite, though still terrifying, can be supplicated to become one's 'ally' in the bittersweet battle of love[2]). Or rather, she thinks she doesn't live in Helen's world. She thinks she lives in a rational society where good women make rational choices and know how to keep their instincts strictly under control. In other words, Phaedra thinks that she has real choices that she can really make (good ones, bad ones), and she feels that she has the capacity to make the good (right) choice. But she also thinks (she *knows*) that "we mortals understand and know what is good and proper, but we don't succeed in doing what we know we should do" (380–81). She proceeds to offer an elaborate, rather messy, and unconvincing explanation for this general failure of rational humans to put their knowledge at the service of their behavior. She wants to sleep with her stepson, and she knows that she mustn't (shouldn't), and she also knows that unless something stops her she will probably try to do just that.

2. See Goff's elegant sketch of Greek erotic theory for this period in Greek culture, 28–29.

What Phaedra—she who prizes rational morality so highly—doesn't know is that she does in fact live in the same world that Helen (and Sappho) lived in, the exhilarating and perilous world in which Aphrodite and her son Eros were, at many times and in all places, the most powerful of gods. She doesn't understand that the rational morality she reveres and trusts in is essentially illusory when Aphrodite enters the equation.³ In this tragedy Aphrodite is even scarier than she was in the *Iliad*. In the tragedy's opening speech the goddess reveals her plan to punish the puritanical stepson for dishonoring her (while overvaluing her rival, Artemis) and, using an economy of effort, she has decided to force Phaedra to accomplish her vengeful design. Though Phaedra worships her and has even built a temple for her, and though Aphrodite herself feels rather friendly to Phaedra, she does not care enough for her to exempt her from the ruin she is about to inflict on Hippolytus.

Ignorant of what Aphrodite has done to her, Phaedra nevertheless has more than an inkling that her passion for Hippolytus will occasion some sort of ruin for her or others whether she acts on it or not. In order to ward off that ruin or to mitigate it she had pondered several solutions to her 'problem' (391–402): 1) to keep silent about it; 2) to master it through self-discipline; 3) to kill herself. The first solution she dismisses because she sees that it doesn't help, indeed it aggravates, the mental torment her passion causes her. The second solution (another attempt at repression) is dropped because she has learned through bitter experience that she is wholly incapable of such self-reform. The third, suicide, is all that is left to her. And that is why she has embarked on self-starvation. All these remedies have been examined, Phaedra says, with an eye to keeping her good name good, for she would, she claims, be overwhelmed with shame if her secret should get out. Many of her readers seem take her at her word, finding that her reputation is more important to her than her chastity. But Phaedra's worries are manifold. It bothers her that she is the daughter of Pasiphae, who mated with a bull, and that she may therefore be, like her mother, inclined (inevitably) to illicit couplings. She frets about what will happen to the children she bore to her husband, Theseus (she doesn't want them to share her punishment or her shame or to be somehow denied their royal prerogatives). Given all these worries, no wonder she has elected self-extinction.

3. For a different, interesting reading of Phaedra's self-deceptions, see Hartigan, 44–51, 67.

But what makes Phaedra argue with herself (and try to explain herself to the world) is the guilt she feels for a passion that frightens her, sickens her, and exalts her. And something else rankles, deeper than shame or maternal anxieties or concerns for the body politic or even guilt. She cannot give up the idea of loving (and being loved by) her stepson. When the Nurse offers her the alternative to the suicide that would preserve her reputation (whether it is a love charm to drug the young man into submission or a remedy for Phaedra's sickness is unclear), after a brief effort to stop her, Phaedra lets her Nurse go off in order to carry out her fatal scheme. Torn, shredded by her conflicts with world, self, and a power she cannot comprehend, Phaedra wants to live and love in spite of everything that tells her she must not. Her excruciating self-analysis reveals the anomalies and the ferocious power of the erotic imperative more fully and more forcefully than anything that had gone before it. It is ready for Dido, but not quite.

Part elegantly condensed epic, part witty burlesque of Homer and of a recently expired, no longer feasible heroic genre, the *Argonautica* presents us with a teenage girl who, struck by an arrow from the bow of Eros, falls in love with Jason, a gorgeous, bumbling young man who has voyaged to her country to fetch the Golden Fleece and take it back with him to Greece. Medea's dilemma, her need to choose between filial devotion to her father, the king, and her new passion (if she uses her witchcraft to aid her feckless lover get hold of the fleece, she must defy her father), is compounded by her total inexperience in matters erotic. Much of the fascination and verisimilar power of Apollonius' portrait of the conflicted young virgin in love derives from how he converts her initial naïveté, through carefully modulated stages, into the final clarities of her self-awareness when she claims her beloved and betrays her father. Her wounding by the love god Eros, which is depicted with a deft artifice that calls emphatic attention to itself, is essentially a plot device conjured up from epical and mythological conventions. It does not explain Medea's passion; it merely sets it in narrative motion. The poet's main concern is with inventing a plausible psychological evolution of his inexperienced heroine's feelings—and her thoughts about her feelings. Once he has established the depth and intensity of her attraction to Jason and his masculine beauty (she has no interest in his mind—one thinks here perhaps of the Julie Brown song, "I Like 'Em Big and Stupid") what concerns Apollonius most is Medea's anxiety about filial devotion endangered by the idiocentric desire that threatens it. These desires are clearly erotic on the surface, but they are fueled by needs at once more complex and more hidden that those that physical passion can account for.

As the narrative unfolds, as Medea flees her native land with Jason and the fleece, as she voyages away to Greece (finding it necessary, on the way, to murder, in a very nasty way, the brother who pursued her), it becomes ever more apparent that what Jason symbolizes to her is escape from her country and from parental authority. What Jason and Greece offer her is emigration from a barbarous backwater and entrance into a civilized society worthy of her intelligence and gifts. What leaving Colchis behind means to Medea is the promise of freedom and a new identity. This theme, in which the erotic merges into and is replaced by the desire, the need, for individuation, for freedom to become what one is, will become in the hands of Ovid a powerful meditation on the meaning of authentic selfhood. In the stories of Scylla, Medea, Byblis, and Myrrha, tragic though they are (except for Ovid's young Medea), a young woman's transgressive passion, though it ends by propelling her toward ruin, illumines for her the possibility of freedom and validates the truth, the rightness, of her desire. The erotic in these stories is revealed as being selfish, but at the same time it is approved of: it reveals the narrowness of a female's life in a patriarchal home and it gestures toward feminine (read, human) life somewhere (as yet undiscovered) outside, beyond, the patriarchal circumference.

These are the two chief literary sources for Vergil's portrait of a woman passionately in love (and one who meets the stringent criteria of Stendhal). Unlike Medea, Dido does not sail off with her beloved, alone, alienated from the society that had become too small for her. A queen in her own right, possessed of an independence and an authority that Phaedra lacks, she is nevertheless circumscribed by a patriarchal sign system that has grown too small for her and her desire.

CATULLUS AND ARIADNE (AND LESBIA AND JUVENTIUS AND MELEAGER)

Dido has one final forebear, one who stands for a class of 'lost ladies' from the poetic generation just before Vergil's, one of those 'neurotic' women in love (to use a now rather old-fashioned label that connotes well enough a quality crucial to this species of dysfunction which comprises the women, and the men, who appear in Parthenius' *Erotika*

Pathemata). A few decades before Dido, when Vergil was just emerging from adolescence, Catullus invented his Ariadne (poem 64). In passing, I must note that Stendhal doesn't include Catullus and his Ariadne among the Roman purveyors of erotic poetry, probably because, in his time, Catullus was only beginning to be thought of as a writer of love lyric. Until the late nineteenth, early twentieth century, the Renaissance model, which Stendhal would have been most familiar with, was firmly in place: Martial's Catullus, writer of epigrams, was acerbic, elegant, political, filthy. The fact that both Propertius and Ovid give him a prominent place, along with Calvus, in their list of elegiac models, was ignored by his readers from the time of his late medieval recovery down to the time when he was pried loose from the clutches of textual critics by Byron and the poets who followed his lead. Emphasizing Catullus' tender broken-heartedness, they began to trace the progress of his passion and his entire life from a handful of what they regarded as his lyric effusions.[4] Only once the hierophants of the Higher Criticism have lost their prey do Ariadne and her erotic sufferings begin to take stage center, where she will remain, even after Romantic Catullus and his opaque life story begin yielding to Alexandrian Catullus, the art-for-art's-sake poetic dandy who, in his metapoetic incarnation, still fascinates us.

Ariadne, abandoned by her treacherous lover, Theseus, whom she had saved from the Minotaur in the fatal labyrinth, is allotted sixty-nine shimmering verses, about a third of the poem (64) whose center she is. In these verses she declaims (to no one in particular) the depth of the despair into which her perjured passion has made her plummet. Unlike Dido, she is less a representation of a human female caught in extreme circumstances than a richly mannered, exquisitely crafted composition of topoi that suit what the kind of woman in this kind of situation would say. What she did for Vergil was to provide him with a superb pattern for what this new kind of (operatic) tirade should sound like when fitted to the new style of 'modern' Latin verse. When Vergil had perfected the verse form Ariadne used, given it greater polish, more fluency, a subtler register, what she says and how she says it could easily be purloined by his Dido.[5]

---

4. For the pre-romantic Catullus, see Gaisser, *passim*; for a thorough defabrication of 'tender' Catullus, one that focuses on his talent for macho invective, see Wray, *passim;* for Byron and the nineteenth century Lesbia, see Vance, 115–18; see also Arkins 2007, 461–78.

5. For the erotic significance of Catullus' other long poems, see Skinner 1997 and Johnson 2007, 183–86, 188.

Catullus' Lesbia, on the other hand, famous though she is as erotic icon, is of little help to Dido. For us Lesbia is, as she has been for two centuries, a beguiling image, the more seductive for being so evasive, so indistinct, of the femme fatale. Helped by the lingering gossip that identified her with Clodia, the aristocratic lady notorious by virtue of Cicero's indelible malice, for Vergil's contemporaries Lesbia was, except perhaps her evocation in the haunting poem 68, mostly a creature of epigram, a female charming and vitriolic by turns, one whom they recreated—as we do—out of the emotions that the poet represented himself as suffering or enjoying because of her whims and moods. Lesbia doesn't talk in Catullus' poems, she doesn't act, she figures only obliquely in scenes that suggest an indistinct story, though many of us can't resist evoking sturdier narratives for her to stride or saunter through. We do this because we want her to make a narrative for Catullus to inhabit along with her, because we want those poems to gather themselves up into a satisfying unity, thus helping to rescue Catullus' poems from what seems the botched, random ordering of the text we have. That decomposition, paradoxically, is part of their charm, for they seem such vivid slices of *la vie romaine,* so persistently and ostentatiously 'in the moment'—rather like the snapshots offered by Frank O'Hara of cosmopolitan life in New York City and its version of Hollywood.[6] But when we read and reread them, we strive to find the pattern they seem bent on hiding, and such efforts provide us with a sort of entertainment beyond that offered by the poems themselves. Lesbia has, in short, no depth to her, she is at least as vague (and addictive) as Marcel's Albertine, and therefore, because she has no story, because we have no notion whatever of *her* perspective on Catullus, she gives Dido no help, because, in a sense, Dido is all story, all stream-of-(un)consciousness. In large measure, though they may have ignored his long poems unfairly, Renaissance readers were correct in assessing where his center lay. If you set aside the long poems and concentrate at their beginning and their end, what Catullus writes is a sort of *vers de société.* What that means is, when he is not producing pictures of the passing scene or commenting on poetry or politics but is instead talking of love, he is, erotically speaking, essentially a poet of *amour de goût* and *amour de vanité.* And that means that, even for a well-bred, well-heeled young man from the provinces Clodia was the most glittering of trophy-mistresses, a very top prize

---

6. For a stimulating commentary on the poems, see Le Sueur's eyewitness account of their contexts and their composition.

in the game of love as it was being played just as Caesar and Pompey were getting ready to square off against each other, just as a teenage Gallus was reading Catullus and Calvus and dreaming of someone like Volumnia/Cytheris, who would presently become his Lycoris, his toy, his trophy and his *vita mea*.

Still less helpful to Dido than Lesbia was Catullus' Juventius. The poems to and about Juventius transform their Greek models (about beloved boys) by making the beloved in question, Juventius, a Roman citizen, a young man about to become an adult citizen. If the poet's adolescent erotic (penetrated) partner had been a slave or a foreigner, there would have been no transgression of the Roman code. Juventius, however, is not Greek, not a slave, but a Roman, perhaps from a distinguished family, and he is, such is the play on his name, in possession of, or about to be in possession of, a beard. What these poems said to Catullus' contemporary male readers is: "I'm going to screw your son—in fact, we're already lovers, just the way the great Greeks of ages past were lovers (and as today's Greeks still are). He may seem a bit young for this sort of thing, but that's better than if he were a bit older, when you come to think of it. I know this relationship—my fervent attraction to your son, a Roman male on the verge of becoming an adult Roman male—may strike you as surprising, even as shocking, but it's a new style of living and loving that's just come to town. It's probably here to stay. Get used to it."

How fashionable it was in fact (or not) is unknowable and, for our purposes, beside the point. But by the time that Catullus and his poetic companions had come on the scene, Meleager's delicate, erotic emphasis on inwardness and rapturous union with the beloved and applicable to love objects of either sex, was ready waiting for them.[7] In its same-sexual guise, this borrowing from Greek culture (and Alexandrian poetics) has become so visible that (as we saw in Cicero's attacks on Antony) it has become part of the common erotic repertoire and figures prominently in both Horace and Tibullus (but it is worth noting that both Propertius and Ovid will acknowledge, almost apologetically, that they are not smitten with boys). In Catullus, however, the delicacy that tends to grace Meleager's pederastic love epigrams, its penchant for soulfulness, gives way to something edgier, more purely carnal. Catullus' poems to or about Juventius depict not so much desire as jealousy; he seems as much

---

7. See the subtle and precise readings of Meleager and his predecessors by Garrison, especially 74–87.

interested in competing for Juventius as he is in possessing him.⁸ This gentler side of pederasty, which Catullus ignores and Meleager refines, owes something perhaps to Plato's charming cartoon in the *Symposium,* where lovers learn to lessen their letchings in order to fatten their spirits, but it is taken very seriously by Aristotle when he uses same-sex sexual devotion as an example of what best defines the intensity and the rarity of true friendships: "Presumably . . . it is not well to seek out to have as many friends as possible, but as many as are enough for the purpose of living together; for it would seem impossible to be a great friend to many people. This is why one cannot love many people; love is ideally a sort of excess of friendship, and that can only be felt toward one person; therefore great friendship can only be felt towards a few people" (*Nichomachean Ethics,* Book 9.10; 1171a; trans. Ross). Aristotle then proceeds to remark that "the famous friendships of this sort are always between two people."

The species of super-friendship that Aristotle describes, its all-consuming intensities and its tenderness, was ignored by Catullus when he imported pederasty into the repertoire of Roman poetry. But, tinged with some of Meleager's delicate yearning for erotic harmony, it found its perfect (and incongruous) poetic incarnation in Vergil's muted celebration of the Roman Empire. His Nisus and Euryalus, the feckless young warriors who rush off into the night to seize glory only to discover their shared doom, are nothing if not fervent in their commitment to one another. Same-sex passion has seldom enjoyed a more successful artistic representation than the one that the poet of the *Aeneid* bestows on it when he provides it with the glamorous (and sentimental) catastrophe that these lovers disappear into. But doomed though they are, their love is not anguished or unrequited. In this they differ emphatically from the other men or women in love whom Vergil imagines.

CORYDON (AND GALLUS)

The poet who created Dido knew a lot about thwarted or unrequited love (which is probably why Stendhal singles him out from all the ancients, except for Apollonius and his Medea). When I say that he *knew* about such love I don't mean to imply that such knowledge came to

---

8. See Arkins 1982, 107; Wray, 73.

him from his personal experience of which we know, aside from gossip we cannot trust, nothing. Poets tend to get much of what they know from other poets whose work they are always pillaging and hoping to improve on—such is that blend of theft and rivalry that perhaps best defines the poetic career. Having granted all that, one is left with the fact that Vergil is remarkably fascinated with those who are unlucky in love and is also remarkably skillful in portraying such lovers. He likes to depict, he likes to imagine, what it feels like to lose what one loves; he likes to contemplate, to meditate on, what it is like to put all one's eggs in the erotic basket, and then to drop that basket or have it snatched out of one's hands (a situation whose significance Dryden cleverly italicized when he revised Shakespeare's sublime version of Antony and Cleopatra as *All for Love, Or The World Well Lost*). Dido is the greatest of Vergil's creations in this mode, but she has predecessors and analogues elsewhere in his poetry, and these are worth a brief glance before we try summing her up, before we attempt to evaluate how she and her beloved reflect both the social milieu in which they appeared and the elegiac project to which they contributed some of their torment and their sparkle.

As we saw, Stendhal eschews notice of Corydon's sexual preference. He ignores the fact that Corydon's model, Theocritus' Polyphemus (*Idyll* 11), is straight. Vergil's shift in the sex of his obsession intensifies the erotic suffering that the original captures so artfully by adding transgression (Romanly speaking) to what was sufficiently bizarre: excessive grief over sexual frustration is funny in the Greek version where the monster's naive misunderstanding of his severe handicaps in the game of love provides his laments with a charming dissonance since we feel for him even as we smile at his delusions and his plight. In Eclogue 2, though we are manipulated into feeling some empathy for poor Corydon, we are aware that his complaints issue from a situation that is not only *contra mores* (real men are not supposed to get that upset over a mere turn-down since there are plenty more where that came from) but also *contra naturam* since Roman men don't screw that way, romantically rather than lustfully (the names and the genre are Greek, but the language is Latin and the puritan codes embedded in it are Roman). Some readers may not feel pity for Corydon, but few will mock his desperation. His excess is irremediable, and his anxiety seems likely to push him steadily toward despair. Polyphemus will probably never quite give up hope of someday being loved by some girl, hopeless though his present case may be. But we don't believe Corydon when he echoes Polyphemus' brave trust in the future: when he cries out, *invenies alium, si te hic fastidit, Alexim,* "You will find another Alexis if this one scorns you." Corydon's monologue, unlike its model, has no framing narrator to insist that, whatever Polyphemus' future luck with the ladies may be, his song, his poetry, brought him relief no money could buy. But Corydon's song, or his tirade, does not put an end to his pain. The line we most remember from his poem is not the final one in which he states his impossible dream (another Alexis), but his cry of anguish four lines before: *a, Corydon, Corydon, quae te dementia cepit,* "O Corydon, Corydon, what madness has taken over you?" He looks about him and sees that his work—and his life—is undone. His love is transgressive (in Rome), and that transgression, instead of liberating him from a meaningless, banal existence (which is the promise of the elegiac ideology), has ruined what life he had and left him in despair. He has all the grief of crystallization, and none of its rewards. In his intensity, his isolation, his obsession, he foreshadows not a little of what Dido will perfect.

Another literary ingredient in the concoction from which Dido will be distilled is the figure of Gallus, as he appears in Vergil's Eclogue 10, the poem that provides his pastorals with their valedictory closure. Judging from the next to nothing we have, Gallus is the pivotal figure in the evolution of the genre, the forms and feelings, of Roman love elegy.[9] Taking what he needed from Catullus and Calvus, and combining those materials with the themes and emotions that he found in Parthenius' little collection of tales of miserable love affairs, he constructed around his beloved Lycoris (who figured so prominently in our previous chapter) a series of poems (very probably not designed as a chronological narrative) in which the spectrum of a lover's experience (from splendor to misery) with a beautiful woman who was as desirable as she was capricious and unkind. This production becomes the model for the poets who take up the genre a half-generation later, in the 20's BCE, just as Gallus, taking a holiday from poetry, goes off to Egypt on the emperor's business and manages (the details here present a tantalizing blank) to make so much of a mess of his career that he decides, perhaps at the emperor's suggestion, to fall on his sword rather than return to Rome and explain himself.[10] In the poem that Vergil shapes around him, he is still an elegiac love poet of mythic stature, suddenly transported from the gaudy, bawdy city where elegy thrives best to Vergil's version of the pastoral landscape, where shepherds bewail their amorous misfortunes

---

9. See the helpful discussion by Crowther, 1639–44.
10. See Dettenhofer, 93–95; Janan, 51–52.

sweetly. So an elegant pastiche of Gallus' complaint to Lycoris is transformed into pastoral measures, with pastoral pictures and pastoral moods to fill them. The result is a delightful, delicately amusing evocation of the elegiac project and the erotic delights and erotic anxieties that sustain it. Gallus, the warrior-lover, becomes a creature of complex artifice, one that his creator both admires and adoringly mocks. When he ends his plaint with the famous *omnia vincit amor, et nos cedamus amori,* 69 ("Love conquers all things, and let us also surrender to Love"), we don't quite believe the solace that the warrior's capitulation offers himself and us, but we have a strong sense of the ideal, the anxious ideal, of self-abnegation that Roman elegy is rooted in (anxious, because men, Roman men, and Roman soldiers in particular, are not supposed to surrender themselves to anyone, least of all women). But if we are not persuaded by Gallus' concluding testament, we feel more confidence in Vergil's own admission which follows immediately on Gallus' final word. Vergil has been writing this poem (and perhaps this entire collection) for Gallus, for his approval, perhaps as a kind of love gift (for which, see Johnson 1984):

> haec sat erit, divae, vestrum cecinisse poetam
> dum sedet et gracili fiscellam texit hibisco,
> Pierides. vos haec facietis maxima Gallo,
> Gallo, cuius amor tantum mihi crescit in horas,
> quantum vere novo viridis se subiecit alnus.

> For the time being, Holy Muses, it will be
> Sufficient that I, your poet, have sung these
> Verses as I sat here, weaving from delicate hibiscus
> This little basket. And these verses you will make
> Splendid for Gallus, for Gallus whom I hourly
> Grow to love as surely as the green alder begins
> Its flourishing with the coming of spring. (10.70–74)

The gift of the basket holding all these verses is small but exquisite. The poet begs the Muses to enlarge them in the eyes of Gallus, make them great, because Gallus is worthy of the love that grows (crystallizes) in the poet's mind, as surely as the world each spring grows green. Did Gallus return that love? We hardly know whether he did, or in what degree or in what kind. What we sense, though, is that the poet's love is so sure and so pure that it requires no reciprocation. That is a love well beyond, or at least different from, Dido's, of course, but perhaps there is, for all its calm self-effacement, some hidden ache in it, a love that couldn't happen or be returned. (It is also hidden perhaps not far beneath the surface of Vergil's definitive retelling of the story of how Orpheus lost his Eurydice forever; this brilliant version of the primal poet's tragic loss was rumored to have replaced the celebration of Gallus which originally closed his fourth *Georgic,* a celebration that Gallus' contretemps with Augustus rendered impossible.) In any case, the theme and the tone, the undersongs, of this final eclogue signal that, against the grain of its pastoral genre, it is, like the poet-lover whom it addresses, at once a product and a reflection of the erotic fashion I have sketched in my first chapter. But, aside from the love elegies that represent that fashion more directly, it finds its most vivid and most unforgettable incarnation in the figure of Dido.

DIDO (AND AENEAS) IN LOVE

She passes every test that Stendhal could set for her, she embodies crystallization. This perfection results from a complex configuration of several dissimilar ingredients. For one, she is the culmination (in antiquity) of the literary models that she borrows from; of these, those provided by Euripides and Apollonius are the most powerful, but she draws also on hints that Meleager, Catullus, and Calvus (and probably Gallus) offered her. Second, she is designed, to no inconsiderable extent, with her contemporary readers in mind, Roman men and women who know both her literary sources and who have some direct experience, in their own erotic encounters, of the erotic codes that she herself relies on. Finally, there is the question of her place (her somewhat anomalous, curiously central place) in an epic that uses Homeric forms to glorify Roman imperialism and the patriarchal virtues and values that called it into existence; a poem that contradicts, at every turn, her erotic identity, and that wants nothing so much as her annihilation. In this it succeeds, for of course she does away with herself—exactly as the poem's plot and Rome's destiny require her to do. But it also fails of its desire, because she has proved herself as forceful (and as perdurable) as the curses she hurls at Rome just before she takes hold of her lover's sword and climbs onto her funeral pyre. She bestows on the first third of Rome's national epic its heartbreaking and dazzling finale, and the concise acceleration of her story, through all its states of exaltation, anxiety, anger, and grief, together with the severe elegance of its construction, gift the poem with perhaps its most finished, most satisfying section. Playwrights and composers (Marlowe and Purcell chief among them) are naturally attracted to *Aeneid* 4 because it begs for dramatic performance, and no other part of the poem better lends itself, even today, to being read aloud when Vergilians gather to share their poem with one another. We see much of the action of this book through Dido's eyes when we are not watching what she does or listening to what she says; and even when she does not stand at or near the primary perspective in any given episode, most of the rest of the book, like filings to a magnet, somehow envelopes her, until, finally, Book 4 entire, her book, seems something like her stream of consciousness, all the actions, scenes, and speeches that she is not party to, being somehow part of what she knows or feels. This aesthetic effect, our constant pull toward the center where Dido herself revolves, goes a long way toward explaining her peculiar triumph, the way she more or less steals the poem before it is half over.

It is Dido, not Juno nor Fortune nor Turnus, who offers Aeneas his greatest obstacle and finally his most irremediable loss. A more than competent ruler of her newly founded city (a woman doing a man's job very well), fiercely committed to preserving her fidelity to her dead husband (and successfully warding off swarms of suitors to do so), she suddenly gives way, her will and her regimen subverted by malicious divine intervention, to an irresistible and incurable passion for a handsome stranger (those who have shied away from Marlowe's Dido, having heard misrepresentations of its plentiful and substantial virtues, might be entertained by Marlowe's brilliant lyrical expansions of Vergil's heroine's response to his hero's masculine beauty). In the grand manner favored by Propertius no less than by Stendhal, her love is as illicit and unpatriotic, as opposed to patriarchal values, as it is intense and joyful (at first) and tragic (at last). In her love for Aeneas she has discovered herself, her real self, and she is therefore willing, nay compelled, to risk everything she has and is in order to obtain what is now the central, indeed the single, meaning and purpose of her existence. In its violent obsession and its ferocious needs, in its almost mystical drive toward a self-immolation wherein extreme selfishness is transformed at last into utter selflessness, this new identity stands in direct opposition to Aeneas and his Roman mission. Dido offers him and his poem their most effective foil. And in leaving her, in leaving her behind him, he becomes everything she is not. It is his rejection of her that fixes indelibly his essential identity, *pius,* pious, The (selflessly) Dutiful, another style of selflessness resulting from a different style of self-abnegation.

Dido, in the perfection of her passion, ends by being at once a suppliant and an aggressor. She begs Aeneas' love and she also demands it. It is she then, elegiacally speaking, who, like Gallus or Propertius or Tibullus, plays the role of lover, which means that it is Aeneas who perforce is cast in the role of the beloved. That is the story that Book 4 of the *Aeneid* seems to tell, but hidden on the surface is that same story very differently told. And that veiled story, one that challenges its own heroic, epical version, deepens it, subverts it, and then reinforces it, is the story of Aeneas in love.[11]

The two great speeches that Dido addresses to her departing beloved have a clarity of emotional precision, a subtlety of shading, and a chilling resonance that only a Verdi could augment. After any rereading of them, they so stick in the mind, they so haunt the ear, that we uttterly forget the speech that her speeches sandwich, that clumsy and futile effort that Aeneas makes to explain, justify, excuse his desertion of her and that goads her into her second speech, which concludes with an explosion of terrifying anger:

> spero equidem mediis, si quid pia numina possunt,
> supplicia haursurum scopulis et nomine Dido
> saepe vocaturum. sequar atris ignibus absens
> et, cum frigida mors anima seduxerit artus,
> omnibus umbra locis adero. dabis, improbe, poenas.
> audiam et haec Manis veniet mihi fama sub imos.
>
>   But I hope
> If there is any power in heaven, you will suck down
> Your punishment on rocks in mid-ocean,
> Calling on Dido's name over and over. Gone
> I may be, but I'll pursue you with black fire,
> And when cold death has cloven body from soul,
> My ghost will be everywhere. You will pay,
> You despicable liar, and I will hear the news,
> Word will reach me in the deeps of hell. (4.382–87; trans. Lombardo, 4.440–48)

---

11. In a subtle, telling discussion of what is at stake in Vergil's transgressions of the form of the epic genre he inherited, see Hinds, 232–36

Having collapsed after speaking these words, Dido is taken away by her maids, leaving Aeneas "hesitant with fear, and with much more to say." And as he stands there, looking after her,

> At pius Aeneas, quamquam lenire dolentem
> solando cupit et dictis avertere curas,
> multa gemens magnoque animum labefactus amore
> iussa tamen divum exsequitur classemque revisit.
>
> Aeneas, loyal and true [*pius*], yearns to comfort her,
> Soothe her grief, and say the words that will
> Turn aside sorrow. He sighs heavily,
> And although great love has shaken his soul,
> He obeys the gods' will and returns to the fleet. (4.393–96; trans. Lombardo, 4.455–59)

Perhaps we can't forgive Aeneas his hesitation (but he is often a hesitant hero), perhaps we want him to chase after, catch her in his arms, sob out his capitulation (as might happen, say, in romance novel or a silent film). Naturally, he does nothing of the kind, for neither his character nor the inflexible demands of the plot would permit him to do any such thing. We must, or should, be satisfied both with the grief he feels for her (and himself) and with the single line, "and although a great love has shaken his soul." That line, and indeed the entire (very brief) passage that encloses it, slip from our memories as quickly as had his shame-faced, plodding speech just a page back from it.

The moment when we next see Aeneas should be harder to forget. As soon as she revives, Dido ascends to a high tower and watches the Trojans prepare to sail. She sends her sister Anna to plead with Aeneas to rethink his abandoning her. Twice Anna essays her mission, but Aeneas "made no response to her words: / Fate stood in the way, and a god had sealed his ears" (4.509–10). Then, describing his state of mind and heart, a superb simile unfolds: Alpine winds buffet "an ancient oak" trying to uproot it, "But the tree clings to the crag, and as high as its crown / Reaches to heaven, so deep do its roots sink into the earth" (4.515–16; trans. Lombardo).

> haud secus adsiduis hinc atque hinc vocibus heros
> tunditur, et magno persentit pectore curas;
> mens immota manet, lacrimae volvuntur inanes.

> So too the hero, battered with appeals
> On this side and that. His great heart feels
> Unendurable pain, but his mind does not move,
> And the tears that fall to the ground change nothing. (4. 447–49; trans. Lombardo, 4.517–20)

The force of this conflict, the pain and the tears that threaten but cannot overturn his resolve, ought to impress us; but, as in the previous passage, it somehow fails to leave much of a mark on our recollection or on the judgment we pass on Aeneas as lover. Dido is dramatized, we see and hear her vividly, we enter her mind, we see things with her eyes. Aeneas is seen mostly from without, and often by her. What Aeneas thinks and feels is here rendered by a flat narration that barely skims his inner life (elsewhere the narrator sometimes describes his hero's feelings less 'objectively'). This choice of narrative strategy by Vergil depends partly on his need to give his heroine (with whom he perhaps has a powerful affinity) throughout her book the full spotlight; and it depends partly on generic requirements that preclude a warrior hero from showing much of his crystallization. Even in Book 6, when he encounters Dido's ghost in hell and their brief encounter is dramatized (but this time it is she who cannot or will not speak), weeping when he first spots her, weeping when she spurns him and departs, even then, Aeneas is not permitted to reveal the full force of his passion. He and his creator are, both of them, determined to temper his emotions, to muffle them, scumble them: because to do otherwise would deeply mar this Roman poem, would threaten to ruin it, with anti-Roman sentiments, and with an anti-Roman (and very un-Augustan) erotic ideology.

But despite generic necessities, and despite the claims of Rome's destiny upon him, Aeneas is (almost) not only an elegiac beloved but also an elegiac lover. That is because Dido herself arises out of and, in a certain way, confirms the values and the perspectives of the new style of Roman lovers in the last century before Christ and of the poetic genre that reflected it and then helped to foster it. Timid, hesitant, otherwise preoccupied as he is (but it takes a couple of forceful divine interventions to jolt him back into full commitment to his patriotic obligations), Aeneas has been dragged by Dido to the outskirts of Boss Cupid's cosmopolis. That he finally will not or cannot enter into it along with her is as bad for him as it is for her. The fact that he hesitates at the gate but then walks away from it doesn't mean that Aeneas was not in love.

CHAPTER 3

TWO PORTRAITS OF THE LADY

> Image-repertoire burns underneath like an incompletely extinguished peat fire; it catches again; what was renounced reappears; out of the hasty grave suddenly breaks a long cry.
> —Barthes, *Discourse,* 108–9

 FOR CENTURIES, AT LEAST since the second century after Christ (and probably before that), readers of Propertius thought they were being granted a glimpse into the poet-lover's exhilarating and turbulent affair with a courtesan (in today's version, a very high-class hooker) whom Apuleius had identified as one Hostia (a name which, by an odd circumstance that feminists might delight in, means "sacrificial victim"). For these readers the first three volumes of the Propertian corpus (plus two poems in his fourth book) contained a somewhat disjointed, if randomly chronological account, as plausible as it was intriguing, of the beginning, the zenith and the end of that affair. They read Propertius' poems, in short, as if they had been intended to comprise a work that was in part a fragment of autobiography and in part a romance, a novel. For them, Cynthia was a real woman who had really tortured Propertius into something like greatness (one thinks here, perhaps, of the wonders Maud Gonne accomplished with the erotic psyche of Yeats). Whatever other charms those poems possessed were, for these centuries of readers, overmatched by the anguished sincerity, the intensity, the unbearable reality they found in the poet-lover's encounter with the truth and fearful beauty of Love (one thinks here, perhaps, of the young Housman as he ponders the mess of Propertius' manuscripts

even as he struggles with that other mess, the one that Moses Jackson, the object of Housman's own unrequited love, had left behind him as he made his way to India and to matrimony).

In such readings, what was central to the poems, what made them cohere and resonate, was Cynthia's (Hostia's) power over the poet on whom she bestowed the erotic identity that, as he himself admitted, fueled both his genius and the poems that it produced. It was this *content* that mattered. It was this *content* that provided the *form* (the illusion of chronological verisimilitude) that the poetry had to take on to be credible as autobiographical representation. Which means that what the poet *intended* (what other choice, in this reading, had he?) was to leave a record, however impressionistic, of how it was, of what had happened to him. It was what had happened to him that dictated the content (his memories of his feelings) that his poetry would have; and that content in turn dictated both the intentions of his poetry and the form that would have to pattern it.

These readings tend to all but ignore what Propertius may have thought or felt about the Augustan settlement, and if they remembered or touched on this aspect of his poetry at all, they converted him into another loyal denizen of the stable that comprised Augustus' court poets (Vergil, Horace, Tibullus, Ovid). That the sincere and powerful patriotism he was thought to share with his fellow poets could be in conflict with his still more powerful (and sincere) erotic obsession (both as poet and as lover, as poet-lover or lover-poet) was a notion that seldom complicated this view of the poet and his poems. Propertius' steadfast refusals to participate in the manufacture of encomiums of the regime were not felt to cast doubt on what seemed his devotion to the man who was in the process of becoming an emperor (and a god). It was sufficient, in these readings, to call attention to the gradual dwindling of Cynthia-Hostia from his third volume and to her violent expulsion from his life and his poetry in its closing poem, then to emphasize his enthusiastic application of himself, in his fourth book, to the task of immortalizing the foundations of the myth of Rome, its monuments, its institutions, its divinely ordered destiny. In constructing this shift—but it is more of a swerve—from lover of an amoral woman to passionate antiquarian, explicator of primordial Rome's humble origins and their connections with its modern imperial splendors, these readers for the most part shied away from the second half of the opening poem of Book 4, where a mysterious astrologer barges his way into the poem and warns the poet that he must not abandon his real strength, the production of love poetry, in order to take up a style of poetry (patriotic effusions) that he is entirely unsuited to. Instead, they concentrated their scrutiny on trying to explain the sudden explosion of Cynthia-Hostia into the middle of the poet's final volume. Just after its midpoint in its sixth poem where the poet is devoting himself to praising the divine force (Apollo's) that brought about the defeat of Antony and Cleopatra, saved Rome from itself, and handed it over to the young man (Octavian) who was soon to become the emperor Augustus, Cynthia, all unannounced, makes her sensational comeback.

A similar willingness to credit the conversion of Propertius from compulsive slave of love to spokesman for the new status quo marks a style of reading him that replaces the confessional poet with a version of him that also evades the possible ambiguities of his patriotism by taking for granted his absorption into the ranks of the Augustan image makers. Beginning roughly at the middle of the twentieth century vigorous doubts started to confront the reliability of what had earlier seemed the solid facts of ancient literary biography. It came to be generally recognized that our paltry information about the lives and careers of the Roman poets were as dubious as they were scanty. This growing sense of uncertainty fostered another kind of skepticism—readers of Roman poetry began to think that poets who had seemed to be writing about themselves, from their own experience, were better imagined as inventing both their literary identities and the experiences those identities recounted, taking their poetic personae and what they said and thought and did not from life but from the books that they had inherited from their predecessors.

As these feelings of discomfort with the autobiographical basis of 'personal poetry' grew, the focus and the expectations of readers of this poetry (not only of elegy but also of lyric and of satire) shifted from the content of the poems and the intentions of the poets to questions about the underlying structures of the poems, about the rules that governed the poetic genres that the poets had chosen to write in, about the formal and stylistic norms that a given genre demanded, about the relations between a given poem and the various literary sources that it was constructed from (its intertextualities). Like lyric poetry, like satire, Roman love elegy ceased to be the representation of a poet's (real-life) experience and became an object to be studied, to be decoded, a piece of evidence that could be adduced to formulate new laws of literary production. The reading of these 'texts' (formerly 'poems') became in short a kind of scientific investigation into the nature of this area (first-person speakers pretending to voice individual experience) of the phenomenon of literature. From here it was but a step, once this species of formalism had triumphed and the ontological preeminence of genre had been securely established, to begin to treat 'personal poetry,' along with all other varieties of literature, as materials for the investigation of cultural practices. Roman love elegy, like other literary genres, became a branch of anthropology in addition to having been transformed into a branch of linguistics.

Which means that Propertius (and his colleagues in making poetry out of the erotic imperatives) became, essentially, a repository of examples and of evidence for the nature and structure of his chosen poetic genre, as well as for the structures, the sign-systems, of Augustan ideology (that is, the Roman individual's imaginary relationship with the real conditions of his existence, as this relationship was designed by Augustus and his chief advisors). What his intentions may have been (why, for instance, he chose the genre he did in preference to other possible genres); what kinds of pleasure, intellectual as well as aesthetic, he was attempting to provide his contemporaries with; what his political attitudes might have been—all these concerns became all but irrelevant by virtue of the quest for the kinds of certainty that formalism hungers for and the kinds of scientific rigor that the social sciences aspire to. Common readers and belle-lettristes alike then had to go elsewhere for their entertainment and sustenance (to the movies, perhaps, but the movies, alas, have also become the property of the new formalism): Propertius and his fellow elegists were no longer available to them. Coterminous with the death of the author, the death of pleasure ensured that no one could or would be enjoying Propertius, at least not in the near future. He, along with his Cynthia, had become a cipher in the landscape of Signs.[1]

THE END OF THE AFFAIR

Suppose a lover of poetry wants more from his poems than the formal principles and the theories that might be thought to generate them? Suppose she finds some solace in the taste and smell of fiction. Where

---

1. Among the most influential versions of Roman love elegy in recent years are Greene (1998), Miller, Veyne, Wyke, and Kennedy (1993); see Fantham's meticulous survey of current views.

should he go to discover some alternative to this style of reading? Maybe, in our need, we should ask the help of Roland Barthes, who atoned for murdering the author by reviving for us the various pleasures of the text. And where would Propertian pleasure be likely to be recovered? Where else but where he himself discovered its origin? Who is she that all the swains do her commend? Let's look at where it all began by looking at where it all ended.

In the final two poems of Book 3, having been overwhelmed by the latest and last straw, an exasperated and exhausted lover-poet finally summons up the courage to, as the vivid saying goes, dump his beloved (capricious Cynthia, more than fickle Cynthia).

> falsa est ista tuae, mulier, fiducia formae
>   olim oculis nimium facta superba meis.

> Woman, the reliance you placed on your beauty has proved to be
> unfounded—it was my gaze—your reflection in my adoring eyes—that
> rendered you arrogant. (3.24.1–2)

So begins a litany of bitter reproaches that spills over from 3.24 into 3.25 (if these are not in fact a single poem) and that will culminate in an explosion of curses (he revels in a premonition of Cynthia's final days when she is old and ugly and alone) that rival Horace's similar vituperations in their impotent misogyny. So shrill is his tone here (he is obviously incapable of the devastating calm that marks Rhett Butler's incomparable dismissal of Scarlett, "Frankly, my dear, I don't give a damn") that one sometimes wonders if it is not *she* who has given *him* his walking papers. In any case, mention of *his* powerful gaze triggers in our memory the very first lines of Propertius' very first poem to Cynthia in his virgin volume:

> Cynthia prima suis miserum me cepit ocellis,
>   contactum nullis ante cupidinibus.

> Cynthia it was who first seized me with *her* gaze [*suis ocellis*]—me,
> wretched me, untainted until then by strong carnal longings.

At the outset of his undoing, his enslavement by desire, it was Cynthia's look that proved powerful over him (a signal instance of the "ravished ravisher"[2]). But now, in this latest (and apparently last) revision of their 'story,' it was the regard that Propertius cast upon her in which her real strength lay. (Newman, in a brief comment on these poems, glides over their complexities, 326.) Far from her having made him the person he became (a genuine lover-poet), it was he who transformed her from mere woman to legendary beauty. He regrets that this prolonged and faithful infatuation endured for five years (*quinque tibi potui servire fideliter annos,* 3.24.23) and produced, in the alembic of his deluded perception of her matchless loveliness, the poems that created both her fame and her megalomania. In one version of the tale, she transformed him from an erotic novice into a connoisseur of passion, from an aspiring poetaster (see 1.7.21, *humilis poeta*) into a supreme craftsman with a resounding message. In the other version of the tale (which the poet claims to be definitive), blinded by his own febrile imaginings, he bestowed on her eternal prominence etched in deathless verse—a gift of which she was entirely undeserving. So, either she was brilliant, powerful, irresistible or she was a two-bit whore, expert perhaps in a few sexual specialties, who somehow conned him into thinking she was his soul mate. Which version is true (or, as Latin wisely allows us to say, which is *verius*)?

One might give Propertius the benefit of the doubt and decide that his final utterance on the subject smacks of something like the truth. Unfortunately, our general impression of him, gradually assembled from these three (or four) volumes (1, 2A, 2B, 3), may well give us pause as we read the "dear Cynthia" letter. He is sincere here, or tries to be, but he is also a moody, querulous fellow, not a little given to small fits of hysteria. We have noticed, in perusing the volumes which this poem closes, that his interest in Cynthia seems somewhat to have abated, to have become increasingly conflicted, and that the ambiguities and neurotic uncertainties that always and already underlay this passion have grown ever more visible. But his increasing anxieties and increasing effort to distract himself from them do not necessarily mean that, in trying to say "goodbye to all that," his prime motive is to be found in his disenchantment with her. Perhaps she was not always a mediocre imposter whom his poetic talents and his erotic hankerings gilded with unreal grandeur. Maybe he was genuinely in love with a woman whose wit and passion and "infinite variety" had more than earned her his humble submission,

---

2. See Barthes, *Discourse,* 188-89; for an ingenious postmodern prespective on the significance of Cynthia's gaze, see O'Neill.

his unqualified devotion, his entire abjection. Propertius' lover-poet, the 'erotic subject' he imagines as the speaker of these poems (3.24, 25), is trying to tell the truth of the whole affair, but he ends by revealing only the complexity of that truth. Try as he may to discard Cynthia, he cannot (as he well knows) do that without erasing much, even most, of his best poetry. To grasp the indestructibility of his love of Cynthia his frequent protestations of undying love (e.g., *semper tua dicar imago,* 1.19.11, "even in hell I will be called the shade that belongs to you alone"; 1.12.19, 1.14.32, 1.15.25f., 1.26B.57f., 2.6.42, 2.9.42, 2.20.17f.) are less crucial than his confession that Cynthia is both the source and the purpose of his poetic genius:

> quaeritis unde mihi totiens scribantur amores,
>   unde meus veniat mollis in ora liber?
> non haec Calliope, non haec mihi cantat Apollo:
>   ingenium nobis ipsa puella facit.

> Dear readers, you ask me how it is that I am constantly writing these love poems, why it is that this tender volume issues from my mouth? It is not Calliope, nor Apollo, who sings me these songs. The girl herself makes of me a genius. (2.1.1–4)

So, in 2.30B, where he suavely responds to the *duri senes,* the puritanical geezers who, appealing to outmoded moral codes (*antiquis legibus*), object to his erotic poetry, Propertius imagines himself and Cynthia whisked off to a utopian spot where poetry holds sway. There, in that paradisiacal place, the Muses sing of Jupiter's delicious adulteries (*dulcia furta,* 28). Thus, divinely vindicated and safe from censure, he asks a question that Ovid, when charged with a similar misdemeanor (by a similar *durus senex,* Augustus), will later borrow and embroider (see chapter 5, passim):

> quod si nemo exstat qui vicerit Alitis arma,
>   communis culpae cur reus unus agor?

> If no one exists who can withstand the weapons of the winged god, why is it that I alone am accused of a crime that is ubiquitous? (2.30B. 31–32)

He then goes on to assure Cynthia that the Muses will not eject her from that sacred spot because she happens not to be a virgin since the Muses, he hints, have themselves tasted love. Indeed, they will invite her to join them in their holy dances while Bacchus takes his place among them at the very moment when Propertius is crowned with the triumphal ivy that great poets claim as their right. This victory he owes to Cynthia alone: *nam sine te nostrum non valet ingenium,* 2.30B.40, "for without you my talent is worthless, my genius is powerless without you."

It is all very well then for Propertius to summarily dismiss Cynthia from his life, from his poetry. But she has defined his identity as a human being (that is, as an eccentric Roman male), and she has, moreover, provided him with the materials and the incentive without which his distinctive poetics and poetry would not have come into existence. He may want, he may attempt, to exorcise his demonic (and rapturous) inspiration. The question is, can he, does he?

A CURIOUS HOROSCOPE

At first blush, a reading of the opening poem of Propertius' final volume suggests that his lover-poet could and did rid himself of his treacherous beloved. In 4.1 the poet proclaims his new poetic project and the new poetic identity through which that project will find its consummation. In this poem he (Propertius or his speaker, as you choose) presents himself as a sort of cicerone who is guiding a nameless tourist (his present reader) through the sights of Augustan Rome:

> hoc quodcumque vides, hospes, qua maxima Roma est,
>   ante Phrygem Aenean collis et herba fuit.
>
> Stranger, whatever you look upon from this vantage was, before the coming of Phrygian Aeneas, naught but a grassy knoll. (4.1.1–2)

So, on the Palatine hill, the place where now stand Augustus' palace and the temple of Apollo, long ago, in ancient days, King Evander, immortalized by Vergil, grazed his cattle. The poet continues expatiating on the theme of Rome's humble agrarian origins, carefully contrasting them with the splendors that now meet the tourist's astonished gaze. Those were simpler times, and one feels not a little nostalgia for their innocence and pristine virtues and values—indeed, nowadays little is left of Rome, the Rome of her founding fathers, but the name itself.

Today's Roman citizen might not credit the story that a wolf had been the wet nurse of Romulus and Remus, whose blood now flows in the body of every Roman:

> nil patrium nisi nomen habet Romanus alumnus:
> sanguinis altricem non putet esse lupam.

> The only thing a Roman has from his city's past is his name. He would believe that a wolf was the wet-nurse of his race. (4.1.37–38)

(The word *lupa*, wolf, is also slang for prostitute, so it's doubly hard to accept the notion that one's own existence, let alone that of one's city, could depend, however remotely, on a woman, Lupa, who once purveyed her wares where modern buildings now shimmer.) Be that as it may, it was Divine Destiny that sent Aeneas and his father and son and household gods to Italy: here the poet condenses, for the benefit of his foreign acquaintance, who may not have read it, the opening of the *Aeneid*. He then alludes obliquely (by now the *hospes* has doubtless lost the thread of the story) to representative Roman heroes (Decius, Brutus) and to Venus' gift of divine weapons to *Caesar* (Aeneas and Augustus are here conflated) and to mysterious but accurate prophecies of Rome's greatness. Having baffled his tourist victim (not to mention his commentators[3]), the poet-guide now turns back to that ambiguous wolf whose dubious ministrations had just bothered the *Romanus alumnus* and which the Vergilian sublimities had for a moment effaced. She returns now in glory:

> optima nutricum nostris lupa Martia rebus,
> qualia creverunt moenia lacte tuo.

> Best of nurses, thou Wolf of Mars, for our Republic, how expansive have our walls become, fed upon your milk! (["Republic" is from Lee's translation].) (4.1.55–56)

Exultantly, the poet proclaims his new intention: to lay out in order, to arrange (*disponere*) those walls in fervent verses (*pio versu*), despite the fact that he is ill-equipped for the task he contemplates: *ei mihi, quod nostro parvus in ore sonus,* "woe is me—so small my voice for such

---

3. See Camps on *rura pianda Remo,* 50.

a mighty sound" (58; here he perhaps has in mind Horace's handsome compliment to Vergil, *Satires* 1.4.43–44, *cui mens divinior atque os / magna sonaturum,* "he has a more than human mind and a mouth destined to sing of mighty matters").

Nevertheless, Propertius is determined to give it his best shot. He wants to bring honor to his birthplace. He wants, like Vergil, to outdo the antique (and venerable) founders of the Roman poetic tradition (Ennius, in particular, with his hayseed garland, *hirsute corona,* 61) by introducing Alexandrian (more precisely, Callimachean) matter and manner into Roman literary production: in this new volume, that wish, that intention, means working to represent the antique origins of Rome in the polished modernist styles that Catullus and his contemporaries began to devise and that Vergil and Horace have brought to near perfection. Such an achievement would make Umbria, the place Propertius came from, proud of him:

> mi folia ex hedera porrige, Bacche, tua,
> ut nostris tumefacta superbiat Umbria libris,
>   Umbria Romani patria Callimachi.

> Bacchus, provide me with some of your ivy so that Umbria may burst with the pride of my books—Umbria, the native land of the Roman Callimachus. (62–64)

He wants Umbria to be proud of his books (the earlier ones doubtless as well as this new patriotic volume, for he had claimed Callimachus as a model for shaping his lover-poet even before his present claim of the Alexandrian as the model for his new role as exquisite antiquarian). He wants Umbria to think of itself henceforth as the native land of the Roman Callimachus. Note that Propertius is divided here in his nationality, signing himself as the *alumnus* of both Umbria and of Rome (the significance of this statement of dual citizenship is clarified by a glance back at the closing poems of Book 1). But it is to Rome that he makes his final appeal (we may have observed that by this time in his oration the bewildered tourist seems to have abandoned the inspired [or crazy] poet, and gone off to find a new tour guide or to purchase himself a guidebook).

> Roma, fave, tibi surgit opus, date candida, cives,
>   omina et inceptis dextera cantet avis.

> Wish me well, O Rome, it is for you this work begins! Give me good omens, my fellow citizens! And may the prophetic bird chant propitiously as I set out upon my labors! (67–68)

The poet then offers a preview of what those labors will entail: "I shall sing of rituals and festivals and the olden names of Roman places, and to elucidate these emblems of patriotism will be the goal to which my sweating horse must hasten." He formally addresses Rome and all its citizens, but his real audience in this poem (and, it would appear, in the poems that follow it in this entire volume) is the Augustan establishment, the *princeps* himself; his wife Livia; Agrippa, his right-hand man; and the various advisers and officials who have helped make the Augustan settlement a reality. It is to these eminences that he announces his change of heart (the one that Maecenas, an eminence no longer, or no longer named, had begged him to make); it is to them that he pledges himself, intent now upon turning a new leaf and finding a new life. It is to them that he promises, with decorous and resonant prayers and with clear-voiced vows, to hunt out and to propagate the meanings of old Rome made new again by its savior and his helpers.

But then a strange thing happens. Either a new poem begins, without prelude or warning, or the poet's guided tour suffers the abrupt and violent intrusion of an importunate astrologer (Horos, by name, as in 'horoscope'), who appears from nowhere, grabs the newly patriotic bard, and chides him for his rash career move. "Why are you rushing off to reveal the working of Fate [*dicere fata*], unsuited though your own destiny has shaped you for the oracular role?" Horos, as he makes clear at the end of his speech to Propertius, has learned the poet's real poetic mission by casting his horoscope (147–50), and he feels compelled to intervene in the poet's unwise and rash decision to switch poetic genres. Having pompously displayed his astrological credentials by recounting his signal success in forecasting the futures of several individuals (89–102), having reminded his victim of the essential nature of astrology, Horos then provides Propertius with a muddled picture of the various and crucial roles played by prophecy (which he slyly conflates with astrology) in the Trojan War. When he has finished defending his profession (which he knows meets with no little skepticism from intellectuals like Propertius) and has demonstrated his own expertise as a practitioner of it, the astrologer moves in for the kill:

> hactenus historiae: nunc ad tua devehar astra.
>   incipe te lacrimis aequus adesse novis.
>
> But enough of anecdotal proofs. I am now impelled to treat of the stars that govern your particular case. Steady yourself, prepare to face up to a new onslaught of wrath and weeping. (119–20)

To ensure that his pigeon understands that he is dealing with the genuine article, Horos rightly identifies Propertius' birthplace, Umbria, which he describes with a touch of charming lyric verve and which, he claims, the poet's own *ingenium* (that word again!) had made "more famous" (121–26). He also flatters the poet with a tactful mention of his distinguished ancestry (*notis penatibus*), and then he further tries to ingratiate himself by recalling that the poet lost his father when he was still quite young and at roughly the same time suffered a decline in his family fortunes when he was divested of much of the abundant farmland that was his patrimony (127–30). Soon after that, continues Horos, as soon as his boyhood was over and his young manhood began with the assumption of the toga,

> tum tibi pauca suo de carmine dictat Apollo
>   et vetat insano verba tonare Foro.
>
> Apollo started to share with you some of his songs, and he forbade you to scream your head off, playing at being a lawyer or politician, in the nutty hubbub of the Forum. (133–34)

Thus, the god saves him, as later Ovid would be saved, from the tedium of an ordinary life devoted to climbing toward a mediocre success as a public servant.

The poet must have been astounded to hear his personal story so accurately (and sympathetically) recounted (unless, of course, he had the wit to realize that Horos, following his usual operating procedure, had done his homework before making his move). His prey thus softened up, Horos can say what he came to say, can deliver the urgent warning that has caused him to seek Propertius out:

> at tu finge elegos, fallax opus: haec tua castra!
>   scribat ut exemplo cetera turba tuo.

> militiam Veneris blandis patiere sub armis,
>   et Veneris pueris utilis hostis eris.
> nam tibi victrices quascumque labore parasti,
>   eludit palmas una puella tuas.

> Just keep on writing those elegies of yours. A slippery sort of job, to be sure, but that's your true métier, that's your genuine bivouac. Do what you do best, and you'll see a crowd of young poets eager to follow in your footsteps. You'll keep on performing your military service employing the seductive weaponry of Venus, and Venus will continue to let her cupids use you for target practice. Of course, whatever medals you end up with in your campaigns [as lover, as poet, as lover-poet], one girl will continue to ridicule them. (135–40)

There she is again: *una puella*. It always was and it always will be—Cynthia. He had said it once and for all way back at 1.12.19–20:

> mi neque amare aliam neque ab hac desistere fas est:
>   Cynthia prima fuit, Cythia finis erit.

> For me, it is prescribed, as if by holy writ: it is impossible to love another, it is impossible ever to abandon her. Cynthia was first, and Cynthia will be last.

At the close of his previous volume the lover-poet had claimed, with all the bitterness his heart was capable of, to be rid of her, and he reveled in the thought of her, alone, in despair, in the wretchedness of full anility. That's what he said then, as he was preparing to escape from Eros (in the tried and true Greco-Roman way, by forcing himself back into sanity), as he was girding up his loins to join the ranks of the efficient propagandists for the *princeps* and his regime (their motto, similar to P. T. Barnum's: "Say it loud, say it often"). But now the astrologer suggests that it may be time to reconsider:

> et bene cum fixum mento decusseris uncum,
>   nil erit hoc; rostro te premet ansa tuo.

> If you manage to shake her hook from your chin, it will do you no good. Her gaff will catch you up by your bloody snout. (141–42)

His manner of talking about the impossibility of the poet's escaping from Cynthia is ugly, almost sadistic, in its image of desperation, helplessness, mutilation. So, now as before, he will dance to her tune. Day and night, he will come and go at her caprice, and he will burst into tears when she tells him to. And he can lock her up, he can station a thousand goons to guard against her sneaking out from the place he has imprisoned her: she will find a way to slip out through a crack in the wall whenever some rival has managed to entice her away from him. Horos closes his reading of the poet's horoscope with a final warning, not about his career or his love life, for he has definitively explained how fate has dealt with Propertius as lover-poet. As a *sanctus amator,* a lover made all but inviolate by his love, Propertius need not worry, says Horos, about death by water or on the battlefield (where he is unlikely ever to be found), but he must be vigilant when Cancer is rising. (We have no idea what this means; perhaps Horos is warning him of the sicknesses that are prevalent when Rome's summer heat is at its fiercest.) The threat is as vague and portentous as the astrologer can make it. A touch of ominous verisimilitude concludes the session and thus confirms its claims to validity.

This poem is, as most of its commentators in some degree acknowledge, a peculiar way to open this new volume and its new poetic project, for it is a programmatic poem that carefully self-destructs.[4] From now on, says the poet, I am going to write patriotic poetry. Then, without warning, without a hint of self-contradiction, the poet lets a ventriloquist's dummy utterly overturn what he has just said: No, I am in fact condemned to write not "what the age demands," but (again, forever) about my humiliating relationship with the venomous bitch whom I recently banished from my poetry and my life.

A REVENANT

Then what does he do? He offers us five poems in a row, four of which (2, 3, 4, 6) deal with some aspect of Roman cult or origins

---

4. See Sullivan's brilliant account, 137–47; for different views of the poem and of Horos's function in it, see DeBrohun, 105–13; Janan, 102–3; for Guenther, 363–64, he performs a "mock recusatio" that in no way subverts the new "commitment to national poetry."

or lifestyle. One of them (5) provides an incisive and vehement meditation, an inside look at, the erotic machinery that a thriving madam manipulates; this poem, in the precision of its minute particulars, recalls, but without its charm or neutral gaze, Lucian's *Dialogues of the Courtesans* and its witty anatomy of the world of the brothel. After a significant hiatus (7 and 8), Propertius returns to his stated purpose for Book 4 and writes three more poems (9, 10, 11) about crucial elements of Roman ideology: the Hercules poem on the Ara Maxima; a poem about the *spolia opima* (and the meaning of triumphant Roman militarism); and the poem on (and spoken by) Cornelia, in which the essence of virtuous Roman womanhood is painstakingly defined.[5] Why is it that this Roman sequence is broken (just after its midpoint, the elaborate celebration, in 4.6, of Rome's victory over Antony and Cleopatra)? What point was Propertius trying to make when he departed so emphatically from his blueprint?[6] These questions about poems 7 and 8 have bothered the commentators of Book 4 no less that those which surround the inconsistencies of its opening poem.

It is a shock, just after the super-patriotic strains of the Actium poem, to find that Cynthia has smashed her way back into the volume that was supposed to exclude her, and she functions here as a superbly ironic example of the return of the repressed:

> sunt aliquid manes: letum non omnia finit,
>   luridaque evictos effugit umbra rogos.
> Cynthia namque meo visa est incumbere fulcro....

> So there *are* ghosts after all! And death is not the end of everything, and sallow specters triumph over the funeral fires that had consumed them. For Cynthia appeared, leaning on my bed. (7.1–3)

Common folk believe in ghosts, modern intellectuals like the poet do not. Nevertheless, Cynthia appeared to him (or seemed to) as he lay in his bed just as he was nodding off to sleep. The bones of Cynthia had only recently (*nuper*) been buried at the side of a loud thoroughfare, and she comes to him now while sleep hangs over him, delaying its full effect because he can't take his mind off "the funeral of Love" (*ab*

---

    5. For an ironic reading of her monologue, see Johnson 1997; for the style and substance of Book 4 as a whole, see Welch, 11–18, 166–70, and Hutchinson, 16–21.
    6. See Nethercut's excellent observations, 1968.

exequiis amoris, 5) and was bewailing the cold kingdom of his lonely bed (*et quererer lecti frigida regna mei*). So, unless he was sleeping and he thought himself awake, this really was Cynthia, or her ghost, come back to haunt him.

At first glance, she looks much as she did in life. Her hair is styled as it was when her corpse was laid out on the pyre, and she wears now the dress she wore then, but the flames have singed it badly, and the beryl ring she had on her finger has been eaten away by the fire. More gruesomely, the waters of Lethe have discolored her lips. So, though she is still recognizable, death has markedly altered her beauty. These dire changes might perhaps have made the poet doubtful as to whether this was his Cynthia or not, but all uncertainty vanishes when she opens her ruined mouth:

> spirantisque animos et vocem misit: at illi
>   pollicibus fragiles increpuere manus.

> The rage and the voice the specter released against me were those of the living, breathing woman as I had known her—still, her hands seemed likely to snap and crumble and her fingers creaked as she gesticulated to emphasize what she had to say. (11–12)

Despite the traces of her beauty, the vestiges of flesh and skin and hair that cling to her ghastly presence, his beloved, as we will be chillingly reminded at the poem's close, is a skeleton.[7]

A DIGRESSION: CYNTHIA'S LOOKS

Before we listen to what the skeleton has to say, let's take a moment to consider the effect the ruined beauty of the revenant might be thought to have on the sleepless poet (and perhaps on us). Roy Gibson, in his elegant and very useful discussion of Roman love elegy (2005), has this to say about Cynthia's beauty: "Some details ... of Cynthia's looks are concentrated in the second and third poems of Book 2, enough at least to build a picture of a tall woman with blond hair, long hands, a snow-white complexion and striking eyes.... But these are generic

---

7. For a subtle overview of the poem, see Hutchinson, 170–72.

looks proper to goddesses and heroines (such as Dido in the *Aeneid*), and elsewhere in poetry. Propertius, like other elegiac poets, is mostly content with general and unspecific references to hair, eyes and looks" (165). This is, at best, something of a half-truth. The other elegists are indeed vague about the loveliness of their beloveds. But 2.2 is rather more elaborate than Gibson's remarks represent it to be. Following "Red-gold hair, long hands, big build" (Lee's delightful translation of *fulva coma est longaeque manus, et maxima toto / corpore,* 5–6) comes a clause that augments these physical traits with luminous clarity: *et incedit Iove digna soror,* "she moves like Juno, fit sibling of Jove himself." This comparison of Cynthia's movement to that of Juno is playful hyperbole, to be sure—if we think of it as part of a sort of seduction poem, it is as guileful as it is charming—but it transforms the flattering clichés (if they are in fact clichés) that Gibson focuses on into something radiant, an impressionistic analogy that teases the imagination and invites the reader to shape this dream girl to his/her own taste. Furthermore, the four opening verses of the poem that precede this description of Cynthia are part of the mythologizing frame that is designed to distinguish this human paragon from all other earthly women:

> liber eram et vacuo meditabar vivere lecto,
>   at me composita pace fefellit Amor.
> cur haec in terris facies humana moratur?
>   Juppiter, ignosco pristina furta tua.
>
> I was at liberty and planning to live my life
> In a companionless bed, but Love,
> Having signed a truce with me, pulled a fast one.
> Why does such mortal beauty remain on earth?
> Jupiter, I forgive you all your antique peccadillos. (1–4)

The poet, in an unusually reflective mood, was lying in his otherwise empty bed, toying with the notion of beginning to live something like a celibate life. But the Love God betrays this momentary truce in erotic warfare. There flashes before the poet's eyes an image of the woman he has been planning, tentatively, to break with. He responds to this image with an astonished cry: "How is it possible that merely human beauty remains earthbound?" That testament to her incomparable good looks leads him to a silly (and rather blasphemous) comment, "Jupiter, I can now pardon you for all your early thefts" (that is, adulteries). Jupiter's countless seductions (or rapes), which might bother anyone trying to make sense of a god whom the philosophers and the theoreticians of the Augustan regime had attempted to cleanse of the filth that poets since Homer, not to mention ignorant worshipers, had immersed him in, can be condoned when they are glimpsed from the perspective that has crystallized in the mind of Propertius as he lies there in his bed, struck by the truth and irresistible power of Cynthia's inhuman loveliness. If the highest god has been swept away (on myriad occasions) by looks that are beyond description, what was a poor mortal to do when confronted with Cynthia, a woman worthy of Jove's attentions?

Having firmly established Cynthia's claim to being rightfully classed among the divinely beautiful, Propertius sends packing Juno and Pallas and even Venus herself, the three goddesses whose naked glories that famous shepherd on Mount Ida (Paris) had once appraised (*cedite iam, divae, quas pastor viderat olim / Idais tunicas ponere verticibus,* 13–14). It is a rash claim, this, that heaven's beauties have been bested by the lover-poet's lady. To ward off celestial ill will from her, he closes this brief poem with an apotropaic prayer:

> hanc utinam faciem noli mutare senectus,
>   etsi Cumaeae saecula vatis agat.

> I pray that old age leaves her loveliness unchanged, even if she should live
> to be as old as the Cumaean Sibyl. (15–16)

This is a far cry from what Propertius will be saying at the close of Book 3. This theme of Cynthia's more-than-human beauty, her divine beauty, returns with exquisite emphasis in 2.28B. In 2.28A Cynthia is represented as being in the grasp of what appears to be a fatal sickness. The poet prays to Jupiter and Juno to save her from death. He wonders if Venus, angered at being compared with Cynthia, has had some hand in bringing on the doom that now threatens her, or is it Juno or Pallas whom she has somehow offended (the trio from 2.2 once again here united)? But here the poet has in mind not his blasphemy in that poem, but Cynthia's own folly:

> semper, formosae, non nostis parcere verbis.
>   hoc tibi lingua nocens, hoc tibi forma dedit.

> Beautiful ladies, you never know when to hold your tongues, and your

rash talk and your good looks alike destroy you. (2.28.13–14)

Nevertheless, dangerous though the boasts and beauty may be to such ladies, when they die they meet with a kinder fate. Io, Ino, Andromeda, Callisto—all these heroines were transformed into divinities of one sort or another. Thus, if Cynthia cannot escape her present peril, she can take comfort in the sure knowledge that she will find herself (we should remember this when the skeleton starts talking) well compensated for her sufferings in life:

> et tibi Maeonias omnis heroides inter
> > primus erit nulla non tribuente locus.

> You will be ranked first among all the legendary women whom Homer sang, not one of them dissenting in the awarding of that honor. (29–30)

At least the equal of the goddesses and superior to the superior women of legend, Cynthia's beauty is incomparable, incontestable.

Cynthia's illness continues to worry the poet in 2.28B. Magic remedies have been of no avail. He wants to die with her if die she must. He begs Jupiter to save her. And then, she begins to rally. In response to this change in her condition, he beseeches Persephone and her husband not to withdraw their mercy. He pleads with them to continue to spare Cynthia because

> sunt apud infernos tot milia formosarum:
> > pulchra sit in superis, si licet, una locis.

> There are among the dead so many thousands of beautiful ladies—please,
> if it be lawful, let there be one of these left here above ground. (49–50)

Propertius then offers a few random examples of these super-lovelies (Antiope, Tyro, Europa, and shameful Pasiphae), lumps together as a class all the beauties of Troy and Greece, and suddenly shifts from the old world to the new:

> et quaecumque erat in numero Romana puella,
> > occidit: has omnis ignis amara habet.

And every Roman girl who belongs in this category has expired, the gluttonous fire has devoured them all. (55–56)

Every divinity, every beautiful mortal, Greek or Roman—Cynthia has bested them all and wins, hands down, beauty's highest crown. We may not believe this (she, in Propertius' fiction of his erotic subject's travails, may not have believed it), but he wants us to believe that he believes it (when his lover-poet writes it). Here, as in 2.3, where he elaborates on Cynthia's intellectual and artistic gifts as well as on her physical perfection, he provides his representations of his response to her manifold and supreme beauties and charms with all the wealth that myth and legend and poetry can provide. In 2.3 we are told that this miracle of pulchritude has, can only have, its source in the divine:

> haec tibi contulerunt caelestia munera divi,
>   haec tibi ne matrem forte dedisse putes.
> non non humani partus sunt talia dona,
>   ista decem menses non peperere bona.

> In case you think a mortal mother bestowed these gifts on you, think again: this beauty was conferred on you by the gods. No, no—such gifts as these no earthly birth conferred, ten months of pregnancy did not bring forth these blessings. (25–28)

It is not easy to ignore the sweetly mocking rhyme of *dona/bona* here. Then (I follow here the line-ordering of Sterke, 29, 32, 31, 30 [see Goold, 126]) the poet reasserts her supremacy among Roman women and the attraction she may have for God himself:

> gloria Romanis una es tu nata puellis:
>   post Helenam haec terris forma secunda redit.
> nec semper nobiscum humana cubilia vises,
>   Romana accumbes prima puella Iovi.

> You were born to be the single glory among Roman girls. This matchless loveliness returns to earth, after Helen's vanishing, for the first time. So, you will not always be coming to our mortal beds, no, you will be the first Roman girl to sleep with Jupiter. (29–32)

Propertius is not surprised, he admits, to see young Roman men ignited by Cynthia since he knows all the troubles that Helen caused for the Trojans and the Greeks and knows, too, how vain were the huge sacrifices that their obsession with her entailed. From these epic hyperboles he then passes to the visual arts. Any painter seeking to put the great painters of the past in the shade need only take the poet's beloved (here, *domina*) as his model. If the painter then exhibits her finished portrait in the East or the West, he will set the world (East and West and everything in between) on fire. These thoughts (and the accumulated weight of his hyperboles) are as much as he can endure. If another more powerful love should ever possess him (*aut mihi, si quis / acrior, ut moriar, venerit alter amor,* 45–46), only death could assuage the torment of that unbearable bliss.

Gibson (2005) had prefaced his remarks on Cynthia's looks by saying: " ... the lover's primary concern is for himself and not for his beloved. ... To approach elegy with the expectation of finding powerful character portraits of beautiful and tempestuous women is to invite disappointment. The focus is instead on how the woman affects the male lover" (165). To this last sentence one can only answer with a hearty, Precisely so. But this lover-poet's response to her, his passion for her (obsessive, neurotic, unquenchable) does not come from nowhere. Some of his matter and manner (and some of his Cynthia) do indeed come from poetry. Perhaps little or none come from life-experiences. But much of it, maybe most, has its roots in Propertius' imaginative recreation of what it is like to be so desperately in love with such a woman, which means that it, his vivid and memorable fictional response to this fictional woman, depends on the precision and power of the relationship between them that he invents for them: that invention has its origins in erotic poetry written previously to his own (and erotic poetry contemporary with his); from his own observations of the world around him (especially as it is in the grip of the fashion of the erotic imperative); from his own capacity (ironic, intellectual) for narrative and for a variety of stylistic experiments suited to rendering that narrative. Cynthia is a powerful collage of erotic possibilities (not excluding perhaps the poet's own experience): to abuse Aristotle's enduring distinction, she is not what *has* happened to a lover like the one that Propertius makes the speaker of his poems; she is rather the sort of amazing lady who *could* happen to that fictional lover, or to any other men bold enough or foolish enough to risk hooking up with her—she who is as "mad, bad, and dangerous to know" as she is "beautiful and tempestuous."

But crucial to reading Cynthia rightly (or 'writerly') is this observable fact: she is nothing like Delia or Nemesis or Marathus, nothing like Lesbia or Juventius, or, most especially, nothing like Corinna. Her presence in the first two (three) volumes (Book 1 and Books 2A and 2B) is as ubiquitous as it is fascinating. She does not get to talk much (until the final book), but we *feel* how beautiful and tempestuous she is from the extensive, tormented, witty, desperate, chaotic moments in which we see and hear how the lover-poet tries to handle his dealings with her, how he is attempting to hold onto both her and his sanity (or what is left of it). We *know* how beautiful she is, in a way we can never know how Lesbia or Corinna looked, by Propertius' unsuccessful efforts to find exaggeration wild enough (think of Shakespeare's strenuous technique of *inventio* in his sonnets) to barely encompass that dazzling sublimity. And we *know* how tempestuous she is as we listen to her lover-poet ransack the lexicon and leave syntax in shreds as he tries to discover how to begin to say how wonderful, how fiendish, and how *mutabile* she is. But her tempestuosity concerns us less at the moment (it will presently be in full view) than the grandeur of her beauty and the misery of its ruin.

WHAT THE SKELETON HAS TO SAY

Some of that beauty all but masks the skull that has accosted the lover-poet just before (or maybe just after) he falls asleep (again, it is uncertain whether she is an apparition or a nightmare, and that uncertainty renders her manifestation all the more uncanny). Cynthia thinks Propertius is asleep, and she berates him bitterly, apparently ignorant of the tearful insomnia she intruded upon, for banishing her from his thoughts so soon after her funeral. In case he has already forgotten her, she reminds him of the numerous times the two of them coupled in various locations. She calls these unions *furta* (a frequent word signifying stolen fornications), which means that her favors to him were purloined from another (nameless) lover. These encounters she also designates as *nocturnis dolis* (nocturnal deceits). She had to sneak out of wherever she was living at any given time, clambering down a rope, out of her boudoir, down to his embrace. Sometimes, often, they ended up "doing it in the road" (*saepe Venus trivio commissa est,* 2.3.19), wrapped in a blanket. Apparently he has let these vanished joys slip from his memory:

> foederis heu taciti, cuius fallacia verba
>   non audituri diripuere Noti.
>
> Alas for the hidden compact we had with one another—its words, mere words, the South Wind has snatched and scattered. (21–22)

"Alas," Cynthia tragically intones (remember, she is well-versed in both reading poetry and writing it).[8] Having reminded Propertius of his betrayal of her and of all the good times they shared, she passes on to more recent history, namely, to her miserable death and worse exequies, and mostly she blames him for the horror and squalor that marked them. He was, as far as she can remember, not there at her deathbed to call out her name and thus grant her one more day of life; he had not provided her corpse with watchers to drive away evil spirits or body-snatching witches; he had not even seen to it that a proper pillow supported her head as her corpse was being borne off to its funeral pyre; he had not donned a black toga when he took his place in her funeral cortege; he had not accompanied her other intimates beyond the gates of the city walls to the spot where her cremation took place; so, ingrate that he was (*ingrate* is what she calls him, 31), he had not been there to pray for winds to whip up the flames of her pyre into maximum efficacy. Nor, of course, had he purchased precious nard to sweeten the flames that consumed her—no, he had not even bothered to bring a few cheap hyacinths to strew, with shards from a broken wine jar, on her pyre.

That's what she claims. But as we will presently see, she is not unwilling to shave the truth to make her point. Cynthia has come upon the poet at his most vulnerable (sleepless, grieving, maybe a little guilty, but not of all the crimes she charges him with). If she is a real ghost, she knows very well how to play upon his peculiar cluster of low self-esteem, narcissism, and masochistic leanings. If she is merely a nightmare, she represents in his dreamwork his grief for her and his anger at losing her, emotions that are masked and displaced by feelings of guilt: the nightmare skeleton voices against him his own self-accusation which, in his waking hours, he admits to only dimly if at all.

Immediately following Cynthia's complaints about the lax treatment

---

8. For Cynthia's admirable cultural attainments, see Hemelrijk, 79–80.

she received from her last breath to the burial of her bones, the poet is confronted with even more serious charges. Cynthia wants his faithful slave, Lygdamus, put to the severest torture. He had, she claims, handed her the fatal goblet, whose wine was laced with the poison that another slave, Nomas, had prepared for it. The instant the wine touched her lips she guessed what was happening to her and who had made it happen. She does not directly name the person who had bribed Lygdamus to do her in, but her candidate for the instigator of her murder quickly emerges:

> quae modo per vilis inspecta est publica noctes,
>   haec nunc aurata cyclade signat humum.
>
> She who was recently on public display at night, trading cheap thrills for cash, she now trails the dust with the golden hem of her gown. (38–39)

This monster, this brazen dime-a-dozen slut, has taken over the establishment that Cynthia, until only yesterday, had shared with her lover-poet. Now the dear slaves who were utterly faithful to her (a *kind* mistress) suffer insult, humiliation, and actual physical abuse from this dreadful interloper. The bitch has even melted down a golden bust of Cynthia to provide herself (the poet's new 'wife') with a fitting dowry.

Something is not quite right here. As it is unlikely that the poet was as negligent in attending to her cremation as Cynthia asserts, so it seems doubtful that Chloris (whose name finally appears at 72) is quite the villainess or exerts quite the force over the poet that Cynthia, in her postmortem paranoia, believes to be the case. For one thing, the poet represents himself as a miserable creature, grieving and chaste, alone there in his narrow bed; for another, Cynthia's suspicions about the cause of her death and her suppositions as to its aftermath in the household she vacated by dying may be entirely delusional. These are the sorts of conclusions that the living Cynthia might jump to, the sort of misperceptions that a newly dead ghost, in her confusion, might be capable of. More important, this is the kind of voice that her lover-poet, in his dreamwork, might endow his guilty memory of Cynthia with: vivid, devious, powerful, incomprehensible, enthralling.

Quite suddenly, Cynthia's mood swings from accusatory to rational. She now displays calm acceptance and offers wise explanations:

> non tamen insector, quamvis mereare, Properti:

>   longa mea in libris regna fuere tuis.
> iuro ego Fatorum nulli revocabile carmen,
>   tergeminusque canis sic mihi molle sonet,
> me servasse fidem. si fallo, vipera nostris
>   sibilet in tumulis et super ossa cubet.

For all that, I don't intend to continue my prosecution of you, much though you deserve it. I swear to you, by the song of the Fates that none can unsing (if I lie may the three-headed dog growl at me as I pass him by)—I swear that I have kept the faith with you. If I deceive you in saying this, let snakes hiss in the mound where my bones are gathered, let them make their nest there. (49–54)

Me servasse fidem. "I was faithful to you (in my fashion)." Cynthia has made that claim before (so, of course, has Propertius). It is a claim that lying lovers tend to make. We know (he knows) from other poems (and we relearn it from the poem that follows this one) that she has a long habit (five years of it) of cheating on him. Had she not been so disposed, the poet's three (or four) previous volumes would have been considerably less intriguing than they are. But now, at a very opportune time (when he is stupid with grief and perhaps a little guilty—perhaps he has tried to cheer himself up a bit with Chloris), Cynthia is eager to set the record straight, and she is in a revisionary and conciliatory mood.[9]

But why, against all the evidence contained in the previous volumes, should her lover-poet believe her, and why should we? For the simple reason that she did not end up, she claims, being confined in the afterlife with the famous bad women (Clytemnestra and Pasiphae, to name only two of them), but was instead assigned a place in that zone of Elysium, the abode of the blessed dead, where Andromeda and Hypermestra (to name only two of them, a nice symmetry) relate to their sisters-in-virtue the steadfastness they showed in the perils they overcame in the name of love, thus earning their places both in legend and among the blessed. Cynthia is right there in their midst where she belongs. But she cannot, of course, join with them in telling *her* story—she must suppress all mention of the many carnal crimes of her lover-poet (*celo perfidiae crimina multa tuae,* 70) and of her long-suffering toleration of his infidelities. This enduring loyalty, preserved even in the underworld, is the final proof

---

9. See the intriguing observations by Dufallo, 167–71.

of her version of their affair. Her love was immutable and pure, his was flawed, wavering, perhaps even spurious.

Cynthia has stated her case, and she has delivered her verdict (she is plaintiff, lawyer, judge, and jury). It only remains now (for she must be returning to the delightful place in the underworld that is now her home) to request that Propertius see to it that her old nurse (73) Parthenie is not uncomfortable in her last years (Parthenie, with its flavor of 'virginal,' is a funny name for someone who was probably less Cynthia's nurse that her madam, her procuress, one whose fees, Cynthia claims, Propertius never found exorbitant). Cynthia also requests that Latris, another funny name since it means, literally, 'slave,' never be required to act as hairdresser to the vile poisoner Chloris (whose name, opportunely, hints of 'green, fresh, blooming,' perfect for her replacement, 'fresh flesh').

Then comes a sudden, unexpected, extraordinary request. Cynthia wants Propertius to burn all of his poems that relate to her. Her reason? *Laudes desine habere meas,* literally, "cease to have my praises," 78. A crabbed utterance that seems to mean something like "I don't want you to continue enjoying the reputation for artistry you gained by writing testaments to my beauty," which would have as its subtext, "Without me you would not be a famous poet, I made you what you are. And I am now unmaking you." After the poet has consigned all his signature poems to the flames, he is, she commands in careful, measured language, to tidy up her final resting place, and there, on the banks of the Anio, he is to set up a column which is to be inscribed with an epitaph which she dictates to him, one that wayfarers, as they depart Rome, may take in at a glance as they hasten past her bones:

HIC TIBURTINA IACET AUREA CYNTHIA TERRA.
   ACCESSIT RIPAE LAUS, ANIENE, TUAE

Here lies, in Tiburtine soil, Golden Cynthia. To your banks, O Anio, glory accrues. (85–86)

She may not be thinking very clearly here. Is she saying that she is so famously 'golden' that she will forever be remembered even if the only durable evidence of her greatness, Propertius' poems about her, have gone up in smoke as she demanded? Perhaps her lucky landing among the good women of Elysium has gone to her head.

Or perhaps the skewed logic of dreamwork makes such questions beside the point. In her last words to Propertius she attempts to confirm her reality, her veracity, by remarking that she has come to him (a nod to Vergil whom she may have read) through the *piis portis* ("the gates of truth," Richardson's plausible rendering of this odd phrase, 461). Like other true dreams, Cynthia is allowed to wander about as she chooses, but at dawn she must go back to the bank of Lethe where Charon waits to row her back to the Elysian shores (as if he hadn't enough to do with new arrivals without having to worry about the comings and goings of ghosts). These statements, like her earlier description of the contrasting abodes of Bad and Good Ladies, show a peculiar ignorance of the traditions of the poetic underworld and do not give us much reason for believing what she says, here and elsewhere in her speech. No matter, she must be off, but not before she tells Propertius one last thing:

> nunc te possideant aliae: mox sola tenebo.
>   mecum eris, et mixtis ossibus ossa teram.

> Let other ladies have you now. Soon you'll be mine alone. You will be with me down there, and our bones will be mingled together and I'll grind mine against yours. (93–94)

This is the skeleton's version of eternal love, their two skeletons fornicating till the end of time. It looks as if Cynthia has forgotten that she is supposed to be found happily ensconced among the heroines of True (Married) Love. Instead, her vision of their (his and her) future felicity is the nightmare of an undying Eros. She lets him go for the time being because very soon she will have him all to herself in erotic hell.

But there is a final surprise in the lover-poet's closing frame to this portrait of his deathless dominatrix. After securing his condemnation in the court of love, she vanishes, *inter complexus excidit umbra meos,* "Her ghost slipped away from my embrace," 96. We might have expected him to recoil from this ghastly apparition, but whether waking or sleeping, he reaches out to hug her to his chest. Even when she appears to him as a grim skeleton, only slightly hidden under the remnants of her beauty, even when she apprises him of what awaits him after his death, he finds her, as ever, as many readers have found her, beguiling, mysterious, irresistible.

A TRIO, A TAVERN BRAWL (BITCH FIGHT!)

When Cynthia's skeleton-ghost vanishes, it seems as though the poet wakes from his delicious nightmare (or rouses himself from her visitation) ready to return to his patriotic *devoirs*. After a brief, opaque statement in which he alludes to a squabble in some low dive, one which somehow involved him, even though he did not participate in it, he drops the story of the mysterious altercation and launches into what promises to be a properly Callimachean investigation into the nature and meaning of a venerable Latin religious ritual. In Lanuvium, a town south of Rome, stood a shrine of Juno Sospita (the Preserver). Here, in a cave, lived a snake that was annually visited by young women who offered it sacred cakes. If a young woman's offering was acceptable to the serpent (which it was, if the young woman was a virgin), her community could expect a good harvest; if not, not. The poet's explanation of the ritual (its origins, its connections with Juno) turns out to be perfunctory to the point of being slovenly and incompetent.

No matter. We quickly learn that mention of Lanuvium was not in fact part of the poet's patriotic program; it was rather an introduction to a lengthy anecdote about Cynthia and the part she ended up playing in the tavern brawl with which the poem opens and which turns out to be almost the culmination of the story that is the real subject of 4.8. Cynthia, it seems, had been on her way to Lanuvium (not, certainly, to offer a cake to the snake); instead, we find her furiously whipping the horse that draws her carriage, racing hell for leather along the Appian Way, while her companion (it is doubtless *his* carriage and it is he who should be grasping the reins) lolls back on his silken seat, fondling his pedigree dogs, a rich kid, smooth and gleaming from a recent wax job. Cynthia's pretext for this journey (the excuse she offered Propertius for her absence) was her need to worship at Juno's shrine on this holy day (the poet sees no need to speculate on the reason for her unusual haste—probably she just likes driving fast). Why, moreover, the young gentleman is accompanying her on this pilgrimage to Lanuvium is left in doubt. One gathers he is her newest boy toy, and, more to the point, he is her new (surprisingly youthful) sugar daddy. Propertius jealously opines that, at the rate he is squandering his fortune, he'll end up eating filthy food at a school for gladiators as soon as he gets his full beard and needs to shave. So, Cynthia's motive for her visit to Lanuvium is probably not so much piety as business or lust or lust combined with business.

Perhaps she wants to get Boy Toy into the sack as quickly as she can (before he changes his mind? because she can barely keep her hands off him? The poet chooses not to consider her intention closely). Whatever her reasons, she has lied to the poet—worse, she has apparently jilted him (if only temporarily, but it has happened before, and doubtless will again).

The poet refuses to take this treachery lying down—or rather, he will take it lying down, in his own fashion:

> cum fieret nostro totiens iniuria lecto,
> > mutato volui castra movere toro.
>
> Since my bed has been dishonored so many times, I decided to enlist in another army and pitch my tent in another camp. (27–28)

He gets out the Roman equivalent of his little black book (which he has retained, for all his protestations of fidelity to Cynthia). There's Phyllis, of course, whose stomping grounds are near Diana's temple on the Aventine. Sober, she's kind of a bore, but with a few drinks in her, a barrel of fun. And then there's Teia, who hangs out in the Tarpeian Groves; very lovely and, in her cups, more than one guy can handle.

> his ego constitui noctem lenire vocatis,
> > et Venere ignota furta novare mea.
>
> I decided to send for these to help me make it through the night and to expand my erotic repertoire with some untried experiments—in short, I thought I'd try a threeway. (33–34)

Here *furta* means "joys stolen from Cynthia"; elsewhere, when it is Cynthia he is stealing them with, the joys are those that belong to someone else, her current 'protector,' for instance: what matters to him is that these encounters break some code or other, for otherwise they lack the seasoning he likes. When the girls arrive and the poet is comfortably sandwiched between them, the party begins in earnest. Few passages in Latin poetry can match, in verve and charming details, its representation of pagan fun. Lygdamus (whom dead Cynthia wanted tortured and sold) is mixing the excellent wine and decanting it into elegant wine cups; an Egyptian piper and an Egyptian girl on the castanets provide the music; there are plentiful roses, ready to have their petals strewn about the happy scene; and there is a dwarf, Magnus, dancing energetically to the Egyptian music.

In the midst of this infectious merriment occur three bad omens. The lamps, just lit and full of oil, begin to gutter, then the table collapses, and, as Propertius is trying his luck at dice (a lucky 'Venus' throw' would presage him a good time with his ladies), he tosses instead the dreaded 'Dog-throw.'

> cantabant surdo, nudabant pectora caeco,
>   Lanuvium ad portas, ei mihi, solus eram.

> They were singing to a deaf man, to a blind man they bared their breasts,
>   I was not there with them, I stood in spirit—wretch that I was—alone at
> the gates of Lanuvium. (47–48)

Line 47 sounds almost as if it had been written by St. Augustine. Propertius' attempt to get back at Cynthia, to take his mind off her faithlessness by amusing himself with these beguiling substitutes, has failed utterly. Isolated, unnerved, existing only in his mind which is totally fixed on nothing but Cynthia, he has been transported to where she had sped away from him, to escape him, to betray him. He is beside himself, is both himself and not himself. This situation is not an entirely new one for him, she has unselved him before: *aut cur sim toto corpore nullus ego,* "why am I, in my whole body, nothing" (1.5.22); *non sum ego qui fueram,* "I am not what I had been" (1.12.11); *non ego sed tenuis vapulat umbra mea,* "not I but my frail ghost is being flogged" (2.12.20). Cynthia gave him his identity, and Cynthia can take it away. Without her, his existence is voided.

But that strange and anxious solitude is suddenly shattered. There is a noise of the front door bursting open, there are dim voices in the hall. Then Cynthia smashes her way out into the garden (*non operosa comis, sed furibunda decens,* 52, "her hair a mess, but lovely in her fury," in Lee's incomparable rendering). The poet, temporarily safe from her anger, vividly describes the epic disruptions of her whirlwind entrance (she certainly knows where he is, but decides to keep his punishment for last, the better to savor it): He dropped his wine cup and his wine-stained lips turned pale.

> fulminat illa oculis et quantum femina saevit,
>   spectaculum capta nec minus urbe fuit.

Her eyes flashed with lightning bolts, she threw a tantrum as only a woman knows how—my love nest looked like a captured town. (55–56)

Cynthia digs her claws into Phyllis' face, while the terrified Teia screams "Fire! Fire!" At this point, wakened by the uproar, people rush out into the street with torches and the whole neighborhood trembles. The two whores flee to a nearby tavern with Cynthia in hot pursuit. She tears at their hair, rips off their clothes, then races back to the house of her cheating man, clutching her victorious trophies. And she proceeds to slap the poet silly, bite his neck, and pound on his eyes. Worn out by these exertions, she catches her breath and then turns her attentions to poor Lygdamus whom she spots cowering behind the adulterous couch. He begs his master to intercede on his behalf, to no avail: *Lygdame, nil potui: tecum ego captus eram,* "I was in no position to help you, I was her prisoner, just like you," 70.

When she has finished with Lygdamus, she pauses before resuming her efforts to punish the guilty poet who takes advantage of this moment to beg for a truce. He kneels before her, his hands raised in supplication, but she will barely allow him to touch her feet, let alone her knees (*supplicibus palmis tum demum ad foedera veni / cum vix tangendos praebuit illa pedes,* 71–72). Exhausted at last, or moved perhaps by what she takes to be his abject sincerity, Cynthia, as merciful a victor as one could hope to encounter, decides to forgive him—on condition. She demands that he desist from the practice of cruising for new acquaintances at Pompey's portico or at gladiatorial shows, to stop ogling ladies in the upper section of the Theater, or to catch their eye as they peer out at him from their litters. And, of course, she requires him to cast Lygdamus into chains and send him off forthwith to the auction block. These are the terms she lays down, and he submits to them instantly,

> indixit leges: respondi ego, 'legibus utar.'
>   riserat imperio facta superba dato.

> She stated her conditions. I replied, "I will abide by them." Magnificent by virtue of the power she had reasserted over me, she laughed in my face. (81–82)

Then, like the priestess of the Religion of Love that she is, she fumigates Love's temple, sprinkling pure water over every spot the vile whores had polluted with their filth and infections. She then commands that all the lanterns be refilled with new oil, and three times she anoints the poet's head with cleansing sulphur. Then,

> atque ita mutato per singula pallia lecto,
>   respondi, et toto solvimus arma toro.

> When all the sheets on the couch had been changed, I reaffirmed my agreement to her condition (with an erection), and we solemnized the treaty by screwing our way over every inch of the newly cleansed lovebed (literally, "we lay down our weapons all over the entire bed"). (87–88)

It is here, in what is arguably Propertius' masterpiece, that we catch our last glimpse of Cynthia.[10] The speeding Amazon charioteer (and cheating beloved) who opens this poem fits neatly with the female Odysseus, ferocious instrument of justice, who all but closes it. This creature, recognizably the Cynthia we have met with throughout the poet's earlier volumes, yet here allowed to reveal herself in all her passion and glory, differs only on the surface from the less self-assured, much more subdued ghost we encountered in the previous poem, a shadow of the living Cynthia we find here, vindictive, triumphant, never more desirable or more beautiful than she is when she goes berserk with self-righteous jealousy. The ghost has been tamed by death perhaps, or, more likely, she has been temporarily weakened by it. But under the whining and the prevarications and the grand renunciations lurks the old arrogance, the old determination to manipulate and to dominate: to have things her way. When the ghost announces that she has plans for Propertius once he arrives in hell, she asserts her mastery over him even as she does when, in the next poem, she forgives the man she has just beaten to a pulp, decides to have mercy on him, to treat his derelictions with a clemency worthy of Caesar, and thus shows her greatness of soul. This ghost of Cynthia, Cynthia juxtaposed with and folded into the living Cynthia at her most theatrical and most formidable, these final Cynthias crown our accumulated impressions of her, the ones that have been gathered in our minds (and in our nerves) from the first poem of Book 1 through the last poem of Book 3. She becomes here, consummately, uniquely herself.[11]

    10. The best introduction to the poem is that provided by Hutchinson, 189–91.
    11. The Cynthias of these two poems are marginalized in different ways by both

CHAPTER 3

ONE IN A MILLION

No other ancient poet wrote anything like her, and it would not be until Chaucer or Richardson, Thackeray or Flaubert or Tolstoy or Proust or Nabokov, that anyone could write another figure of the erotic female to rival her. These writers would be employing wider canvases than Propertius' and more sophisticated psychological codes than were available to him; they had the novel to play with, whereas Propertius had a form, a pattern, a genre that let him let us see what his 'erotic subject' was tormented by and blessed with only at scattered moments, in random snapshots, until, in Book 4, totally by surprise, when we could least expect it, he thrust into view two portraits of the lady that permitted us finally to see her steadily, clearly, vividly. When that composite image has fixed itself in our mind, we can begin to understand what we had more feebly guessed before: why it is that this "woman affects her male lover" with such irresistible force, in such unforgettable ways; how Cynthia, the poet's version of the *femme fatale* of his Rome, could crystallize in the mind and heart of the lover-poet that Propertius imagined to pair with her and so, his imagination fired by the two of them, be able to write what amounts to a Roman version of *A Lover's Discourse, Fragments*.

When Propertius came to Rome, a young man from the provinces, Gallus and his Lycoris were the embodiment of erotic fashion, at the zenith of their brief splendor, both in papyrus scrolls and in life. They were, the pair of them, the incarnation of the erotic imperative, and the naïve young man, whatever else he made of these exciting novelties that the metropolis offered to his attention, may well have found them (the people and the books that seemed to mirror them) beyond fascinating. As would be the case with Ovid a little while later, Propertius quickly ceased to have any interest in the career that his mother (and doubtless his older male relatives) had in mind for him. He found the legal profession as tiresome as he found other kinds of public service that might procure him a pigeonhole in Rome's newly reinvented bureaucracy. He had a flair for verse, he had a taste for leisure and wine and womanizing. He was hardly surprised when he found his several interests merging and realized that he was experimenting with the possibility of becoming a

---

DeBrohun, 146–47, 151–57, and Janan, 102–12, 118–27; Warden offers a very useful insight into how the two poems illumine one another.

poet, somewhat in the manner of the era's most dashing poet, the author of the *Amores,* Gallus. This version of his early years is speculative, to be sure, but it is perhaps no more fragile a guess than those provided by other versions: 1) in which Propertius falls in love with a flesh-and-blood Cynthia and becomes a poet solely in order to write about their 'love,' 2) in which his poetic ambitions for one reason or another—none of them obvious—fasten on love elegy, and his Cynthia is essentially a metaliterary symbol of his poetic activity, of his *écriture*.[12]

After publishing his first volume, the so-called *Monobiblos,* he continues to refine his personal poetics and the poems that exemplify it, but as his oeuvre develops it takes a turn that might at first have surprised him. We lack here any decent chronological evidence, a problem which 'the damage to the text,' only exaggerates,[13] so it is hard to say anything very meaningful about the causes and effects of this swerve in his poetic production; but we do know that two important events occurred sometime not very long after the appearance of his first volume. First, Gallus died, probably a suicide after his having managed to greatly displease the princeps. Second, one of the princeps' most powerful advisers (or handlers), Maecenas, himself something of a poet and a connoisseur of poetry, begins to suggest to Propertius that he think of turning his talents to patriotic verse (of the sort that Gertrude Stein would one day label "patriarchal poetry"). With the living model for his poetry deceased (under unpleasant circumstances) and with an attempt to shift the direction of his poetry now threatening to distract him from his original inspiration, the nature of his material begins to alter and his attitude toward it begins to grow complicated. These tensions dismantle the harmonies that had been achieved in the first volume. The poet is forced to reorder his fiction of himself as 'amorous subject'; he must ponder and reinvent his perspective vis-à-vis his Gallan inspiration. That perspective becomes increasingly ironic toward itself and the enterprise it was shaped to serve. What it initially took as sincere, ideal, romantic, transcendent it now views as problematic, in need of deeper scrutiny. At the same time, far from feeling the call to abandon the erotic imperative in order to take up the banner of the new ideology that Maecenas and his colleagues are devising and espousing, the poet feels more than ever called upon to defend it. That imperative is, after all, the origin of

---

12. For a bold, fascinating sketch of the beginnings of this poetic career, see MacKay.
13. See Richardon, 10

the poetic vocation he had chosen (or that had chosen him), it inspires the idea of poetry, of love, of poetic and of human identity, that have nourished the production of his verses.

These reformulations of Propertius' poetic project and of his poetic (and existential) identity inform and manifest themselves in what is now Book 2, which was (probably) originally separate volumes, 2A and 2B.[14] Cynthia is therefore now forced to share the limelight with other concerns in Books 2A and 2B, and our sense of the lover-poet's distraction from her, what seems a lessening of his obsession with her, is increased by the mishaps that overtook the transmission of the text of these volumes (and effected their conflation into a single volume). Nevertheless, Cynthia remains the chief focus of these volumes. In Book 1's twenty-three poems (counting 1.18 as two poems), she is directly addressed nineteen times, and in two poems where she is not named (2.1, *vita* and 14.9, 17, 19, *illa*) it is she to whom the poet is clearly alluding. In Books 2A and 2B, out of thirty-four poems she is mentioned in fourteen poems and she is addressed by name fourteen times; the incidence of indeterminate reference to the poet's 'amorous object' (twenty-five of them) is much higher than was the case in the previous volume, but a substantial number of these (*mea vita, mea lux, pulcherrima cura, domina, cara puella*), in particular the magnificent *cinis hic docta puella fuit* ("this dust was once a learned girl," 2.11.6) clearly move in Cynthia's orbit. In Book 3's twenty-five poems, though Propertius gives her a vivid speech in 6, her name appears only in three poems, at or near the end of the volume (21, 24, 25), in which he is busy celebrating his permanent break with her. Nevertheless, unnamed though she is, she is the subject or addressee of nine poems (5, 7, 6, 10, 11, 15, 16, 19, 20), and one concludes from this that the rumor of the poet's disinterest in her, even before he condemns her to outer darkness in his final poem of this volume, is considerably exaggerated.[15] She remains, until the moment he curses and abandons her, the core of his poetry, the reality, exquisite and terrifying, that has called his poetic identity into existence and has sustained it, constantly, cruelly, wonderfully.

---

14. For the complications that surround these intractable difficulties, see Butrica, 199, 208; Heyworth, passim; Murgia; Lyne (1998).

15. See, for example, Richardson, 11.

WHAT CYNTHIA MEANS

Without her—he has said it again and again—without her, no poems, no poetic identity. Who or what was she then? It's the fashion nowadays to say that she is a metaphor for love elegy itself, or, beyond that, a sort of signifier of the erotic or amorous sign-system that governs the literary repository of vocabulary, images, themes from which the genre of love elegy draws its sustenance.[16] In feminist versions of this metaliterary style of reading love elegy, Cynthia or any other amour (including perhaps Juventius and Maranthus) becomes a metaliterary mirror in which male narcissism may preen, prance, and strut; before which it may glory in and worship its phallocentric aggression, its dominance (over anything it feels like penetrating), a vainglorious dandy performing his victory dance despite his habit of whining and his attempting to gain our sympathy by mimicking the rejected lover who suffered death—he, the humiliated votary of Vagina Dentata: in Housman's definitive description of such abjection, "The brisk, fond lackey to fetch and carry, / The sick, true-hearted slave." This construction of Cynthia represents a useful and perhaps inevitable displacement of the older, romantic readings in which a very real-life woman drives an autobiographical Propertius to distraction, then to his poetry notebooks.[17]

The version I offer here is not inspired by the desire to find some sort of middle ground between these two positions, but it does allow each of them a grain of truth. Propertius, as I read him, takes his materials both from life (though perhaps not much from his own life) and from books, especially those by the Roman poets who came just before him and who had been reflecting and revisiting in their poems the erotic imperative that they had inherited from Greece; that had begun to come into fashion just before they were born; and that would continue to exert its influence, in life and literature, for some decades after their heyday. Viewed from this perspective, Cynthia as poetic metaphor is an amalgam of the Roman erotic imperative both as it was lived by various Romans at the middle of the last century BCE and as it was written (recorded and reimagined) by Roman poets of the decades in

---

16. The crucial proponents of this perspective are Kennedy, 1993, and Veyne.
17. For the essential formulations of this powerful strategy of interpretation, see Wyke's invaluable collection of her essays on this crucial topic.

question, who presented themselves in their poems not just as poets but also as lover-poets. With this formulation in mind, Cynthia reveals herself as a worthy successor of Volumnia-Cytheris-Lycoris (woman, actress, poetical erotic object): that is to say, she *stands for* a real woman who really was engaged in the activities proper to the erotic imperative and, at the same time, she *is,* not stands for but *is,* (like) Gallus' Lycoris, a creature of fiction, one of whose functions is to symbolize Propertius' particular poetic enterprise (his obsession with the nature of the erotic imperative, his anatomy of love elegy and its codes and their cultural contexts). Cynthia, then, as a way of dramatizing the process of the erotic imperative, is a complex hybrid, part fact (because she signs the manner in which some real lovers are really engaged in 'being in love' or really following the current fashion for 'falling and being in love'), and she is also part fiction (because, even if some traces of his real-life encounters maybe tinge the poet's psyche and his poems, she is, mostly, a product of his imagination).

If that were all she is (means), the task of peeling away her layers would be at an end. But she is more complex still. As an emblem of the erotic imperative, she stands for much more than the services that a highly skilled (and highly paid) sex-worker can provide for her customers.[18] The gifts she bestows (or withholds) are very much carnal in nature, but they are not merely carnal. If she proffers her trick or her long-time companion delights that he cannot expect to get at home from his wife or his slaves, she is no less lavish in her willingness to awaken in him emotional energies, psychological pleasures, and expanses of imagination that are as vivid as—and sometimes more vivid than—the bodily thrills that accompany them. She (or such women as she symbolizes) cannot fabricate for him a new identity, but she can help liberate him from the codes, the sign-systems, the ideologies, that he was born into and that have, until she got hold of him, prescribed for him not just who he thought he was and thought he ought to be but also what he valued and chose and did. This freedom allows him and indeed encourages him to assume a new identity, one that requires him to fashion for himself a new set of ethical norms, ones that provide his existence, his daily life, his sense of himself and the world, with new directions, new meanings, new purposes. Whether as an ideal or an illusion or a bit of both, she is the catalyst of a new style of self-fashioning.

Propertius may have taken up, for reasons which must remain mys-

---

18. For a thorough examination of this aspect of Cynthia, see James, 71–107.

terious to us, the genre of love elegy *faute de mieux*. He seems to have felt entirely unsuited to epic (as he never tires of telling us); he was apparently not much interested in drama, whether comic or tragic; and was not stupid enough to try writing satire (which might have been a very possible choice for him) once he saw what Horace had sublimely accomplished in that vein.[19] However he may have found his way into love elegy, once he got inside it, he let it possess and feed his imagination. He discovered that it gestured to a realm of thought and feeling, of forms and feelings, that transcended mere lust (which seemed to be its core, however fancy the euphemisms that had collected around it) and that also outpaced mere pleasure or the mere masculine yearning to dominate everything it encountered. Love elegy offered to a young Roman from Umbria and to his coevals an alternate style of living, another way of being oneself. In a society that was just recovering itself from its spiritual and cultural ruins, one in which the emerging ideology offered mostly patched-up facsimiles of antique Roman virtues (Cato the Elder's ideology of hypermasculinity and unselfish self-sacrifice to the State) that were all but useless to and severely incompatible with the new world order and its Hellenizing, cosmopolitan, monarchy—in such a society the values that informed the erotic imperative seemed more than attractive. When the new regime began to express its displeasure with the erotic imperative and the poetry that celebrated it, Propertius was faced with a complex choice, and his Book 2B and his Book 3, as we are about to see in the next chapter, reflect, ponder, and question the tensions that choice brought with it.

Cynthia provides Propertius with various blessings: 1) thrills and pleasures, both carnal and emotional-mental; 2) the possibility of a new (un-Roman) identity that *frees* him from a cluster of codes that he finds oppressive and unattractive and unreal (because, the more he imagines his Cynthia, he becomes, through Cynthia, everything a Roman male must not become: he becomes willing, and more than willing, to be mastered and humiliated); 3) poetic forms and feelings that suit his genius and that guarantee him the freedom to refuse genres that he dislikes, that encroach upon his freedom; 4) freedom itself, an ethical or existential freedom that derives from his poetic freedom and from the sexual/gender freedom that his passion, whether real or fictive, has endowed him with: the freedom to do with his mind and his genius as

---

19. For a brilliant discussion of the nature of the 'conflict' between Propertius and Horace, see Ferri, 15–33.

he pleases is linked to and derives from, both in life and in books, his freedom to do with his indocile body as he pleases.[20]

Propertius' is a complex but coherent consciousness that is bent on a passionate and honest exploration of itself and of the context of its making, of its self-remakings (the growth, so to speak, of a poet's mind). At the end of Book 3 he may give Cynthia the gate; but when, at the beginning of Book 4, his horoscope tells him he has made a mistake in trying to rid himself of her, if we have been listening carefully to him in Books 1–3, we are not much surprised by this pronouncement, which amounts to a palinode inside a palinode. So, when Cynthia bursts into the middle of what was supposed to be a volume devoted to patriotic forms and patriotic feelings, when she scares her lover-poet out of his wits and roughs him up and then has her way with him, both her macabre visitation and her brutal interruption of his swinging bachelor soiree seem, on reflection, anything but astonishing. Propertius cannot get rid of Cynthia because she is his worse and better half, she is his fate and his salvation, she is his Id and Super-Ego. She is the source and the shape of his poetic identity.

---

20. For Cynthia as allegory for poetry, see Miller, 63–66; for a subtle exploration of Cynthia's polyvalences, see Gold, 87–93.

CHAPTER 4

PROPERTIUS AND THE POETICS OF DISGREGATION

> ... Or to disuse me of the queasy pain
> Of being loved or loving ...
> —Donne, "The Calm"

> Yet this is my singularity: my libido is entirely enclosed. I inhabit no other space but the amorous duel: not an atom outside, hence not an atom of gregarity: I am crazy, not because I am original (a crude ruse of conformity), but because I am severed from all society.
> —Barthes, *Discourse,* 121

IN HIS FIRST BOOK of poetry, the *Monobiblos,* Propertius concerns himself only tangentially with political matters. At the outset of his career he is, rather like a new dog in the neighborhood, mostly interested in marking off his territory. He accomplishes this task by defining himself with the help of four foil figures, four other Roman males of his generation whose temperaments, pursuits, and lifestyles he sharply contrasts with his own. In his first volume, the poet busies himself with telling us who he is by telling us who he is not, thus sketching the outlines of the figure who, as we have seen, will obsess him through most of the rest of his career and whose domination over his imagination he will attempt—or pretend to attempt—to throw off. The *Monobiblos* is shaped by the poet's effort to validate his choice of poetic career and poetic identity by constructing his mask, the one that represents him as a credible erotic subject, from four fragments of negative identity.

The first of these, Tullus, is the addressee of poems 1, 6, 14, and 22.

Tullus was a young patrician with good prospects for satisfying careers both in the army and in politics, the kinds of career Propertius probably could not expect would likewise fall into his lap. Some have thought of Tullus as a well-heeled, well-connected and sympathetic young fellow, more than ready to help a promising young man from the sticks find his footing in the big town. When Tullus' uncle goes off to govern the province of Asia in 30 BCE and takes his nephew along with him (a sort of apprenticeship in the mysteries of high bureaucracy), Tullus kindly invites his less privileged new acquaintance to come with him and share some of the education in soldiering and administering and some of the fun that a tour of duty in the province of Asia holds in store for him. The poet uses this occasion to proclaim his absolute devotion to Cynthia (and, obliquely, to boast of her boundless passion for him). He thanks Tullus for the helping hand, but he fervently affirms his allegiance to a destiny utterly opposed to Tullus':

> me sine, quem semper voluit fortuna iacere,
>   hanc animam extremae reddere nequitiae.
> multi longinquo periere in amore libenter,
>   in quorum numero me quoque terra tegat.
> non ego sum laudi, non natus idoneus armis;
>   hanc me militiam fata subire volunt.

> Fortune has always chosen me to be among the losers in the world's lottery, so let me give myself up to a life of what the world regards as utter degradation. A lot of people before me have gladly perished in longterm love affairs, ones they couldn't extricate themselves from, and I hope to be numbered among them when it's time for me to go to my grave. I was not born for a life in the Roman military; rather, Fate has decreed that I must serve in the army of Love. (1.6.25–30)

Tullus, then, though he seems to have regarded the poet as a kindred spirit, is defined here, as in 1.11 (where his material wealth is contrasted with the poet's proud poverty) as a counter-persona, the poet's complete opposite both as regards their destinies and their value systems and worldviews. It is by virtue of his being the poet's anti-self, of his being everything that Propertius is not, that he is the ideal figure to open and to close the poet's maiden volume of verse (just how important Tullus is in designing the Propertian persona will be clear when we look at how his presence in 3.23, a poem that takes its place just before the end of

Book 3, just before Propertius attempts to say "goodbye to all that," to Cynthia and to all she represents).

A second addressee, Gallus, also figures in four poems (5, 10, 13, 20), which occur in an almost regular, almost musical sequencing. Gallus apparently imagines himself the poet's rival for Cynthia's attentions, but he is by and large rather unlucky with the ladies (perhaps, as we learn in poem 20, because he is as interested in boys as he is in women). Having witnessed, somewhat voyeuristically, Gallus' style of lovemaking (10.5ff; see also 13.13ff.: for which, see the acute observations of Miller, 183–94), and after congratulating him on his current luck, the poet feels called upon to offer him some friendly and expert advice on how to keep his love object's affections (Cynthia's instructions to him as to what to do and not do have been marvelously efficacious). His suggestions center on Gallus' need to learn to be tactful, considerate, submissive, loyal—to be more like Propertius himself:

> et quo sis humilis magis et subiectus amori,
> > hoc magis effectu saepe fruare bono.
> is poterit felix una remanere puella,
> > qui numquam vacuo pectore liber erit.

> The humbler you are, the more you abase yourself to love, the better the outcome will be. The man who resists the impulse to keep to his own ways (fancy free to pick and choose), that man will find true happiness (at last) with his one and only. (1.10.27–30)

It is generally acknowledged that this Gallus cannot be the Gallus whom we've already encountered in earlier chapters, the famous poet, lover of Volumnia/Cytheris/Lycoris and friend of Vergil, that Gallus who was immortalized in *Eclogue* 10 and who, having somehow run afoul of Augustus, committed suicide in Egypt in 26 BCE.[1] But to call this amatively challenged lover Gallus, to name him with the name of the celebrated master of the style of poetry one is oneself beginning to write—what could be the reason for that clumsy misstep or embarrassing forgetfulness?—unless of course it was deliberate; unless this was a young Turk's way of claiming that he had new wine for new bottles, that the heyday of the poet of the *Amores* and his Lycoris had faded, that it was now Cynthia and Propertius (and not Tibullus and his Delia

---

1. Janan offers a useful sketch of him, 51–52; see also Janan, 29–31

either) who were about to become the talk of the town. The figure of this Gallus augments the new brilliance of the new lover-poet on the block by his deficiency as lover (and by his passing out of poetic fashion). A tactic as brazen as it was unkind, this—but understudies (think of Eve Harrington of *All About Eve*) are not known for tact or tenderness.[2]

Ponticus, the third addressee (poems 7 and 9), a friend of Ovid's (*Tristia* 4.10.47), is an epic poet who falls helplessly and hopelessly in love, even as Propertius had warned might happen to him; then, caught up in the anguish of that passion, he discovers, as again Propertius told him would be the case, that ladies loathe epics and love both love poetry and the lover-poets who write it (for them). That Ponticus would wish desperately and vainly for the ability to write love poems when he belatedly (*serus Amor*, 1.9.20) became enamored and gravely needed to poetize amorously, was Propertius' accurate prediction. So, while the epic poet suffers acute writer's block, he endures the added indignity of watching the triumph of Propertius:

> tum me non humilem mirabere saepe poetam,
>   tunc ego Romanis praeferar ingeniis;
> nec potuerunt iuvenes nostro reticere sepulcro
>   'Ardoris nostri magne poeta, iaces.'
> tu cave nostra tuo contemnas carmina fastu:
>   saepe venit magno faenore tardus Amor.

> Then you will often be forced to admire me—no longer a second-rater, then I will be prized beyond Rome's best poets. And young men gathered at my grave will burst forth with their praise: "Great poet of our passion, here you lie!" Therefore, take care not to belittle my poetry; when Love delays his coming he often charges excessive interest for the transaction (you risk nemesis in insulting my genre and me, its servant).
> (1.7.21–26)

This is a quick and effective way of trivializing epical grandeur and, in so doing, of advertising, rather disingenuously, the splendor of the poet's own investigations of the erotic life.

Bassus, who is addressed in 1.4, is another poet and another friend

---

2. See Bramble, 87; Janan, 36–39; Crowther, 1637–38; Miller, 70–73, 80–85, 251 nn41 and 42; for an especiallly intriguing analysis of the problem, see Pincus, 171–87.

of Ovid's (*Tristia* 4.10.47), one who specializes in invective and has unpleasant things to say about Cynthia. Propertius advises him that Cynthia's gift for revenge is memorable and suggests he look for other, safer targets.

Viewed, or better, felt, as a whole, these four men conjure up a milieu for the poet, one which is at once his matrix, his workshop, and, in part, his audience. What matters about his relationships with these four figures is not what joins him to them but what distinguishes them from him. He, Propertius, is not distracted by traditional pursuits: making wars and speeches, subduing the natives and governing them. He is not a naïve beardling trying, hit or miss, to get laid. Rather, young though he is, he is already skilled at seduction—or perhaps at being seduced and dominated. He, Propertius, does not waste his time writing epic verse or misogynistic verse; he writes only the kind of poems that women in general and his Cynthia in particular admire (not to mention those curious young men who study his poetry for clues to their own erotic styles). He is, in short, the right man in the right place at the right time. He is worthy of—and worthy to write of—the ravishing, irresistible, and dangerous woman who is addressed, pondered, and praised in most of the remaining poems of Book 1, the creature who more than Tibullus' three rather shadowy beloveds or Ovid's vague pastiche, Corinna, and more even than Catullus' Lesbia, incarnates what is really at stake in the erotic idea and ideal that we glimpse in Latin love elegy.[3]

MAECENAS INTERVENES

That is the sort of thing, the sort of poetic persona, that we encounter in Propertius' Book 1, a poetic identity composed of a handful of rejected personae and a torrent of loud, passionate assertions of rapturous erotic bedazzlement. This peculiar concoction derives much of its force and vividness from the clarity of its poems' formal patternings and from the elegance of the ordering of the poems. The notorious textual problems that bedevil the poems in Books 2A and 2B are all but absent here, where, despite occasional doubts and setbacks, a cocksure, hectoring, essentially unified voice shouts his luck and mastery to the

---

3. For a different perspective on the thematic center and the structure of Book 1, see Manuwald, 226–31.

world. That loud self-assurance, that swagger and arrogance (which are as fragile as they are naïve), manifest themselves in the finished structures of the poems, their clear endings and beginnings and, comparatively speaking, their lucidly articulated middles.

That clarity (of self and purpose) and that confidence (in the verisimilitude of the poet's fictive erotic object, and in his fabrication of himself as erotic subject) gradually dwindle in Books 2A and 2B. To account for these alterations, an older style of reading would have recourse to biographical speculation and the dim chronologies that it feeds and is fed by. What did Cynthia do to him, and when and where and how and why did she do it? These questions are as unanswerable as they are irrelevant.

What we know for sure about Books 2A and 2B as we peruse them is the arrival of a new and crucial ingredient in the mix: for the first time and in the first poem of 2A, we encounter Maecenas, the figure who comes to define for us the poet's new milieu and who denotes a change in, a widening and complication of, his audience. With the coming of Maecenas, a topic that had been handled in a slighter and less urgent manner in the poems addressed to Ponticus and Bassus, namely, the nature and function of erotic poetry and the erotic poetic vocation, suddenly take on a new and troubled resonance. The self-sufficiency, the poetic and erotic harmony and autonomy, that Propertius had proclaimed and performed in the dramatic speech acts of Book 1, is now contested. If, as Bakhtin says, each utterance is an answer to a question, one could say that in Book 1, glorying in his youthful energies and his new-found erotic power, Propertius had not heard or had perhaps refused to listen to any questions that might have been asked him about himself or his poetry—its eccentric self-regard, its dismissals, both implicit and explicit, of civic responsibilities. Suddenly, at the outset of Book 2A, there comes a question he cannot ignore.

> quaeritis, unde mihi totiens scribantur amores,
>   unde meus veniat mollis in ora liber.
> non haec Calliope, non haec mihi cantat Apollo,
>   ingenium nobis ipsa puella facit.

You ask me, Maecenas, why it is I'm constantly scribbling loves poems, how it is that such tender sentiments issue from my lips. Well, it's not the queen of Muses nor the poetry god himself who dictates these poems to me. No, it's my girl herself, she alone, who has transformed me into a poetic genius. (2.1.1–4)

We don't know why or when or in what manner Maecenas first asked the question that followed hard upon this first question (namely, when are you turning your hand to court poetry?), but Propertius, who in his first volume was accustomed to ask all the questions and give all the answers, now encounters a question he cannot easily brush aside (though he tries to, though he pretends to). Maecenas wants (Augustan) epics from him? Well, as he said, Cynthia is both his Muse and his *materia*. He can write epics, indeed he could write an *Iliad,* about *her:* whatever the state of her coiffure, whatever she wears or doesn't wear, whether she is plucking her lyre or snoozing (so ubiquitous and efficacious is this poetic crystallization):

> seu quidquid fecit sive est quodcumque locuta.
>   maxima de nihilo nascitur historia.

> In short, whatever she does, whatever she says, a mighty legend comes into existence out of (what may seem to others) a mere nothing. (2.1.16–17)

The poet, then, in an ironically conciliatory mood, ventures that if he had the epic knack (but he doesn't), he wouldn't waste his precious gifts refurbishing various hoary and outworn topics from Greek and Roman legend and history. No, he would hymn the glorious deeds of Augustus, and after that of Maecenas himself:

> bellaque resque tui memorarem Caesaris, et tu
>   Caesare sub magno cura secunda fores.

> I would recount the wars and deeds of your dear Caesar, and you would be, after great Caesar, my focus. (2.1.25–26)

(This sly in-house joke is brazenly reprised at 35–36: the virtues of Maecenas were varied and many but military prowess was hardly among them.) Yet for all the witty bravado that informs this poem, it marks a severe alteration of the poet's program. The moment Maecenas tactfully broaches his questions, Propertius discovers that he is no longer the master of the only game in town. He discovers that he is now (as he should have known from the outset) a player among other players, and he must learn some new rules, must learn anew to justify what he does and to explain who he is.[4]

The poems of Books 2A and 2B come to us in an unusually and irremediably messy text, perhaps in part because Propertius is now engaged in answering questions, in arguing with Cynthia and the world and himself. The project of proclaiming the unique veracity of the Propertian version of erotic ideology has now given way to the more painful—and more interesting and exciting—task of questioning, of meditating on, the complexities and inconsistencies, the incompatible goods and unintended consequences, that make up erotic experience. This new project, which constitutes a sort of analysis of the varieties of amative stimulus and response, is presented in kaleidoscopic fashion: the poet seems to change his mind and his mood almost randomly. In any case, the know-it-all of Book 1 has all but disappeared by now and has left behind him a more fragmented speaker, one more exposed to and more aware of the vicissitudes of loving and being loved.

LYNCEUS ADMONISHED (AND ADVISED)

That total impression is at once challenged and confirmed in the long, meandering poem that closes Book 2 (34), where the poet assails another poet, Lynceus, who has tried to steal Cynthia from him.[5] Boucher has made a plausible though by no means certain case for identifying this poetic rival with the poet's contemporary, Varius, who wrote both epic and tragic poetry and became one of the editors of Vergil's epic. Lynceus, it seems, an unusually austere character and one entirely given over to thinking philosophic thoughts and translating them into lofty verses, has somehow made a pass at Cynthia while he was, against his wont, deep in his cups (*errabant multo quod tua verba mero*, 2.34.22). Fond of the grape himself, that is the kind of lapse the poet can overlook, even from someone whose puritan façade never fooled him

---

4. Greene 2005, 67–68, minimizes the reality of Maecenas' proddings and Propertius' response to them; instead, for her, Maecenas becomes a marker in a poem whose chief feature is a sort of gendered textuality: "a fiction within a creative universe."

5. For this poem's text and its possible unity, see Butrica, 201–4; see also the arguments for its unity by Syndikus, 315, n211, and most recently, by Heyworth, 262–65.

(*sed numquam vitae fallet me ruga severae,* 23). In any case, after Lynceus has blown his own cover and revealed himself as just another ordinary mortal (lover), Propertius welcomes him to the club:

> Lynceus ipse meus seros insanit amores!
> > solum te nostros laetor adire deos.

> At last, my chum Lynceus has gone off his rocker, a late-bloomer in amour. Gladly I welcome him, him above all, into the cult of my gods. (2.34.25–26)

Propertius immediately advises Lynceus to get off his high horse, forget all his philosophical and scientific studies, and busy himself with the lighter genre of love songs, an activity much closer to his mental and emotional condition, that of bemused, distracted apprentice lover. The girls of Rome, whether native born or imported, don't want to listen to rehashed Homer or warmed-over Hesiod. They want to hear about lovers sick with love, and it is writing in this style that has made Propertius, a kid from the provinces, without money or family, the King of Love, the guy whom the girls flock to and love to party with and to adore.

> aspice me, cui parva domi fortuna relicta est
> > nullus et antiquo Marte triumphus avi,
> ut regem mixtas inter conviva puellas
> > hoc ego, quo tibi nunc elevor, ingenio!

> Just look at me. Left with only a modest inheritance and with no victorious granddad from ancient wars to point to—look how, at all the parties, I'm treated like a king, surrounded by swarms of girls—and all because of the talent that you're in the habit of ridiculing. (2.34.55–58)

And because he is admired by those readers who matter (girls able and willing to read what's good for them and for him), Propertius is more than content to assume what might seem—from the perspective of the dominant ideology—a demeaning, even decadent, posture:

> me iuvet hesternis positum languere corollis,
> > quem tetigit iactu certus ad ossa deus.

It's my delight to lazily languish amidst the fading garlands of all of yesterday's parties, I whom the god's unerring arrow has pierced to the marrow. (2.34.59–60)

So much for any epic ambitions he might harbor in some foolish mood, so much for any officials come to badger him into epic production. Sprawled there with the rotting flowers, probably with a bad hangover, he is definitely not an epic poet. Which hardly matters, because, luckily for the age and what it demands, the right poet has popped up at the right time:

Actia Vergilium custodis litora Phoebi,
    Caesaris et foris dicere posse ratis . . .

Vergil is capable of doing justice to the shores of Actium that Apollo protected and to the valiant fleets of Caesar. (2.34.61–62)

Greater than himself, greater than Lynceus, greater than anybody (even Homer?), a true *vates* has arrived: Greater than Homer, though? Yes:

cedite Romani scriptores, cedite Grai!
    nescio quid maius nascitur Iliade.

Give place, you Roman writers, and give place, too, you Greeks, for something incomparable, something greater than the *Iliad,* is coming to its birth. (2.34.65–66)

Vergil is in the process of writing an epic that will end by putting even Homer into the shade. Which is wonderful, to be sure. But he also wrote, on a smaller scale, his agriculture poem, and furthermore, in an even lighter vein, his pastorals, which are crammed with lovers and beloveds. So, even the greatest poet ever, unlike Lynceus, shared the themes that Propertius has made his own (we will see in chapter 5 how Ovid kidnaps this clever ploy and touchdowns with it). Propertius, who here again defends his erotic poetic and defends it even more forcefully than he did in the poems to Ponticus and Bassus in Book 1, closes Book 2B with a thundering *sphragis,* his seal, his mark, his Propertius-Was-Here. He stands proudly (and rightfully) in the (somewhat new yet splendid) tradition of Catullus and Calvus and Gallus (and Vergil). His Cynthia will be immortal if Poetic Fame decides to rank him with his predecessors, those Latin poets of love who prepared the way for him.

> Cynthia quin etiam vivet laudata Properti
> hos inter si me ponere Fama volet.

> How will Cynthia praised by Propertius not live if Fame will deign to place me among them? (2.34.93–94)

This is a testament of triumph, to be sure, but it is marked, just faintly about the edges, with a hint of irritation. If Lynceus is Varius, next in line after Vergil to become Rome's poet laureate, then two representatives of the new regime and its official poet assume the roles of Propertius' newest foil-figures. Though he cleverly tries to convert the more formidable of the two into his ally in the poetry wars, what designs the poem's rhetorical path is the poet's awareness that Lynceus and Vergil and the powers they represent are encroaching on his private artificial paradise and that what he had made the center of his identity and existence is now shifting back to where it in fact always was, to the periphery of Rome's collective consciousness. The negative identity fragments that he challenged and defeated—on paper at least—in his opening volume have returned, in new shapes, from their long repression, at the end of this third volume, 2B.

THE WORM CONSIDERS TURNING

Book 3 opens not with one but with five programmatic poems, none of them addressed to Maecenas, who will finally turn up in poem 9. Exactly one-fifth of this fourth volume, published probably in 22 BCE, just after Maecenas' mysterious withdrawal from the prince's cabinet, is devoted to that clustering of apologies, excuses, rationalizations, protestations of possession of a minor talent unsuited to the higher grandeurs, to all the plentiful and transparently flippant alibis that mark the two *recusationes* in Book 2A: the one addressed to Maecenas which opens the volume and the other (10), coyly addressed to Augustus himself, which promises eventual assistance in spreading the emperor's message (*bella canam, quando scripta puella mea est,* 8, "I'll hymn your battles when I've finished writing up my girl"). What functions in the orators mostly as rhetorical legerdemain and in Horace as ironic flourish becomes in these poems, in this avalanche of passive-aggressive fandancing, almost a genre of its own. These poems are, with a single exception, addressed to no one in particular. No mere mortal is asking him, as Maecenas once had asked and will again (though perhaps more faintly in 3.9), why he is frittering away his talent on un-Roman topics. In poem 3.3, however, no less an authority on poetry that Apollo himself will ask the big Callimachean question: Why should this featherweight contemplate wasting his frail gifts on matter much too huge for him? The judgment implicit in this nearly rhetorical question is seconded by Calliope, who commands Propertius to get back to his proper duties, which include inciting his male readers to covet their watchful neighbors' wives successfully: *ut per te clausas sciat excantare puellas, / qui volet austeros arte ferire viros,* 49–50.

But despite the intervention of the poetry god and the muse, Propertius seems, in the opening poems of Book 3, to be seriously reconsidering (or pretending to reconsider) his commitment to poetizing the erotic imperative. At the time Book 3 appears it is still four to five years before the passage of laws that will outlaw several kinds of unpatriotic sexual activities, recommending severe punishments for those who persist in directing the erotic urges of their indocile bodies to unprocreative behaviors or in failing to marry those they should marry, thus refusing to produce new babies for the new, newly restored Roman state. Propertius had written a funny, naughty poem (2.7) a few years back when the idea of stringent marriage laws was first being floated (for which, see Badian's persuasive analysis). In that poem he had boldly proclaimed that Jupiter himself could not part lovers who do not wish to be parted (*quamvis diducere amantis / non queat invitos Juppiter ipse duos,* 3–4). When someone who overhears this blasphemy offers wise correction ('*at magnus Caesar,*' "but Caesar is great"), the poet brushes earthly power aside as easily as he had just done the powers of heaven: *sed magnus Caesar in armis: / devictae gentes nil in amore valent,* 5–6; "Sure, Caesar is great in his wars, but vanquished nations mean nothing where love is concerned." This daring affirmation of the power of love leads him to venture the utterance of a supremely un-Roman speech-act:

> unde mihi Parthis natos praebere triumphis?
>   nullus de nostro sanguine miles erit.

> What reason do I have to furnish sons whose valor will defeat our worst

enemies, those damned Parthians, so forcing them to march in our generals' victory parades? I'm not about to father any soldiers. (2.7.13–14)

Such was the extravagance of his salad days. Now a bit older, maybe a bit wiser, he wonders if perhaps he should discard a fashion that was maybe beginning to wear a little thin, abandon a style of singing that celebrated a lifestyle that was beginning to fray about the edges—and that was, in a few years, very likely to become against the law.

The anxieties and uncertainties of Rome in the early and mid-20s had not ended by the time Propertius composed his next to last volume, and they would all but disappear only in the opening years of the next decade with the celebration of the Secular Games (celebrations performed roughly every hundred years, commemorating the power and endurance of the city of Rome and its citizens; the games were produced with special magnificence and ideological symbolism by Augustus in 17 BCE). However, the chief outlines of the regime when it had found its real stability were already sufficiently clear when Book 3 was made available for dissemination.[6] In this volume Propertius surveys the regime's claims to a steady improvement in its ideology and reshapes his response to continuing hints that he should participate in its ornamentation. The five poems that open Book 3 and the poems that variously echo them (9 to Maecenas, 11 on Cleopatra, 12 to Postumus, 13 on luxury, 14 on Spartan women, 18 on Marcellus, 22 to Tullus) constitute his answer to what the age is ever more insistently beginning to demand of him. Hence, some of the time and space that would once have gone to praising and blaming Cynthia are now devoted to bickering with the brave, new Zeitgeist in its emerging perfection.

A FRIEND SHOULD BEAR
HIS FRIEND'S INFIRMITIES

This pattern of the poet's ubiquitous self-defense and his growing sense of the meaning of his separation from the flock, his 'disgregation' (I borrow the term from Antonio La Penna) seems to have endured a sharp reversal in 3.22, the poem to Tullus that almost reads,

---

6. For a succinct and compelling account of Augustus' situation in the 20s, see Cartledge.

on its surface, as a sort of palinode, one which harbingers the poems, immediately after it, in which Propertius gives Cynthia her final walking papers (or, perhaps, marks the moment when he gets his Dear Propertius missive from her). In any case, in 3.22 we encounter the return of the poet's first and most crucial foil-figure, the one who opened his first volume and closed it. More than Maecenas or 'Lynceus' or Augustus or Vergil, Tullus represents everything Propertius is not and does not want to be. What would happen if Propertius should transevaluate himself and embrace, ardently, the things that make Tullus Tullus? Wouldn't that mean that Propertius had come to a place in the road where he would no longer say "no" or "maybe" to being all Roman all the time, for the rest of his life; when he would finally jettison his erotic identity and would, against all odds, at long last, say "no" to Cynthia and "yes" to Maecenas and "yes" to Augustus?

Back in Book 1 Tullus was about to go off and help his uncle govern the province of Asia. Propertius had declined an invitation to join him there and, in 1.14, had further been at pains to contrast his own modest means with his friend's conspicuous consumption, pointing out, somewhat disingenuously (the poet was very far from being penniless), that he who has love hasn't much need of money:

> nam quis divitiis adverso gaudet Amore?
>   nulla mihi tristi praemia sint Venere! . . .
> quae mihi dum placata aderit, non ulla verebor
>   regna vel Alcinoi munera despicere.
>
> Is there anybody who really enjoys his money if Love has it in for him? If Venus is pissed at me, why should I worry about getting my share of the booty? . . . But when Cynthia favors me, I will instantly disdain a kingdom or the fabled wealth of Alcinous (1.14.15–16, 23–24)

But in Book 3 some changes have occurred. For one thing, Propertius has found out, definitely, that Love and money are by no means incompatible since it turns out that girls, even Cynthia, tend to be greedy.[7] For another, Tullus has not returned from his Eastern travels. Why he has remained 'out there' after his uncle's job was finished and his own tour of duty has apparently ended is unclear. Perhaps he has just grown used

---

7. For a description, thorough and imaginative, of the dynamics that govern this aspect of the genre, see James, *passim*.

to, perhaps too fond of, near-oriental pleasures (think of Antony and the ruinous fleshpots he had stumbled on in those humid climes); or perhaps he got involved in lucrative business transactions that required his continued presence. Whatever the reason, Propertius, who in 1.22 had spoken of the unending friendship between Tullus and himself, really wants, he claims, to see him again, back in Rome, where he belongs. Hans-Peter Stahl, who doubts that Propertius is all that desperate to be reunited with his long outworn foil-figure, offers another possibility for Propertius' pleading letter-poem: now more amenable than in the past to making himself useful to important people, Propertius has yielded to the requests of Tullus' family and written a poem to urge the prodigal home (205–9). Which is it then? A sincere, heartfelt plea to a friend whom he much misses? Or a more pedestrian product, an impersonal service rendered to his friend's influential clan?

Or is it a parody of Vergil and of the imperial project in which Vergil's poetry was by now, willy-nilly, inextricably enmeshed? The baroque verbiage of the poem's exordium (this is an oration, after all, a *suasio* shaped by *comparatio*) proliferates its fusion of pompous mythological allusions and elaborate geographical fillers to represent, to evoke, the fascination that may have seduced Tullus into lingering in those storied, glamorous locales:

> frigida tam multos placuit tibi Cyzicus annos,
>   Tulle, Propontiaca qua fluit isthmos aqua,
> Dindymis et sacra fabricata in vite Cybebe,
>   raptorisque tulit quae via Ditis equos?

> Have you delighted all these years in cold Cyzicus, there where the isthmus is bathed by the waters of Propontis, where stands that statue of Dindymian Cybele, carved from sacred vinewood, and where winds the road traversed by the horses of the King of Hell? (3.22.1–4)

The ornate style of this question is briefly merged with a slightly plainer style:

> si forte iuvant Helles Athamantidos urbes
>   nec desiderio, Tulle, movere meo . . .

> But if perhaps you are enthralled by the cities of Athamantid Helle [she, that daughter of King Athamas of Thebes, who was drowned in the Hel-

lespont, which is part of the nexus of my abstruse geographical ornaments] and are in no way touched by my telling you how greatly I miss you. . . . (5–6)

The burden of his letter-poem is *desiderio, Tulle, meo,* "Tullus, I really miss you." That laconic utterance (whether heartfelt or, as Stahl reads it, rhetorical, impersonal) sets up a second stylistic register which, though sparingly employed in the poem, nevertheless emphasizes, by the extreme contrast it offers, the absurd extravagance of the baroque style—it verges in fact on the rococo—that dominates the poem and undermines the 'message' it purports to help deliver.

After the single distich in plain style, the baroque style is immediately resumed and lavishly magnified in the next section of the poem, which quickly swallows itself up in a vortex of violent images of monstrous faces and dangerous places: Atlas, Medusa, Geryon, Antaeus, Hercules, the Argonauts are all jumbled together and spewed out from a bizarre cornucopia of inflated language and chaotic images. This strange passage ends by being, as the poet intended, as unintelligible as it is pompous and grandiloquent—*in se magna ruunt,* or "great edifices collapse on themselves," as a poet who knew such matters well happily put it. This rotten magnificence ends with its stylistic antithesis:

omnia Romanae cedent miracula terrae:
    natura hic posuit, quidquid ubique fuit.

The Roman world beats all the wonders of the world. Here, in this single spot, Nature has placed all of them from everywhere. (3.22.17–18)

This is Voice of the Father, it is the words and the music of Cato the Elder. *Miracula*—wonders, tourist attractions, miracles, freaks. Myth or strange fact, amazement or monstrosity, that near-eastern, Greeky world and its enticing, decadent culture are a snare and a delusion. Nature, which is to be found at her essential best only in Italy, in an Italy now and forever Romanized (and Augustinized), has wisely situated all good things, right where she has made her real home.

This return to *Romanitas* signals the arrival of the poem's core, which turns out to be an elegant hybrid created from some of the loftiest sentiments to be found both in Vergil's *Georgics* and in his *Aeneid:*

armis apta magis tellus quam commoda noxae:

>   Famam, Roma, tuae non pudet historiae.
> nam quantum ferro tantum pietate potentes
>   stamus: victrices temperat ira manus. (3.22.20–22)

Guy Lee's translation is hard to beat:

> Fitter for war than friend of felony this land.
>   Fame is not ashamed of Roman history,
> For strong we stand through duty no less than by steel,
>   In victory our anger always stays its hand.

The probity of Rome's wars, sustained as they always are by a force of arms that *pietas* and *clementia* have tempered, confronts Greek violence and the fraudulent splendors of its legends, legends in which dim fact vanishes into brilliant fiction. The Greeks have their myths, the Romans have their history, and all the truths that Anchises tells Aeneas down in the underworld resound in the spare, proud verses that here find themselves memorably rephrased by, of all people, the dandified, elegant aesthete, by the irreverent elegist who has previously disdained them.[8] These verses immediately give way to an *homage,* as concise as it is lovely, to Vergil's *laudes Italiae,* in which suave rhythms mimic the play of water in motion, of Italy's rivers and lakes (the passage ends, as if Propertius had already heard or read a draft of the end of *Aeneid* 12, with a mention of Juturna's pure and patriotic fountain):

> hic Anio Tiburine fluis, Clitumnus ab Umbro
>   tramite, et aeternum Marcius umor opus.
> Albanus lacus et socia Nemorensis ab unda
>   potaque Pollucis nympha salubris equo.

Here flow your waters, Tiburtine Anio, and here wash the waves of Clitumnus, fresh from its Umbrian watercourse, here splashes the water from the venerable Marcian aqueduct, here are the Alban and Nemorensian lakes, and here is nymph Juturna's curative fountain where her brother, godly Pollux, watered his steed. (23–26)

Abruptly, this core of Roman truth makes way for another heavy

---

8. Newman, 340, is briefly amused "to find the poet assuming the role of *patruus,* elder statesman," but is not sufficiently engaged by this entertainment to probe its complexities.

dose of Greek horror show phantasmagoria—Snakes, Dragons, Thyestes, Althaea, Maenads, pitiful Iphigenia, Io, sadistic Sinus—they're all here, a copious Hellenic nightmare zoo dumped haphazard into the by now unmistakable message of this campy cautionary tale: the Graeculi glory in their monsters, we glory (humbly) in our simple traditions and simple virtues. Come home, Tullus, back to your roots, back to the truth and purity of Italy and Rome.

> haec tibi, Tulle, parens, haec est pulcherrima sedes,
>   hic tibi pro digna gente petendus honos,
> hic tibi ad eloquium cives, hic ampla nepotum
>   spes et venturae coniugis aptus amor.

> Back here, Tullus, back here is the land of your birth and your homeland, the most beautiful place on earth. It's here that you should be looking for a public office that's worthy of your clan's glory. Here you will find an audience of free citizens capable of appreciating your eloquence, and here you have waiting for you ample hope of grandsons and a wife whose appropriate love is also right here, ready for your taking. (3.22.39–42)

Aptus amor: love as defined by Cato's code. His homeland's love of him (or his for her) is "suitable, convenient, appropriate": it (she) will produce children and grandchildren. That is Roman marriage and Roman Love.

Once again, it's five or so years before the emperor's marriage law, which, in the pipeline for a few years now, will see formal passage. It's in the air, people are probably talking about it, particularly the men and women of Propertius' class and generation who have watched Antony and Gallus as Mad Lovers in action and who have read the poetry that helped shape them and that they in turn helped to shape. But now, ironically, it's Tullus, who should be a prime representative of the Roman Way, who is found to be derelict in his conjugal and procreative duties and who is being urged to take on the venerable and rewarding responsibilities of citizen, husband, and father; who is being lectured on citizenship and morality by—of all people—the feckless whoremonger who has made the theory and practice, and the advertisement of, random and frequent lechery his life's work. And it is this purveyor of fancy, decadent, modernist (that is, neo-neoteric) style who has usurped Cato's own plain style (*rem tene, verba sequentur*), mockingly mingled with its stylistic antipodes, to do it. No wonder readers of the poem have been hard pressed to come to grips with what seems an astonishing change of heart and mind.

Both those for whom the change of heart and the letter-poem that expresses it are sincere, and for Stahl for whom the change is unreal and the letter written under constraint, have mostly ignored the poem's stylistic loop-the-loop and its wild polarities. They have missed as well its peculiar omission: both its broken tone and the deliberate failure of its rhetoric's logic evade them. The crucial line is: *Famam, Roma, tuae non pudet historiae,* 20: "Fame, Rome, is not ashamed of your history." For rhetorical balance and for logical consistency, it is the history, not the mythology, of Greece—the history of Athens, say, or better of Sparta—that ought to be played off against the history of Rome. Furthermore—in a tactic which would be hardly less crucial to the poem's apparent aim and one which would be considerably more honest—there should be some discussion of Rome's own history rather than this pious and abstract paraphrase of Anchises' version of how the Roman Empire was won and his celebration of the virtues that marked it uniquely. Such a gesture would be particularly appropriate in this circumstance because Tullus may very well remember (and so ought we remember) the observation the poet had made about one moment in Roman history in the ferocious *sphragis* poem that closed his first volume:

> qualis et unde genus, qui sint mihi, Tulle, penates
>   quaeris pro nostra semper amicitia.
> si Perusina tibi patriae sunt nota sepulchra,
>   Italiae duris funera temporibus,
> cum Romana suos egit discordia civis,
>   (sic mihi praecipue, pulvis Etrusca, dolor,
> tu proiecta mei perpessa es membra propinqui,
>   tu nullo miseri contegis ossa solo),
> proxima supposito contingens Umbria campo
>   me genuit terris fertilis uberibus.

> You're always asking, Tullus, What's my station,
> My parentage and where it is I come from?
> Dear friend, you know perhaps Perusia's tombs,
> Perusia, where our countrymen reside
> In graveyards, dead when Italy endured
> The infamies of Roman fratricide?—
> Etruscan ground! you are my chiefest grief,

For it is you that keep my cousin's bones,
Scattered, unhallowed—there, where Umbria,
My fertile mother, gazes down upon you. (1.22.1–10)

This linking of the poet's birthplace, Umbria, with a moment in his history that Octavian/Augustus and his handlers in the 20s would like to see buried deep in the collective unconscious borders on insolence.[9] At the time this closure was written and put into circulation, the regime's ideology was, to be sure, still in the process of being constructed. As Paul Cartledge has reminded us (163 ff.), the evolving principate was by no means secure in the 20s, and Fergus Millar (2002, 321) has even suggested, accurately to my mind, that the term 'Augustan poetry' misrepresents the poetry of the 20s because the Augustan Age, as we term it, was not safely in place until the middle teens, that is to say, about the time that Propertius published Book 4, his fifth and final volume. In that brief, explosive, final poem to Tullus in Book 1, three emotional utterances roil about in the tangled syntax that attempts to shape them: 1) the poet is, proudly, not a Roman patrician like "the friend" who has asked him for his credentials; 2) he is a sort of naturalized citizen, both Roman and Italian-Umbrian; 3) he feels somewhat conflicted, somewhat alien in the city that brought death to his kinsman, for whom and for whose cause he still grieves (and this would mean that he has not forgotten the ugly role that Octavian/Augustus played in the never-ending wrong of Perusia). It is a bitter, defiant way of knotting up a poem about who he is and who he intends to remain, as a human being, as a citizen, and as a poet.

In 3.22, Greek evil is balanced against and overwhelmed by Roman good. This sleight of hand succeeds from the effacement of the dark side of Roman history, especially of recent Roman history, the Social Wars and the civil wars (*cum Romana suos egit discordia civis*), a clustering of internecine crimes that does not exclude the part played in those horrors by Augustus and his circle, a part Augustus is anxious to consign to national amnesia. The poem's rhetoric collapses, on purpose, when the mythologizing legends of Rome's origins and evolution, which were enjoying a splendid transfiguration in *Aeneid* 6, find themselves caught in the distorting mirror that Propertius fashions in that poem. In this reading of 3.22, with its echoes of the final poem in Book 1 and echoes

---

9. For a discussion of the significance of the poet's attachment to his native place, see Bradley, 239, 243; see also DeBrohun, 105–13.

there of Perusia's horrors, Propertius has not been converted to the new regime and its claims; he has not abandoned what he took to be his own poetic mission, the investigation of the splendors and miseries of love as they were now being experienced and enacted in the divided psyches of the Roman men and women who were likely to be his most attentive readers. And he has not pretended, out of some kind of craven ambition, to have been so altered in mind and heart that he finds himself abandoning the poetic task he has taken on. Instead, he turns the claims of the regime inside out, transforming their demands and their boasts into materials for satires on what threatens the kind of poetry he was born to write, that he had devoted his young life to writing.

DARTS DIPPED IN ACID

The technique that shapes 3.22, whereby the poet arranges for antitheticals to collide, recurs in other poems in Book 3. In the body of the elegy for Augustus' heir apparent, Marcellus, a severe Stoicism chants of death's inevitability and, with raw emphasis, of its impartiality:

> quid genus aut virtus aut optima profuit illi
> mater, et amplexum Caesaris esse focos?

> What good did he get from his high birth or his own virtues or his wonderful mother? Or even from his having been nurtured in the bosom of Caesar's family? (3.18.11–12)

Supremely favored by fortune, power and glory seemed to be his destiny, his right, but then in his twentieth year, he dies:

> i nunc, tolle animos et tecum finge triumphos.
>   stantiaque in plausum tota theatra iuvent.
> Attalicas supera vestis, atque ostra smaragdis
>   gemmea sint Indis: ignibus ista dabis.

> Go now, exalt your spirit and let your imagination construct for you triumphal marches and a packed theater giving you a loud, standing ovation. As you daydream, dress yourself in the fanciest clothing you can conjure

up, cover their purple and gold with emeralds from India: all that you'll be consigning to the flames of your funeral pyre. (17–20)

That is the voice not of a eulogist but of a satirist (compare it with the voice that informs the grief for Marcellus toward the end of *Aeneid* 6). Caesar's heir (and by extension, Caesar himself) is, finally, a mere mortal:

> sed tamen huc omnes, huc primus et ultimus ordo:
> est mala, sed cunctis ista terenda via est.
>
> Despite all such expectations, to this end everyone, high and low, must come. It's a bad, hard path, but no one can evade it. (21–22)

Not what one expects to hear, not with the elaborately sardonic detail that Propertius uses to decorate his threnody, not the tone one wants for the funeral of this (or any) young princeling, certainly not what the Prince himself wanted to hear. Beautiful Nireus, brave Achilles, stinking rich Croesus—all of them go down, down, down into darkness. And Marcellus goes with them, it seems.

But suddenly the tone and topos swing in the opposite direction. It turns out there are exceptions to the dreadful rule: Charon is sometimes cheated of his fare in very special circumstances, as is the case here. This body being carried to its funeral pyre is empty of its soul (*hoc animae corpus inane suae,* 32); like the soul of Marcus Claudius Marcellus, conqueror of Syracuse, and that of the great Julius, the soul of Marcellus escapes its mere carnality and, abandoning the road of mortality, it zooms off into the heavens (*ab humana cessit in astra via,* 34). It is a pious thought, as comforting here as the similar piece of imperial propaganda about Julius' catasterism (remember the use Propertius makes of this image in his Actium pastiche[10]). But some of the poet's initial readers are less likely to have been comforted by this observation or the sudden switch in rhetorical logic that permits it than they are to have been amused by its effrontery.[11]

In 3.14, a sly meditation on the relativity of erotic mores and the sexual legislation they give rise to, Propertius pits classical (fifth-

---

10. For which, see Johnson 1973, 168; Welch, 106–11; Hutchinson, 152–55. For a parallel moment in the Cornelia poem, 4.11, see Johnson 1997, 171.

11. See Nethercut 1970 for excellent readings of 3.22 as well as of 3.13, 3.14, and 3.18.

century BCE) Sparta against modern (Augustan) Rome. He likes the idea of women being required to exercise naked in the same space time as their naked menfolk (*inter luctantis nuda puella viros,* 4) nor is he displeased by what he imagines to be a Doric sexual utopia, one where girls are not locked up away from the men who might interest them, and one where jealous husbands don't cause you trouble (*nec timor aut ulla est clausae tutela puellae, / nec gravis austeri poena cavenda viri,* 23–24); where you are free to say what's on your mind or groin (*nullo praemisso de rebus tute loquaris / ipse tuis,* 25–26). And you don't have to guess at what you're going to be getting, and you won't have to buy her expensive perfume either (*nec Tyriae vestes errantia lumina fallunt, / est neque odoratae cura molesta comae,* 26–27). In Rome, they order things quite differently. It is not so easy for the elegiac lover in his own city to obtain a little of what he fancies as it would be in that quondam Spartan paradise. Once again, there are rumors of the coming marriage and adultery laws, and this incipient, homegrown draconianism is wryly juxtaposed with a silly sketch of Doric fun in the sun. At the heart of the poem is the poet's yen to see men and women, covered in dust and sweat, wrestling one another, as they train for their erotic pancratium. Which is not what fuels the Augustan reformulation of the sexual instinct in the interest of improved family values.

In 3.13 the traditional Roman loathing of luxury, combined with a call for a renewal of old-time frugality and old-time religion, culminates in a lapidary warning: *frangitur ipsa suis Roma superba bonis,* 60, "Proud Rome is imploding from her own prosperity." But this admonition is spoken by Propertius as he impersonates Cassandra in one of her whiniest avatars. The topos that Livy and Horace, not to mention Augustus and Livia (he with his farmer's luncheon, she at her spinning wheel), had successfully embellished here encounters a poet who decides to turn it on its head. In an earlier poem the poet had linked luxury (and the prosperity that fuels it) with the emperor and his empire: *arma deus Caesar dites meditatur ad Indos,* 3.4.1, "The god Caesar is planning to attack India and its riches." Though he is certain that Caesar's project will be successful and though he hopes to see the day when the emperor returns, laden with spoils, in triumph from his eastern campaign, he himself intends to be standing on the sidelines with his dear girl at his side, cheering and praying for the enduring felicity of Caesar's clan. But he wants no share in the profits, which belong solely to those who have earned them (Caesar and his soldiers); he is content to be part of the adoring crowd of spectators who line the Sacred Way (*praeda sit haec illis, quorum meruere labores: / me sat erit Sacra plaudere posse Via* [3.4.21–22]) In 3.13, the poet, who has not shared in the influx of imperial riches, protests that it is Rome's passion for luxury that encourages high-class hookers (and their society-girl imitators) to charge higher prices (*quaeritis, unde avidis nox sit pretiosa puellis, / et Venere exhaustae damna querantur opes*, 1–2). Once again, the orthodox platitudes dissolve in acidulous irony.

In 3.11 the poet begins with what promises to be a rationalization for the enormous ruin of his life, for his having become so abject, so degenerate, a Roman male—enslaved by his lust for a commanding woman (*quid mirare, meam si versat femina vitam / et trahit addictum sub sua iura virum*, 1–2). Beginning with Jason and ending with Jupiter who *infamat seque suamque domum* (28, "disgraces himself and his family"), the poet catalogues better males than himself, great heroes all, who have found themselves shamed exactly as he has been shamed. But the ruined males of poetic myth are not sufficient to explain his real self-debasement. He turns, inevitably, to recent history, to the greatest of the great Roman lovers, to Antony and to the abominations that Cleopatra had prepared for his destruction. To depict that tragic action and its monstrous architect, Propertius avails himself of every slander and half-truth that Augustan propaganda had been able to devise against the glamorous and doomed pair. Luckily, of course, this story has a happy ending—not for Antony of course, but for Rome, which Augustus, a real hero, greater than all the heroes of Greek poetry or Roman history put together, has saved from its bad fate. The poet's thanksgiving is so intense that he slips into a jingoistic blasphemy which most commentators tend to sweep under the carpet (for example, Newman, 344): *vix timeat salvo Caesare Roma Iovem*, 66, "While Caesar lives Rome hardly need fear Jove." It makes perfect sense, poetically speaking, for Propertius to identify himself, elliptically, with Antony, for Antony was the larger-than-life Mad Lover who gave Latin love elegy its definitive figure. But, of course, after Actium, the equation is awkward: it invites the poet to try out-Vergiling Vergil and out-Horacing Horace in representing the wicked dominatrix (*et famulos inter femina trita suos*, 30, "A woman whom even her slaves had screwed"), and it tempts him to connect this theme with that of Augustus the Savior of the World. The logical progression is reasonable enough, but the juxtaposition of grand panegyric (*cape, Roma, triumphum / et longum Augustum salva precare diem!*, 49–50, "Sing, Rome, sing a song of triumph! Saved you are, so pray that Augustus' life may be a long one") with his own erotic servitude creates a funny, indecorous dissonance. Here as elsewhere in this group of poems, the poet is inept or insolent. Take your pick.[12]

Finally, in 3.9, to Maecenas, the poet indulges himself in an elaborate double-speak of humble aporia (can't do it) scrambled with tentative, eventual capitulation (someday perhaps I can) to what the age and its makers demand. He begins by insisting that Maecenas is asking too much of him and reminds him that, particularly with artists, different kinds of talent suit different kinds of endeavor (*omnia non pariter rerum sunt omnibus apta,* 7, and *naturae sequitur semina quisque suae,* 20). Take, for instance, Maecenas himself. His services to Rome's common good equal those of Rome's greatest sons (Camillus, for instance, 32), and he will take his place in history alongside Augustus himself (33), even though he hasn't bothered with military service or making himself conspicuous in the forum and elsewhere in public life. Instead, he is modest, he hides his light under a bushel: he is not a man of action, not someone you would put in an epic if you happened to be writing one. So, thinks Propertius, he will imitate his friend, the host of Rome's choicest poetic soirees, and he will follow his own bent and not embarrass himself trying to write epic, and he will continue to delight young men and young women who are desperate to read about erotic bliss. That special audience, his very own, may well come to regard *him* as a god and offer *him* divine worship (*haec urant pueros, haec urant scripta puellas, / meque deum clament et mihi sacra ferant!,* 45–46). Then, with no transition whatever, he says: *te duce vel Iovis arma canam.* With you as my leader, better, with you as my general, I shall sing of War in Heaven and then go on to sing of Roman wars and Rome's empire, war by war, century by century, until I get to—of course, Antony: *Antonique gravis in sua fata manus,* 56, "Antony's hands fierce in shaping his own destruction." And then, having once again offered his ironic submission (I'll be a soldier, if you will), the poet asks leave to pursue his present path for a little while longer.

> mollia tu coeptae fautor cape lora iuventae,
>   dexteraque immissis da mihi signa rotis.
> hoc mihi, Maecenas, laudis concedes, et a te est
>   quod ferar in partis ipse fuisse tuas.

---

12. See Nethercut 1971 for an exemplary reading of 3.11; see also the useful discussion by Fantham 2006, 196–98.

Partisan of my career (which is still in its early stages), while I speed onward in my poetic chariot, rein me in gently, I beg you. So much esteem you proffer now me, Maecenas, and it is because of your kindness that I will be said to have achieved a place among your circle of friends and poets. (57–60)

The gratitude is delicately (and carefully, and slyly) expressed. And once again, the regime's worldview and the poet's, though they seem about to fuse, finally fail to mesh, with the result that the regime is diminished (as I see it, the regime has all the power and nevertheless loses) while the poet's integrity (and poetic power), though feeble, remain (ironically) intact.

THE TRIUMPH OF DISGREGATION

Antonio La Penna, in his marvelous book, *Properzio e l'integrazione difficile,* shows, better I think than most of the poet's readers, how fiercely Propertius confronted various efforts to get him to alter his poetic vocation. La Penna, as his book's title reveals, takes the poet's *recusationes* seriously. He thinks, however, that in the end Propertius found it impossible *not* to be integrated into Rome's society in its Augustan reformulation. I am arguing that the integration was not just difficult but impossible. We don't know how it was that Propertius first began writing his love poems (maybe he just felt drawn to the subject for unknowable reasons, maybe he fell in love and then wrote poetry; maybe—in the manner of Yeats and not a few other poets—he wrote poetry and then, subconsciously, fell in love in order to write intenser poetry). However it happened, however he became a poet of love, that became his vocation, that became how he lived, how he lived for the sake of his poetic identity and its poetry. And this happened just at the time that something new was taking shape in the world around him. Antony and Gallus, the great Mad Lovers who had been the icons of young lovers and young poets of love, died a decade and a half from one another, just in that period of time when their nemesis was cobbling together the values and the institutions that would define the state he would end by governing for over four decades after Antony died. It is inside that drastic change of climate that Propertius begins and ends his poetic career, his poetic mission. Whoever or whatever Cynthia was, she, her figure, symbolized for Propertius and in his poems the freedom and the integrity of his poetic identity.

He could not write about 'something else' because, for him there was nothing worth talking about except his vision of a way of being liberated from outworn styles of living, a vision that had become fused with the shaping of a poetic craft that could represent that vision, make it visible, almost tangible, to the young men and young women who would become his readers, make it always new for them, make it always real for them. At the end of Book 3 he does in fact foreswear Cynthia, and at the beginning of Book 4 he claims he will finally begin writing the kinds of patriotic poetry that Maecenas and his friends have been begging him to write. But Cynthia, as we've seen, returns to dominate the center of that final book of his, thus confirming the prophecy of the strange astrologer who disrupted the poet's avowals of his change of heart in 4.1. The astrologer warns him that he won't succeed at this new undertaking, and this resonant echo of what Apollo and Calliope had said to him in 3.3 strengthens our doubts about the likelihood of the poet's capacity for carrying out his new design, for successfully performing his new role as celebrant of the triumphant regime. Not a few of the poems in Book 3 confirm the accuracy of the warnings from the god, the muse and the stargazer: they mock the regime's platitudes mercilessly, and they affirm the constancy of Propertius' identity both as poet-lover and as a *disgregatore;* as someone whom his Cynthia had shown the path to disgregation, away from Rome's dream of empire, back to Callimachus and to Umbria and to poetic freedom. The heir to whom he passed his torch—or who snatched it up where he had put it down (the when, how, and why of this event ancient gossip is silent on)—would find himself facing—and taking—greater risks than those Propertius had met with, but his own style of constancy and his courage were more than equal to the task.

CHAPTER 5

WHATEVER HAPPENED TO LATIN LOVE ELEGY?

> That fine fellow who when I was young castrated so many beautiful ancient statues in his City so as not to corrupt our gaze ... ought to have recalled that ... nothing is achieved unless you also geld horses, donkeys and finally everything in nature.
> —Montaigne, 3.5

> It is through disobedience that progress had been made, through disobedience and through rebellion.
> —Wilde, *The Soul of Man under Socialism*

WE DO NOT LIKE the fact that some artists die young, before they achieve their promise, and we are equally unhappy when mature artists find themselves and their art crushed by arbitrary and unjust Power. Ovid's exile from Rome to one of its empire's wilder peripheries, his punishment by Augustus, remains a problem as fascinating as it is mysterious. As will quickly appear, I am in the firm grip of my own private certainties in these matters, but I must nonetheless admit how dim and slippery, how fiercely resistant to proof and resolution, the whys and wherefores of the poet's fate have always been and how likely they are to remain so. With these caveats in place, let me glance briefly at two recent and influential perspectives on the conflict between Augustus and the most talented poet writing in the final decades of his long reign before I try my hand at recontextualizing the production of *Tristia* 2 and then–what concerns me most–at offering my version of the meanings that generate its aesthetic design and the pleasures that design has to offer.

For many of his readers, the thought of Ovid's opposition to Augustan ideology is all but unthinkable. To challenge the emperor, they say, or even to lightly twit him would have been too dangerous even if it were something a poet of the time might have felt like doing. A poet in that time and place would, after all, have had, could have had, no political agenda, except the emperor's. Moreover, leaving aside the question of whether the emperor would read or come to hear of the peculiar verses that seemed to allude to him in a perhaps unflattering way, what sorts of audience could a steadily dissident and lonely voice hope to capture and retain then and there? Questions such as these construct the perspective from which a satirical Ovid becomes a flat impossibility. And once that impossibility is defined and its truth secured, it's not a hard task to show that what might otherwise appear to be witticisms at the expense of the imperial ideology can instead be viewed, and were best viewed, as the natural and intricate workings of the semiological process that Power is always in control of.[1]

Alessandro Barchiesi's version of Ovid's perspective on Augustus calls for a sign system in which the emperor's ability to manipulate all the signifying practices in his empire, not least of all those of the plastic and verbal arts, constrains everyone, not least of all artists, to implicate themselves in the process of replicating his own self-representations, thereby contributing, willingly or not, to exponential expansions of his ideological web and its reflecting and reflected glories. In this scheme Ovid's ambiguities and ironies, far from being deliberate spitballs hurled at an unmoving target, were best perceived as strategies of escaping headlong clashes with the emperor and his more powerful partisans. This formulation of the Augustan sign-system allows Barchiesi to have his cake and eat it too: that is, as Barchiesi imagines that milieu and moment, it was impossible for Ovid to mock the emperor explicitly, but, nevertheless, mock him he perhaps did anyhow, slyly and obliquely, or at least with the sort of fruitful (and entertaining) indeterminacy that the postmodern hermeneutics find useful and admire.

A similar if subtler belief in the ability of Augustus and his handlers to control the game of signs, indeed, to design the game board and thus determine how the game has to be played, by all players, anytime

---

1. See Habinek, 155–58, for a neat summary of this style of reading. This style is perhaps best characterized by 'optimistic' interpretations of Augustus, his renovations of Rome, and his entire regime. For a good analysis of what this optimism consists of, see Kallendorf, v–vii and passim.

and anywhere, is offered by Duncan Kennedy in his influential essay, "Augustan and Anti-Augustan: Reflections on Terms of Reference." For Kennedy, the conflict between Augustus and Ovid is something of a fiction since the once fashionable terms "pro- and anti-Augustan" would seems to cancel each other out. Thanks to the "dynamic, dialogic framework" that constitutes Augustan discourse, "no statement (not even those made by Augustus himself) can be categorically 'Augustan' or anti-Augustan" (40–41). Either pole of this antinomy (those who favor Augustus versus those who don't) can seize the other's argument and turn it upside down. "The degree to which a voice is heard as conflicting or supportive is a function of the audience's—or critic's—ideology, a function, therefore, of *reception*" (40–41; emphasis in original). So far, so good: what seems to be said in blame of Augustus reminds us that what he demanded was praise, but, at the same time, his obsession with being praised, with having himself favorably represented, *semper, ubique, ab omnibus,* reminds us that there were reasons for blaming him (and that some people might even have busied themselves in such a pursuit). But Kennedy then continues his argument in this way: "Power is successful in so far as it manages not so much to silence or suppress as to *determine the consumption* of the oppositional voice within the discourse. Critics' responses to Augustan poetry are a measure of the *continuing* capacity of Augustan ideology to determine its reception (41; emphasis in original). What this seems to mean is: not only when the Power in question is still in physical/temporal existence can it silence or not silence the opposing voices that are coeval with it, but also, even after it survives only in historical memory, it can still shape the ways in which both it and the voices that opposed it are received by posterity and judged by it. As Kennedy frames his proposition, the ghost of Power not only can influence how it is received and judged in its afterlife, but is also, in fact, very likely to do so.[2]

Nevertheless, barely half a century after Augustus died, Pliny the Elder, while meditating on the mutability of human fortune (*Natural History* 7.147–50), singled out Augustus as a prime example of human beings who are apparently possessed of fortune's richest gifts but whose lives are nonetheless shot through, from beginning to end, with diverse griefs and humiliations and crimes (he lists, copiously, everything that, glaringly, does *not* find a place in Augustus' own version of who he was and what he did, the *Res Gestae)*. In Kennedy's reading of how

---

2. For an incisive critique of Kennedy's arguments, see Davis 2006, 9–22.

Augustan power functioned and continues to function, any opposition to that power exists chiefly to validate it, to prove its capacity to structure both how it will be seen and represented by its contemporaries *and* how those representations will be received by those who seek in aftertimes to understand it and its workings. In this version of the discourse of power, Pliny's ferocious emphasis on the opposing voices who trumpeted what went wrong with Augustus' life and reign merely serves to demonstrate how inevitable was the triumph of Augustus (and his spin-doctors) over his would-be detractors.[3] But what Pliny's remarkable pages actually show is that, even before Tacitus had perfected the topic, Pliny expected his carefully crafted distillation of voices in conflict with Augustan triumphalism to find sympathetic eyes and ears. After Pliny, after Tacitus, from Dio Cassius down to Gibbon and beyond, the receptions of Augustus and his ideology are marked not so much by his capacity to control how his images will be viewed, but rather by the variety of contingencies that are utterly beyond his control and that in fact determine the pattern of "dynamic dialogic framework" between his admiring and disdainful receptors. Different temperaments in different times and different places for different reasons examine the fragments of Augustan ideology in different ways.

It's true that the reception of Augustus tended to be favorable while the notion of regal divine right (which his ideology had done much to establish) retained its hold on the mind of Europe; but even before it became fashionable to execute kings and thus abrogate their celestial warrants for dominion, there were times and places when students of the Augustan Vision paid attention to, were persuaded by, the voices that opposed him and that survive in Pliny, Tacitus, and Dio Cassius, the voices whose relevance and enduring power Kennedy's formulation seeks to diminish.[4] So, in certain places and at certain times, certain kinds of temperaments receive Augustan ideology much as he intended it to be received by his contemporaries *and* by posterity; but at other times, and in other places, certain temperaments are proof against the emperor's devices and seductions, and then the voices that opposed his ideology sound out loud and clear. (This zigzag pattern of the ups and downs of great men's reputations tends to be ignored by them when they fondly hope to be Judged by History.)

Finally, when casting our yea or nay votes on the meanings of the

---

3. An excellent discussion of this Augustan strategy is provided by Davis 1999.
4. For an illuminating sketch of the receptions of Augustus, see Carter.

Augustan Solution, we want to bear in mind that the evidence on which we base our judgments remains, though meretriciously plentiful, pitifully meager and hopelessly fragmentary. Recall here that Dio Cassius, the writer who provides us with our fullest account of the reign, tells us forthrightly that "much that never occurs is noised abroad and much that happens beyond a doubt is unknown, and in the case of nearly every event a version gains currency that is different from the way it really happened." He goes on to remark (53.19.4–6) that so vast now is the Roman Empire that "there is something happening all the time, in fact, every day and concerning these things, no one except the participants can easily have correct information, and most people do not even hear of them at all" (Ernest Carey's Loeb translation). Dio is writing of his own time in this passage, but the situation that he finds himself in as he ponders the dearth and unreliability of his evidence has not changed, he insists, since the moment Augustus formalized his control of Rome in 27 BCE. It was then that the public began to be disinformed by those who governed in their name (53.19.2): "most things began to be kept in secret and concealed, and even though some things are perchance made public, they are distrusted just because they can not be verified; for it is suspected that everything is said and done with reference to the wishes of the men in power at the time and their associates" (3). Dio goes on to say that he will, of course, sift as best he can through the abundant evidence he has gathered, unreliable and contradictory though it often is, but he makes it very clear, most especially when he comes to deal with the various plots against Augustus (54.15ff.), that the official versions cannot be trusted. So, though the information is abundant, he is aware that too many pieces of the puzzle, some having been deliberately mislaid, are missing for good. "Dio accepts the Empire," says Fergus Millar, "as the only stable form of government, but this in no way blinds him to the gap between political realities and constitutional forms" (93). For all his acceptance of the necessity of empire and his willingness to record the official version of its birth and growth, Dio was not prevented by the official version from "writing in an ironical, not to say cynical, tone of the political structure which Augustus erected. For to Dio this political structure was a mere façade, masking the simple reality of the rule of one man" (Millar, 97). In Dio, therefore, the pro and anti portions of the Augustan debate find an ironically harmonic disharmony, in which the supportive and the conflicting, the praisers and the blamers, almost succeed in sharing the same space time. For all his defects, which seem fewer now than they did before Fergus Millar reread him, Dio stands as a cautionary emblem for us when we evaluate the first modern European king, rating his achievement, examining his motives, grading his character. We know much less than Dio knew, and our biases are, on balance, less sophisticated than his were. Aside from a few facts, what we know that Dio didn't know is how the palimpsest of reception and its complex genealogies thicken steadily and how endless and inevitable and inconclusive revisions and re-revisions of Augustus must be.

WHAT AUGUSTUS HAD IN MIND

So much for the ongoing dilemma of praise and blame that festers when moderns look into their ancient classical mirror. What I want to do now is try to imagine the perspectives of Augustus from the years 16 BCE down to 2 BCE, that is to say, from the years after he celebrated the Secular Games, the *Ludi Saeculares,* down to the time when his daughter, Julia, was banished for her dubious entertainments and possible political intrigues (see below, 133); that is to say, from the year in which the first edition of Ovid's *Amores* appeared in five books down to the year before the *Ars Amatoria* appeared, which is roughly the time when the revised edition of *Amores,* now distilled into three books, began to be circulated. I entertain little hope of getting inside the emperor's mind (which of his historians, pro or con, does not, whatever objectivity they may aspire to, end by doing exactly that?); but, as an experiment in literary criticism, I want to see if I can look at Ovid's early career through the eyes of the person who would eventually feel constrained, very possibly with some reluctance, to give him a one-way ticket to the Black Sea.

The five books of Ovid's first edition of the *Amores* appeared in 16 BCE or shortly thereafter. In the previous year Augustus had celebrated the Secular Games, an action, a spectacular religious event, which commemorated both the renewal of the Roman Nation and its preservation and salvation *by* the beneficence of the gods and *through* the courage and purity of will of their human agent, Gaius Julius Caesar Octavianus, the man who had received, from the senate and the people of Rome, just a decade before that, the splendid title Augustus. The decade that separated the gift of his new name from his celebration of and thanksgiving for the survival of Rome and its empire (and himself) had been rather more hectic than one might infer from glancing at the emperor's own version of his reign or Karl Galinsky's *Augustan Culture* or even at the pages of Velleius Paterculus (2.88–91), who mentions plots against Augustus in order to emphasize both their futility and the emperor's luck and leadership.[5] A huge portion of the Roman citizens who had survived the last wave of Rome's civil wars grew ever more willing to shut out the grim, ruinous past and to concentrate on a calm and ordered present that promised, after nearly a century of savage turmoil, a sustained abundance and an uncommon tranquility. This large and unsilent majority were delighted to have found an Augustus to protect them both from the barbarian hordes and from each other. But not everyone was dancing in the streets. A small but vigorous minority found their leader's settlement in some degree unacceptable; they were disaffected, they disliked his style of rehabbing Rome's buildings and statues, his revival–or rather reinvention–of Roman religion, his tinkering with its maps and calendars, his showy restoration of the censorship and of senatorial powers, his professionalization of the army—in short, his restoration of the republic as he claimed it had formerly been. So there were grumblings and protests (for instance, by M. Licinius Crassus and his dispute over who deserved the *spolia opima;* for which, see Cartledge, 36–37), and even some plots to overthrow the savior, though of these we hear little and know much less for reasons that Dio, as I've mentioned, makes clear.[6] So, in these years 27–25 BCE, Augustus gets out of town and attends to various matters in Spain and Gaul; and he repeats this remedy for unrest again from 22 through 19 BCE in Sicily, Greece, and Asia Minor. He is, moreover, gravely ill both in 25 and in 23 BCE; in this latter fateful year he also endures one of the most serious of the plots against his throne and his life, as well as the death of Marcellus, his nephew on whom his hopes for his dynasty were pinned and whose loss, famously, Vergil would choose as the poignant, grieving closure for the first half of his epic.

In the year 16 BCE, therefore, Augustus must be feeling pretty well. He has weathered a swarm of dangers and difficulties, his opponents seem mostly to have perished or to have worn themselves out or to have been won over; both his retooling and his invention of the machinery of government are keeping pace with his fabrication of a viable and highly visible ideology for a distinctly Augustan Roman Empire. There is still

---

5. For an acute reading of Galinksy's erudite and laudatory representation of the emperor's reign, see Henderson.

6. See Seneca's pious remarks on these plots, *De brevitate vitae,* 4.5.

a lot to do, but it looks as if he now has both the means and the time to do it all, that is, to accomplish the aims of his quiet 'revolution.'

A DOMESTIC SCENE

Then one day, someone—I like to think it's his daughter, Julia—my inspiration for this piece of prosaic license is some of the Julia's witticisms as they come down to us in Macrobius[7]—enters her father's study carrying a bagful of scrolls. "Daddy," she says, "have you heard about these swell poems by this wonderful new poet named Ovid, they are *so* funny." No, he answers, he doesn't know anything about any new poems. Aside from Vergil and Varius and Horace, he doesn't, as she perfectly well knows, read much current verse. He does, though, have a vague memory of some Ovid or other—maybe it's that bright young kid from Paelignia that Maecenas has been blathering about. His folks had sent him to study law, but apparently he ended up with the wrong crowd, so now he was doing what lots of idiots like that often did—he started scribbling so-called poems. "Couldn't I read you a few of them, Daddy?" wheedles Julia, "just a few of them, just one?" "Sure," says Daddy, "read me one." When she's finished the first one and starts a second, he stops her. "Ho hum," says Augustus, "are people still writing that kind of stuff?" Julia attempts to counter his disdain by telling him that everybody is reading Ovid these days, that he's all the rage, that everyone's just crazy for him. But it turns out that by everyone she means, naturally, her cronies, those throngs of her lazy, stupid hangers-on who, having squandered their parents' money, avoid the normal pursuits of grown-ups, the army, the law courts, government service, and, of course—despite his new laws!—marriage. These poor dismal creatures, having failed to make the transition from childhood to maturity, had latched on to an antiquated lifestyle under the illusion that it had never died or that this Ovid and other young whippersnappers like him had invented it. When Julia was barely out of diapers, her Daddy tells her, various people were still writing that sentimental crap. They called it love poetry but it was just timid smut. Catullus and his pal Calvus had started the craze back in the old days when Catiline was running amuck. This smarmy junk was fashionable for a while (he doesn't, for obvious

---

7. See Richlin's witty account of these delightful fragments of history—or gossip.

reasons, mention Gallus in this context; he skips over Tibullus; he forgets to mention Propertius or suppresses him). But nowadays, Daddy assures her, the love fad is dead as a doornail. So, her bright new discovery had better learn some new tunes or he's out of luck—he very much needs to make another career choice.

Julia rolls up her scroll, stuffs it back in her poetry bag and departs, convinced, of course, that her father is—she always knew it—a dinosaur and a Philistine and a party-pooper. Utterly ignorant of poetry, wholly lacking in a sense of humor, totally out of touch with what the age demands, with the new styles, with fashion.

But Julia is mistaken. Her father is himself a master craftsman of fashion, and there is little about it that he and his image makers don't know. In her circle and in the circles that ripple from them, Ovid's glittering fecklessness may have discovered its proper space time, and he may have stumbled upon his first and, in a way his ideal, audience in the silly creatures who cluster like moths about the flame of the emperor's daughter, people among whom the gospel of an erotic imperative that is beyond good and evil may survive and thrive. But in the vast population of Rome and Italy and the known world, among her father's multitude of supporters, though adultery and salacious celibacy by no means lose their attraction, love poetry and its worldview have all but faded. Their grandfathers (and grandmothers) and fathers (and mothers) may have found, some of them, their true selves in yielding or trying to yield themselves to un-Roman passions, but the disordered world that gave rise to that mode of what now seems—to Augustus and his loyal subjects—merely sentimental lust in pursuit of a glamorous self-destruction, that world has passed away; the times have changed and changed much for the better. Those who survived those old days and their erotic illusions, these sober, purposeful citizens, are more than satisfied with the new ideology (though not the practice) of moderation and its mild austerities.[8] It is Julia and her Ovid and their friends who, deluded by ghosts from a vanished amative Utopia, are behind the times. It is Augustus and all the people, noble and plebian alike, who have kept him and keep keeping him in power, it is they who are on the cutting edge. So it might have seemed to Augustus if he had taken any notice of the first version of the *Amores* in 15 BCE. And, essentially, he would have been right.

---

8. See Clarke's shrewd caveat on the degree of popular acceptance of Augustus' resuscitated morality, 89–90.

WHEN SORROWS COME

We skip ahead now a decade and a half. During this period (15 to 1 BCE), Augustus has his downs and ups, but, for a while, on balance, more ups than downs. The stability of his regime grows steadily more secure, his vision of a new Rome and of his own role in shaping it shines constantly ever clearer. Ovid, meanwhile, has written an estimable tragedy and invented a new genre, the letters of lost ladies, and he has busied himself with revising, with winnowing and distilling, his first work, the *Amores*.[9] Whether Augustus knew or cared anything about what the poet was up to during this period is utterly unknown, but it's not improbable that he heard reports of his daughter's continuing giggling, now over passages in one of Naso's works in progress; he may have heard rumors that there were some new poems that contained a few passages packed with snide remarks about Rome and its renewal, bits that smacked of Propertian insolence. Augustus would have paid little attention to this information. He was starting to have other things to worry about. He had begun to hear grim rumors, about Julia and her friends. Not about their taste in poetry but about their other diversions, about their taste in sexual entertainments, perhaps about their penchant for political intrigue. Finally, he would be forced to banish his daughter, and Antony's son, one of her playmates, and/or political cronies, committed suicide and the gilded soirees vanished. The next decade showed more downs than ups. There were continuing, accelerating worries about the succession, there were financial and military troubles. And then, Julia's daughter, another Julia, the emperor's granddaughter, showed that she had inherited her mother's flair for disobeying the Voice of the Father. We have no information about whether, like her mother, she combined a yen for subversive verse and treasonable politics with hankerings for illegal fornication. Whatever her infractions, she followed her mother into exile, on a different island. That same year Ovid also boarded a ship, his to Tomi at the end of the earth.[10]

Here too we have no information about what Ovid did wrong. Maybe Augustus had heard that there were possibly slanderous passages in the strange new epic Ovid was said to be undertaking, or in the patriotic poem that he'd also begun about the Roman calendar in

---

9. For a persuasive account of this process, see Tarrant, 16–17, 20–21, 28.

10. For a lively account of these events, see Balsdon, 82–89; for a more elaborate discussion, see Meise, 1–46.

its new imperial incarnation. Maybe the granddaughter's crimes made him decide, irrationally but explicably, that the infamous poem that was said to be a sort of sexual instruction manual was an incitement to adultery; maybe both Julias had read it once too often, the mother in rough drafts, her daughter in the deluxe edition. If so, the Emperor had been patient or indifferent long enough. And he was old and angry and tired, and these were the last straws (and with or without the poem, it would have been enough for a jealous informer to claim he had heard that Ovid was somehow complicit, however indirectly, in one of young Julia's dalliances). In any case, the last Julia and the smart-aleck poet both disappeared from the scene they loved best.

A POET IN AND OUT OF LUCK

But a quarter of a century before, back in 16 BCE, himself just over a quarter of a century old, in the flower of his young manhood, his first love elegies just being put in circulation, Ovid had looked at the world as his oyster. Of the poets who shone brightest in the glamorous 20s—Vergil gone, Tibullus gone—only Propertius, his mentor, and Horace, that sacred monster, remained, but both of them were in semiretirement, the one pretending to fiddle with antiquarian researches, the other immersed in playing gentleman farmer whilst dabbling in literary theory. There was the solid, stolid Varius Rufus, of course, but he was soothing his dotage by editing, at the emperor's request, Vergil's noble poem about pious Aeneas. And there were a host of others who were versifying, some good, some not so good, but Ovid had felt back then that he had the knack and more than the knack—and the feeling began to grow that maybe he would end up having the field to himself. His music was copious and fluent, it floated on its lilt and swing like feathers in a breeze, the poems all but sang themselves, their rhetoric was easy and deft, almost transparent, and they were brittle and bright and fun. He had stumbled on an affable if ironic pose that let him pump a bit more genuine life into the fading forms—he could do little with their content—that Propertius had exalted and then abandoned. He was on his way.[11]

Some of Ovid's elders and not a few of his coevals were not much

---

11. See Harrison, 80–82, for a good account of Ovid's treatment of love elegy.

taken by his poems, but these were people who, for one reason or another had bought into—or given lip service to—the Augustan grand renewal of antique mores, old Cato's Rome magically and paradoxically revived right here in modern Rome, the new metropolis, Alexandria on the Tiber. The revival, the revival of law and order and prosperity and reliable public services—all that was indeed spectacular. But its success hardly meant, so Ovid and his readers thought, that individuals should abandon their cultivated pleasures and diverse delights; that they should instead start trying to live their lives as if they had actually been transformed into those sweaty, stinking peasant farmers of olden times. Surely Augustus had not really intended that Romans should abandon everything that made modern life decent and livable; surely it was enough to give (or feign) tacit approval to the new (old) morality and the divine monarch's new emphasis on duty and citizenship. Certainly the charming people Ovid was beginning to encounter, the fashionable circles into which he had gained entrée—those people had no intention of divesting themselves of sophisticated entertainment and luxurious leisure in order to devote themselves to the well-being of the hive. Julia was hardly a convincing advertisement for her father's antique austerities. What was good enough for Julia was good enough for Ovid.

He was not much interested in what some of his new acquaintances had to say about lost liberty—they were a bit too earnest, these people, they sentimentalized idiotic old Cicero and the rotten republic as well. He had no time for that sort of conviction, and idealists tended to bore him. His only real ideal was the perfection of his art. And the more he focused on that perfection, the less he bothered himself with the gap between Julia's worldview and the emperor's. He was bubbling with ideas, and, as harsh, perhaps jealous, critics were quick to point out, he could scarcely dictate his verses fast enough.

Fast forward now (again) a decade and a half, to 1 BCE. Ovid is forty-two years old, smack in the middle of what was for a Roman advanced middle age; he is about to begin circulating his masterpiece, the *Ars Amatoria* (there will be, of course astonishingly, two more masterpieces after that, both of them completed in the desolation that was Tomi, certainly a testament to the purity of Ovid's poetic will). He has arrived at the place he guessed might be his, at the pinnacle of the Roman Helicon, but the world is no longer his buffet, the world has changed again. In the previous year, Julia had been banished. The emperor, now beset by a variety of difficulties, is less inclined to tolerance for the foibles of others or indifference to what he or his loyal courtiers take to be disesteem for the regime. The *Ars* shows all the familiar wit and dazzle and ease, but its undersongs glow with something mordant, something complexly dissonant. The emperor is no longer a remote, beneficent oddity; now he and his ideology and its ubiquitous iconography have invaded the air the poem breathes. The gap between the emperor's vision of civic tranquility and the poet's vision of libertarian innocence, never bridgeable, is no longer ignorable. A simultaneity of multiple causes, which may be conveniently symbolized by the punishment meted out to Julia and her friends, brings about a change in Ovid's thinking: he has begun to take the emperor's ideology personally. He has begun to think of liberty, not as a lost political reality but as an endangered personal, that is to say, poetic, necessity. Like Propertius before him, but in a very different way, he has begun to feel that the autonomy of his art, frivolous perhaps in the world's eyes yet precious in his own, has been threatened by the republican alibi for absolute monarchy.[12]

We will probably never know what moved Augustus to exile the last of the great poets who would come to be associated with his reign. But we do have, in the closing lines of *Tristia* 3.7 (43–54), the poet's most eloquent response to his emperor's anger:

> singula ne referam, nil non mortale tenemus
>   pectoris exceptis ingeniique bonis—
> en ego cum caream patria vobisque bonoque,
>   raptaque sint, adimi quae potuere mihi,
> ingenio tamen ipse meo comitorque fruorque—
>   Caesar in hoc potuit iuris habere nihil.

> Of all we hold most dear there nothing is
> That wards off perishing save only goods
> The intellect has garnered. Look on me,
> Stripped of my country, of my friends and home—
> Whatever can be stolen, I have lost,
> Am destitute, alone, and yet I have,
> As comrade and as constant joy, my gift
> For fictions and for verse—and that I keep
> Where Caesar's jurisdiction cannot seize it.

This full-voiced challenge to Power from the spirit that Power had

---

12. For the pressures of Augustan ideology at this time and Ovid's response to them, see P. Johnson, 13–21, 39–40.

sought to annihilate ends with the defiant claim to immortality that echoes a similar claim made at the end of the *Metamorphoses*. But a subtler and, in a sense, more ferocious rebuke to Augustan ideology shapes the content *and* the form of *Tristia* 2, that long and elaborate poem in which brazen recriminations against tyranny masquerade as humble appeals for understanding, forgiveness, compassion.[13]

THE MEMOIRS OF ICARUS

The poem opens with an exordium in which the sincerity of the poet's spectacular abjection finds its validation in his passionate, irrational statement of complete aporia. Here he is again, he says, driven by madness to take up his pen and write in the treacherous elegiac meter, using the same medium to try to win mercy that had brought him to ruin:

> at nunc—tanta meo comes est insania morbo—
>   saxa malum refero rursus ad ista pedem.

> But now—so great is the madness, companion to disease—I carry the evil meter back to those rocks. (*Tristia* 2.15–16)

The poet is like a defeated gladiator who returns to the arena's fatal sands or a ship that escaped being wrecked only to venture back into the sea's tempests. (This latter simile, the wreck of the ship of poetry, recurs five times more—99, 330, 470, 496, 547—and becomes a prime thematic marker for the poem as a whole.) What knots the poem's exordium together is the word that we have just seen glorified in the proud boast of *Tristia* 3.7:

> quid mihi vobiscum est, infelix cura, libelli,
>   ingenio perii qui miser ipse meo?

> My notebooks, accursed obsession, what am I doing, picking you up— again? Haven't I already let my genius destroy me? (1–2)

So reads that poem's first distich: It was his *ingenium*, his gift, that

---

13. For a good account of this aspect of Ovid's finales, see Williams.

enabled Ovid to write his poetry, and it was his poetry that led glamorous Roman ladies and gentlemen to wish to know him better, or, more specifically, it was that infamous volume of his, the *Ars Amatoria*, his *The Joys of Seduction*, that caused his emperor to want to suppress his book and remove him from the city his songs had polluted. This confession occurs toward the beginning of *Tristia* 2.12–13:

> hoc pretium curae vigilatorumque laborum
> cepimus, ingenio est poena reperta meo.

My crime and punishment were my reward for my poetic labor, the exquisite revision and sleepless nights given over to the search for artistic perfection. Once again, it is to my genius for verse that I owe my condemnation:

No wonder, caught in this torrent of despondency, that the poet abjures his art so fiercely. But if one shape of poetic madness propelled him into criminal poetic licentiousness, another now takes hold of him, and he becomes first a gladiator and then a ship, both of them marked for doom. He thinks of Telephus, whose wound could be cured only by Achilles, who had inflicted it. On the surface of this equation, the poetry that wounded Ovid must heal him, but turn it on its other side, and it is Augustus, who dealt the wound, who must cure it. Another hopeful example of a miraculous salvation occurs to him: poetry is not always injurious, since Augustus himself had asked *matresque nurusque* (chaste Roman wives and their daughters-in-law) to perform choral songs at the Secular Games and thereby propitiate Ops, the goddess-wife of Saturn, as well as the emperor's own patron god Apollo (23–24). There is a nice irony lurking in this example of innocent and propitious poetry since it was to protect these very wives and daughters-in-law from his salacious Muse that Ovid and his poem were condemned; and not a few passages in the poem suggest that, for all Ovid's elaborate disclaimers, at least some of the ladies in question were among the dangerous poem's most avid readers.[14] Be that as it may, seemingly self-convinced by these exempla, Ovid turns his opening line of argument inside out:

> his precor exemplis tua nunc, mitissime Caesar,

---

14. For a telling analysis, see Roy Gibson 2003, 25–35; see also Hollis, 97.

fiat ab ingenio mollior ira meo.

> Won over by such precedents as these, most compassionate Caesar, I pray that your anger grow gentler by virtue of my genius (and so, what ruined me may yet rescue me). (27–28)

There is, granted, a certain logic to this line of argument: If my poetic skill moved you to hate me, perhaps that same skill, more wisely employed, may cause you to relent. And indeed perhaps it might have done so had this letter, *Tristia* 2, been sent. Or rather, perhaps it might have been successful (had it been sent) if its poetic skill had been employed with more ambiguity and less sarcasm. But the genius that condemned Ovid to the miseries of Tomi is not deployed in this poem for the purposes of begging for a pardon that was always unlikely to come. It is used not to implore clemency, but to celebrate the purity and the indomitable autonomy of the poetic vocation. With an insolence that is both breathtaking and hilarious, the poem's structures and rhythms zigzag from what present themselves as whimpering pleas to what reveal themselves, as the poem gathers its momentum, as corrosive innuendoes.[15] What some readers of the poem take as discreet or politic or timid indeterminacies or as blank sheets on which Augustan ideology inscribes itself inevitably, indelibly, eternally (one thinks here perhaps of Kafka's *In the Penal Colony*) or as the inept fumbling of servile flattery, I hear as a meticulously crafted assertion of a great poet's claim not to innocence but to the intellectual and spiritual freedom that hard-won mastery brings with it. I hear it as a ringing vindication of the transforming power of poetry, its capacity for creating nurturing beauties that endure even in the face of the forces of untruth that crave to erase them. Maybe poets don't legislate for humankind, maybe they don't always purify the language of the tribe. But if they haven't been co-opted into aiding in the replication of the status quo's official doctrine, in advertising the values of its sign-systems, they do help us to liberate our minds from the clichés we're born into and inculcated with, and they do, again and yet again, enable us to free our imaginations.

This is a modern, rather romantic way of paraphrasing what I take to be the gist of this letter to an emperor that was in fact a letter to the world. The manner of the poem is, as we expect from this poet, slyer,

---

15. Both Nugent and B. Gibson furnish cogent and lively readings of this aspect of the poem; see also, Hinds, 230.

more devious, more Mozartian, more ingenious than my prosaic encapsulation of its matter can suggest. 'Ingenious' is the key term here. A little more than halfway through the poem's meandering, shifting patchwork of antitheses (guilty and unguilty/ crazy and sensible/ inexcusable and extenuatory), Ovid slips into Propertian mode (329ff.). A tiny rowboat, adequate on a lake, dare not venture out into the epical ocean. His frail talent is barely suited to trivial themes in trivial styles. Had he undertaken to represent, *allegorice,* per request, the Augustan Gigantomachia, he would have fallen flat on his face. Indeed, he did once try his hand at Augustan grandeur and flopped miserably. So he went back, like a dog to its vomit perhaps, to the erotic style he knew best, and he dearly wished he hadn't because that's exactly when he landed himself in hot water. So, lines 341–42, in the nice translation of S. G. Owens:

> non equidem vellem: sed me mea fata trahebant
>   inque meas poenas ingeniosus eram.

> Like a failed Stoic dragged unwillingly to his destiny I lavished my talent on my own destruction.

A naïve, regretful artist, then, hoist with his own petard.

It was a theme that Ovid was perhaps a bit too fond of. We remember in the *Metamorphoses* the fate of Marysas when he vies with Apollo in a music contest or the punishment of the daughters of Pierus who were tranformed into magpies by the Muses whose artistry they had challenged, or—in a tale that unfolds with a peculiarly sinister beauty—the vengeful transformation of Arachne after she triumphs over Minerva as a weaver of tapestries. More spectacular than these punishments, and more complex, is the tale of Daedalus and his son Icarus, which Ovid recounts in both the *Metamorphoses* and the *Ars*. Daedalus, the ingenious master engineer, had been summoned to Crete by King Minos to design and build a labyrinth to contain the monstrous Minotaur. When he completed his work, the king refused to let him and his son Icarus leave the island. In order to provide himself and Icarus with a means of escape, Daedalus constructs flying machines for himself and the boy (feathers held together by wax are strapped to their bodies). When he has fitted his son into the winged contraption and demonstrated how to operate it, the pair of them fly off to freedom. But Icarus, who fancies himself a sort of artist of the air, forgets the instructions his father had carefully given him, surges upward too near the sun, melts the wax that holds his wings together, and plunges into the sea to which he thus gives his name. Icarus doesn't anger the gods with an artist's vanity like Arachne or Marysas (he is merely youthful, naïve, impetuous); but like them he is an overreacher, and he transgresses authority in another way: like Phaethon, extravagantly overestimating the degree of his skill, he disobeys parental instruction, he defies the Voice of the Father. In this story, like father, like son. Daedalus, himself something of an overreacher, challenges both the authority of the king and laws of nature. Too much *ingenium,* too much confidence in the powers of one's genius, too little respect for one's limitations. Both of them, then, father and son alike, are in different ways emblems of the capacity of art for self-destruction. Fused together, the artist and the victim of his art unite to symbolize both the power of art and the dangers of that power.

The poet as transgressive artist, the self-destructive artist as criminal, that is the unambiguous confession that Ovid makes when he characterizes himself as fatally and wickedly *ingeniosus.* But then *Tristia* 2 takes a strange turn and subtly modulates into an ingenious and incontrovertible defense which renders Ovid innocent of salacious intent even as it reveals Augustus as guilty both of astonishing and almost systematic misreadings of Greek and Roman poetry and of what can only be thought of as a malicious or stupid misuse of his legal powers, namely, his wanton condemnation of an innocent man, one who is the faithful servant of the Muses, who stands squarely in the great tradition of Greco-Roman poetry.

Never, Ovid insists, had he tried to lure decent women into indecencies; his amatory poems were not really improper. Furthermore, taking a leaf from Catullus that Martial will also borrow, he claims that his personal life has been virtuous (*vita verecunda est, Musa iocosa mea,* 354) though his Muse has liked to fool around. You can't judge a book by its covers—if you do, you might end up thinking that writers of epic were serial killers. In any case:

> denique composui teneros non solus amores:
>   composito poenas solus amore dedi.

> Finally, I am not the only poet to compose delicate love poems, but I am the only poet to have been punished for writing such verse. (361–62)

Ovid begins his long list of the unindicted with Anacreon and Sappho and Callimachus and Menander—love poets all of them, a predictable selection, though one not without its dangers for this line of argument since these poets, even if they are read Horatianally, that is, by boys and girls, *pueris virginibusque* (370), might seem to some readers a bit racy. So, suddenly he shifts gears. His next example is the *Iliad,* which, like the *Odyssey* that follows it on the list, turns out to be essentially concerned with erotic entanglements hardly less suggestive than those featured in Ovid's own volumes. He then devotes twenty lines to the illegal passions strewn throughout Greek tragedy before he breaks off from citing these instances, overwhelmed by that embarrassment of riches. He next passes on to satyr plays and to various authors who write overtly pornographic works, sometimes with a distinctly autobiographical cast to them. Works like these find their place beside the lyric and epic and tragic authors in public libraries where they are ready to be opened by all and sundry.

Cross over to the Latin section of the superb library on the Palatine that Augustus himself had built and stocked with classic volumes and you find, to be sure, high-minded poets like Ennius and Lucretius, but—and these by far outnumber their sober opposites—you also come upon those poets who, like Ovid himself, offer their readers *multa iocosa,* lots of laughs. In defining these poets with whom he classes himself, Ovid heads their list with Catullus and Calvus, founders of Roman love elegy, then breezes through other poets whose works are lost to us, then briefly and bizarrely mentions the infamous and tragic Gallus whose crime was not the composition of amative verse but drunken slander of his emperor (445–46). Oddly, having characterized the major themes of the genre by describing them as they appear in the corpus of Tibullus (447–64), he relegates the poetry of his chief model Propertius to a single distich, emphasizing the fact that Propertius, even Propertius, who closes this list of frivolous poets of eros, suffered no disgrace from writing the kind poetry he wrote (*destrictus minime nec tamen ille nota est,* 466). Slyly, Ovid then moves away from the topic of erotic verse to take up other frivolous poetic genres, instructions for games of chance and skill, poetry about physical training, cosmetics, throwing parties. He admits that he indulged in composing this sort of trivia when he wrote a book on cosmetics (instead of slaving away at imperial epic as the age demanded). Having confused the issue thusly (and transparently) by mixing eros with other trivial pursuits, he again remarks that he alone has been singled out for punishment from all the unepical poets (as though writing a sexual manual were the same as writing a manual for playing monopoly or poker). He then compares his own style of frivolity with the filthy frivolities of mime shows (which the emperor delights in witnessing and which he handsomely funds). Ovid briefly remarks that there is nowadays a taste for smuggling lascivious representations into serious paintings of mythological scenes. Then, having added, apparently, the last ingredient to this bewildering stew of extenuating circumstances, he suddenly veers back to poetry and presents his final and unannounced witness for the defense. It is Augustus' own personal poet, the author of the epic that proves the claim of the Julian clan to unending hegemony in Rome even as it proves the claim of Rome to unending world empire.

Others sing of war, some of the victories of your clan, and some of your personal victories. I can't do that, repeats the poet for what seems the hundredth time, because nature has provided scant powers to my *ingenium* (that fatal word again). But the lucky poet of your *Aeneid* (yours now, not his) conducted "weapons and the man" (*arma virumque*) right into the boudoir of that Carthaginian temptress. And no part of the poem is more eagerly read and reread than this section, the one that centers directly on *non legitimo foedere,* 536, "on an unlawful compact," as Owen dryly renders the snickering euphemism. Dido and her new friend, that heroic pair, were fornicating, they were committing adultery. A few centuries later, St. Augustine, no partisan of fornication, will memorably, as we have seen, confirm Ovid's judgment on the best-loved book of Vergil's epic. Not everyone will agree with those judgments, but quite a few readers will. In any case, it is the last thing that Augustus would want to hear about *his* poem, and Ovid underlines this final intertextual zinger by reminding his most prominent intended reader that Vergil had been prone to romantic notions from the very first, when, in his *Eclogues,* he imagined his very close friend, Cornelius Gallus, and others of his erotic ilk, yearning for bucolic embraces.

Having gathered together this mass of exculpatory evidence from classical literature and from the emperor's own aesthetic predilections, Ovid reverts, in his peroration, to the groveling abjection that informed his exordium. The crime is old, he says, but the punishment is new (540): *supplicium patitur non nova culpa novum.* He has had a good record up to now, he says, the work in question was written when he was a young man, and his recent work shows a change of heart; it is no longer, *remissum,* flippant, easy going. The poet is now sailing the epic ocean in a sturdier boat, he is at work on a patriotic poem on the Roman Augustan calendar and a long narrative of huge philosophical and patriotic import, a new style of epic, a sort of universal history that gestures to the inevitability of the Augustan settlement. These protestations and pleadings judder and speed their way to a respectful and decorous finale—Ovid was not for nothing trained as a lawyer—in which he advances, rather in the manner of Socrates apologizing, a modest proposal. The poet doesn't expect to be recalled from exile, but in exchange for dreadful Tomi, he would appreciate a safer, slightly more tranquil and more civilized spot for his chastisement, one more suitable to his misdemeanor—or to his rotten luck in attracting the hostile gaze of an elderly autocrat.

WHEN WORLDS COLLIDE

The poem amazes for its brilliant display of sustained improvisation and for its torrent of daredevil tactics. But of course the letter was not written to be sent to its addressee, nor was it really composed to establish the innocence of its writer, nor even, very much, his desire to define and fix the malice of his tormentor. Instead, it celebrates what happens when two irreconcilable sign-systems collide and the feeble energies of art smash into the seemingly irresistible yet curiously inefficacious brute force of governments that are desperate to usurp the strengths of art and direct them to their own designs. Very much of the time in such collisions it is art that shatters into oblivion, and sometimes the artists who confront despotisms are noble, or if you like, naïve: they are idealists who put their art in the service of truth and martyr themselves and their art in the eternal name of truth. Ovid was not noble and he was not naïve, nor did he shatter.

It was chance or temperament or a bit of both that caused him to take up and don the mantle of Propertius and so become the standard bearer of a threadbare residual ideology, that of the glamorous libertarianism of Catullus and Calvus, of Antony and Gallus and of their companions. At some point, maybe just after he had published his first version of the *Amores,* he may well have begun to sense that his poetic manner and matter were becoming not only passé but increasingly ill-suited to the ideology that was now clearly dominant and that was likely to remain so, barring various accidents or miracles, for the foreseeable future. And soon after that, like Propertius before him, he began to discover that his poetic and his civic ego were all but identical, and by that time—like Lucan or Marlowe or Blake or Byron or Hugo or Wilde or Pound or like Mandelstam, who called his second volume of poems *Tristia*—by that time he had realized his talent lay both in imagining extravagant beauties and in dissecting, with a keen, quick scalpel, a smug grandiloquence that wants to control beauty and to expropriate it for its own needs or, failing in that attempt, to expunge it. By the time this coherence of identity had become not only a dawning reality but a conscious choice, Ovid had been taken up by Julia and her pretty friends. And that cursed blessing seems to have provided him with an enthusiastic audience and a quite false sense of security.

In any case, at this time (we are now roughly between the publication of the first edition of *Amores* and the first Julia's banishment), when the emperor is still anxious to perfect the façade and perhaps the reality of his great-uncle's legendary clemency and tolerance, the loudest critics of his regime, Labienus, Cassius Severus, and Cremutius Cordus, are still flying safely under the radar.[16] So, Ovid in his heyday finds himself imitating the bravado and the hijinks of his Icarus without much concerning himself with how that story invariably ends. *Tristia* 2 looks back at the moment when its poet gave into the temptations of Icarus, and it does so with an exuberant mixture of small regret and giddy rejoicing. Like Icarus, Ovid had defied the Voice of the Father and he had crashed and burned in the process; but, unlike Icarus, he was not annihilated—shipwrecked, yes, but, amazingly, still alive and kicking, with his self-respect and his genius and his poetic integrity intact.[17] And the bravado that had landed him there on the Black Sea at the fringes of civilization, far forever from his wife and friends and the city he loved, that bravado survived to nourish the last perfections of his art and gave him the strength to announce that his art would outlast the empire whose emperor had inspired him and also tried to destroy him; that when the empire was gone and its first emperor existed mainly as a ubiquitous yet ghostly memory, stored in the history books which tried to piece its puzzles together, the complete beauty of his art would continue to flourish and, century after century, to seed new beauties, not least among them, his testament, his own version of the erotic imperative whose core meaning, freedom, he had learned from his mentor, Propertius.

---

16. For the state-sponsored suppression of intellectual and artistic freedom at this time, and for what little we know about these orators and historians who bravely celebrated the ideologies that challenged "the Augustan settlement," see Forbes and Dettenhofer; for an excellent discussion of the significance of Phaedrus' *Fables* 3.10, see Langlands, 220–23; for a different version of these matters, see Raaflaub and Samons.

17. For judicious estimations of his final stance, see Newlands and also P. Johnson, 122–24.

CHAPTER 6

CODA

Mercy, madame! Alas, I die, I die!
—Wyatt

Man's love is of his life a thing apart,
'Tis woman's whole existence.
—Byron

THE MAD LOVER IS perennial and ubiquitous. He and she manifest themselves now alone or in clusters, now in mobs and movements, in all times and all places (they comprise, in fact, one of those 'universals' we have been admonished to disbelieve in). How and why this phenomenon occurs in the Near East, in India, in China, in Japan (and elsewhere) I leave to historians and sociologists who concentrate on the rise and fall of erotic fashions, scholars who are equipped to handle the complexities of a comparative erotics. What I have offered in this book are speculations about the appearance of passionate, obsessive love in Rome in the last century of its republic and observations on how this style of loving and being loved functions in the poetry of the writer whom I take to be its most successful (extant) exponent. What especially interests me about the Mad Lover in his Propertian avatar is the manner in which his unalterably fixed idea is mingled with and nourished by a powerful distrust of the uses of society and a no less powerful drive to individualism and a fierce need for personal freedom and for artistic autonomy.

Most patriarchal versions of the ideal erotic code have some correspondence with the verses of Byron quoted above (that they occur in a letter written by a woman provides a nice ironic twist to them: *Don Juan* 1.194.1551–52). From this perspective the male animal is an excellent multiple-tasker: he falls in (and out of) love when he chooses (or needs) to, while pursuing other ambitions and other triumphs, and it is women, the objects of his mutable, moveable attentions, who remain constant in their love—because that is their nature, their reason-to-be. But when Sir Thomas Wyatt cries "Mercy, madame! Alas, I die, I die!" or Shakespeare describes the lover he impersonates as "Mad in pursuit and in possession so, / Had, having, or in quest to have extreme," the patriarchal code they inhabit has somehow faltered and the myth of male erotic self-control and of the female erotic compulsion on which it depends has begun to crumble. What contributed to reshaping of the social contexts in which Wyatt and Shakespeare could write these verses—whatever the contributing factors to this reshaping were, they were not restricted to shifts in literary conventions or mere intertextualities—I cannot say. But when I think of these poets and their poems (or later, of Goethe and Heine, of the Brownings and Tennyson and Hardy, of Baudelaire and Yeats and Rilke), what comes to mind is the transformation of a traditional (patriarchal) sign system which permits some males to imagine themselves as being permanently consumed by their loves for a woman (or a man) and which allows some women to contemplate the possibility of finding the core of their lives outside the bedroom. Whatever caused these transvaluations of erotic values in Europe's sixteenth and nineteenth centuries, in the last years of ancient Rome's republic the erotic components of the traditional codes of masculinity began to undergo a severe alteration when the citizen-soldiers and the untrammeled orators were replaced by a professional—and increasingly mercenary—army and by imperial bureaucrats and courtiers; when the world of Cato widened to give way to the worlds of Petronius' Trimalchio and of Statius, Juvenal, and Martial; when the city-state of Rome became the Greco-Roman cosmopolis, capital of "the known world." In that new spacetime, just at its onset, mad (Latin) lovers flourished in ancient Rome.

Propertius provided that strange, brief era with its most vivid representative, and Ovid straddled that era and the one that closed it. After his own ambivalent elegies (honoring the genre, mocking it), Ovid went on, in the *Ars Amatoria,* to perform a satiric autopsy on the Mad Lover, and then, in the *Metamorphoses,* his tragicomic counter-epic that would vie with the greatest long poems of antiquity and would influence Europe's poetry and art century after century, he examined erotic obsession in the wide spectrum of its splendors and miseries. He wrote exquisite short stories about love that exalts its devotees and often destroys them. He wrote stories about mad lovers that were sometimes critical of them but were more often empathetic with them. He wrote stories in which lovers collide with reality and are, mostly, overwhelmed by it.

The Mad Lover speaks best for himself in first-person poetry, in love elegy, in lyrics, in sonnets, where the energies of his passion are distilled to their essence by a process of extreme concentration. But, as Ovid saw, the intricate dynamics that fuel the Mad Lover are most intelligible when they undergo the rigors of complex narrative, when they are subjected to the scrutiny of multiple perspectives and are viewed in the contexts of the societies that contain them and seek to limit and constrain them. Propertius would find his most fluent heirs among the writers of sonnets and love lyrics; Ovid would find his subtlest heirs among the great writers of the novel: Austen, Goethe, Stendhal, Flaubert, Charlotte and Emily Brontë, Tolstoy, Hardy, Schnitzler, Proust, Wharton, Colette, Lawrence.

Sometimes the Mad Lover becomes a Stalker or a Black Widow, sometimes he or she becomes a splendid longtime companion or a splendid spouse. He or she can be dangerous, but societies cannot get rid of him or her, nor can societies get along without the erotic ideals that "younge, fresshe folkes, he or she" (Chaucer, *Troylus and Criseyde* 5.1835–36) confer on them. Among the surest repositories of those ideals and their erotic imperative are poems and novels wherein the Mad Lover survives and thrives and the accents of Propertius and Ovid continue to re-echo.

BIBLIOGRAPHY

Ancona, Ronnie. "(Un)constrained Male Desire: An Intertextual Reading of Horace's *Odes* 2.8 and Catullus Poem 61." In Ancona and Greene 2005, 41–60.
———, and Ellen Greene, eds. *Gendered Dynamics in Latin Love Poetry*. Baltimore, 2005.
Aristotle. *Nicomachean Ethics*. Translated by Sir David Ross. Oxford, 1925.
Arkins, Brian. *Sexuality in Catullus*. Hildesheim, 1982.
———. "The Modern Reception of Catullus." In Skinner 2007, 461–78.
Appian. *The Civil Wars*. Translated by John Carter, Penguin, 1996.
Augustine, St. *The Confessions*. Translated by R. S. Pine-Coffin. Penguin, 1961.
Badian, Ernst. "A Phantom Marriage Law." *Philologus* 129 (1985): 82–98.
Balsdon, J. P. V. D. *Roman Women: Their History and Habits*. London, 1962.
Bardon, H. "Q. Lutatius Catulus et son cercle littéraire." *Les Études Classiques* 18.2 (1950): 145–64.
Barthes, Roland. *A Lover's Discourse: Fragments*. Translated by Richard Howard. New York, 1978.
Benedikston, D. Thomas. *Propertius: A Modernist Poet of Antiquity*. Carbondale, 1984.
Boucher, Jean-Paul. "L'oeuvre de L. Varius Rufus d'après Properce 2.34." *Revue des Études Anciennes* 50 (1958): 307–22.
Bradley, Guy. *Ancient Umbria: State, Culture and Identity in Central Italy from the Iron Age to the Augustan Era*. Oxford, 2000.
Bramble, John. "Cui Non Dictus Hylas Puer: Propertius 1.20." In *Quality and Pleasure. In Latin Poetry*. Edited by Tony Woodman and David West. Cambridge, 1974. 81–93.
Butrica, J. L. "Editing Propertius." *Classical Quarterly* 47 (1997): 176–208.
Cairns, Francis. *Sextus Propertius: The Augustan Elegist*. Cambridge, 2006.
Camps, W. C. *Propertius, Book IV*. Cambridge, 1965.
Carter, John M. "Augustus down the Centuries." *History Today* 33 (1983): 24–30.
Cartledge, Paul. "The Second Thoughts of Augustus on the Res Publica in 28/7 B.C." *Hermathena* 119 (1975): 30–40.

Clarke, John R. *Looking at Lovemaking: Constructions of Sexuality in Roman Art 100 B.C.– A.D. 250.* Berkeley and Los Angeles, 1998.
Conte, Gian Biagio. *Latin Literature: A History.* Translated by Joseph B. Solodow, revised by Don Fowler and Glenn W. Most. Baltimore, 1994.
Courtney, Edward. *The Fragmentary Latin Poets.* Oxford, 1993.
Crowther, N. B. "Cornelius Gallus: His Importance in the Development of Roman Poetry." *Aufstieg und Niedergang der Römischen Welt* II.30.3 (Berlin 1983): 1622–48.
Davis, P. J. *Ovid and Augustus: A Political Reading of Ovid's Erotic Poems.* London, 2006.
———. "Since My Part Has Been Well-Played: Conflicting Evaluations of Augustus." *Ramus* 28 (1999): 1–15.
DeBrohun, Jeri Blair. *Roman Propertius and the Reinvention of Elegy.* Ann Arbor, 2003.
de Rougemont, Denis. *Love in the Western World.* Translated by Montgomery Belgion. New York, 1956.
Detternhofer, Maria H. *Herrschaft und Widerstand in Augusteischen Rome. Historia,* 140. Stuttgart, 2000.
Dio Cassius. *Roman History, Books 51–55.* Translated by Earnest Cary. Cambridge, MA, 1917.
Dufallo, Basil. "Elegy as Restored Behavior: Evoking Cynthia and Cornelia." *Helios* 30.2 (2003): 163–78.
Evans, Dylan. "From Lacan to Darwin." In *The Literary Animal: Evolution and the Nature of Narrative.* Edited by Jonathan Gottschalk and David Sloan Wilson. Evanston, 2005. 38–55.
Fantham, Elaine. "L'histoire littéraire immanente dans la póesie latine." *Entretiens sur l'Antiquité Classique* 47 (Geneva 2000): 183–212.
———. "The Image of Woman in Propertius' Poetry." In Guenther 2006, 183–98.
Fedeli, P. "The History of Propertian Scholarship." In Guenther 2006, 3–24.
Ferri, Rolando. *I dispiaceri di un epicuro: uno studio sulla oraziana delle Epistole (con un capitolo su Persio).* Pisa, 1993.
Fischer, Robert Alexander. *Fulvia und Octavia: Die beiden Ehefrauen des Marcus Antonius in den politischen Kämpfen der Umbruchzeit zwischen Republik und Principat.* Berlin, 1999.
Forbes, Clarence A. "Books for Burning." *Transactions of the American Philological Society* 67 (1936): 114–25.
Gaisser, Julia. *Catullus and the Renaissance Reader.* Oxford, 1993.
Galinsky, Karl. *Augustan Culture: An Interpretive Introduction.* Princeton, 1996.
Garrison, Daniel. *Mild Fenzy: A Reading of Hellenistic Epigram.* Hermes Einzelschriften 41 (Wiesbaden, 1978).
Gavinelli, Simona. "The Reception of Propertius in Late Antiquity and Neo-Latin and Renaissance Literature." In Guenther 2006, 399–415.
Gibson, Bruce. "Ovid Reading. Reading Ovid. Reception in *Tristia* II." *Journal of Roman Studies* 89 (1999): 19–37.
Gibson, Roy. *Ovid. Ars Amatoria Book 3, Edited with Introduction and Commentary.* Oxford, 2003.
———. "Love Elegy." In *Companion to Latin Studies.* Edited by S. J. Harrison. Oxford 2005, 160–73.

Goff, Barbara. *The Noose of Words: Readings of Desire, Violence and Love in Euripides' Hippolytus.* Cambridge, 1990.

Gold, Barbara. "But Ariadne Was Never There in the First Place." In *Feminist Theory and the Classics.* Edited by Nancy Rabinowitz and Amy Richlin. New York, 1993. 87–92.

Goody Jack. *Islam in Europe.* Oxford, 2004.

Goold, G. P. *Propertius: Elegies.* Cambridge, MA, 1990.

Greene, Ellen. *The Erotics of Domination: Male Desire and the Mistress in Latin Love Poetry.* Baltimore, 1998.

———. "Gender-Identity and the Elegiac Hero in Propertius 2.1." In Ancona and Greene 2005, 61–71.

Gregory, Paul. "Personhood and Erotic Experience." *Philosophy Now* 5 (1993): 8–12.

Griffin, Jasper. *Latin Poets and Roman Life.* Chapel Hill, 1985.

Gruener, Andreas. *Venus Ordinis. Der Wandel von Malerei und Literatur in römischen Burgerkriege.* Paderborn, 2004.

Guenther, H. C., ed. *Brill's Companion to Propertius.* Leiden, 2006.

———. "The Fourth Book." In Guenther 2006, 353–95.

Habinek, Thomas. "Ovid and Empire." In Hardie 2002, 46–61.

Hallet, Judith P., and Marilyn B. Skinner, eds. *Roman Sexuality.* Princeton, 1997.

Hardie, Philip, ed. *Cambridge Companion to Ovid.* Cambridge, 2002.

Harrison, Stephen. "Ovid and Genre: Evolution of an Elegist." In Hardie 2002, 79–94.

Hartigan, Karelisa V. *Ambiguity and Self-Deception: Apollo and Artemis Play of Euripides.* Frankfurt am Main, 1991.

Hemelrijk, Emily A. *Matrona Docta: Educated Women in the Roman Elite from Cornelia to Julia Domna.* London, 1999.

Henderson, John. "Exemplo Suo Mores Regit." *Hermathena* 101 (1998): 101–17.

Heyworth, S. J. *Cynthia: A Companion to the Text of Propertius.* Oxford, 2007.

Hinds, Stephen. "Essential Epic: Genre and Gender from Macer to Statius." In *Matrices of Genre: Authors, Canons and Society.* Edited by Mary Depew and Dirk Obbink. Berkeley and Los Angeles, 2000, 221–46.

Hollis, A. S. "The *Ars Amatoria* and *Remedia Amoris.*" In *Ovid.* Edited by J. W. Binns. London, 1973. 84–115.

Hutchinson, Gregory. *Propertius, Elegies Book IV.* Cambridge Greek and Latin Classics. Cambridge 2006.

James, Sharon L. *Learned Girls and Male Persuasion: Gender and Reading in Roman Love Elegy.* Berkeley and Los Angeles, 2003.

Janan, Micaela. *The Politics of Desire: Propertius IV.* Berkeley and Los Angeles, 2001.

Johnson, Patricia J. *Ovid before Exile: Art and Punishment in the Metamorphoses.* Madison, 2008.

Johnson, W. R. "Angst in Arcady: Vergil and his Theocritus." *Atti del convegno mondiale scientifici di studi virgilio* I. Milan 1984: 76–84.

———. "Final Exit: Propertius 3.11." in *Classical Closure: Reading the End in Greek and Latin Literature.* Edited by Deborah Roberts, Francis Dunn, and Don Fowler. Princeton, 1997. 163–80.

———. "Imaginary Romans: Vergil and the Illusion of National Identity." In *Poets and Critics Read Vergil*. Edited by Sarah Spence. New Haven 2001. 3–16.

———. "Neoteric Poetics." In Skinner 2007, 175–89.

———. "Propertius and the Emotions of Patriotism." *California Studies in Classical Antiquity* 6 (1973): 151–80.

Kallendorf, Craig. *The Other Virgil: Pessimistic Readings of the Aeneid in Early Modern Culture*. Oxford, 2007.

Katz, Jonathan. *Complete Elegies of Sextus Propertius*. Princeton, 2004.

Keaveney, Arthur. *Sulla, The Last Republican*. London, 1982.

Kennedy, Duncan. "Augustan and Anti-Augustan: Reflections on Terms of Reference." In *Roman Poetry and Propaganda in the Age of Augustus*. Edited by Anton Powell. London, 1992. 26–58.

———. *The Arts of Love: Five Essays in the Discourse of Latin Elegy*. Cambridge, 1993.

Knox, Peter. "Propertius and the Neoterics." In Guenther 2006, 127–46.

Konstan, David. *Sexual Symmetry: Love in the Ancient Novel and Related Genres*. Princeton, 1994.

Langlands, Rebecca. *Sexual Morality in Ancient Rome*. Cambridge, 2006.

La Penna, Antonio. *L'integrazione difficile*. Torino, 1977.

Last, Hugh. "Family and Social Life." In *The Legacy of Rome*. Edited by Cyril Bailey. Oxford, 1924. 209–36.

Lee, Guy. *Propertius: The Poems*. Oxford, 1996.

Le Sueur, Joe. *Digressions on Some Poems by Frank O'Hara*. New York, 2003.

Lewis, Thomas, M.D., Fari Amini, M.D., and Richard Lannon, M.D. *A General Theory of Love*. New York, 2000.

Lightfoot, J. L., ed. *Parthenius of Nicaea: The Extant Works*. Oxford, 1999.

Lombardo, Stanley. *Aeneid*. Introduction by W. R. Johnson. Indianapolis/Cambridge, 2005.

Lyne, R. O. A. M. *The Latin Love Poets: From Catullus to Horace*. Oxford, 1980.

———. "Propertius 2.10 and 11 and the Structure of Books '2a' and '2b.'" *Journal of Roman Studies* 88 (1998): 21–36.

MacKay, L. A. "Umbrian Rimbaud." *Greece and Rome* 17 (1970): 177–83.

McDonnell, Myles. *Roman Masculinity: Virtus and the Roman Republic*. Cambridge, 2006.

Manuwald, Genise. "The First Book." In Guenther 2006, 219–44.

Meise, Eckhard. *Untersuchungen zur Geschichte der Julisch-Claudischen Dynastie*. Munich, 1969.

Millar, Fergus. *A Study of Cassius Dio*. Oxford, 1964.

———. *The Roman Republic and the Augustan Revolution*. Chapel Hill, 2002.

Miller, Paul Allen. *Subjecting Verses: Latin Love Elegy and the Emergence of the Real*. Princeton, 2004.

Murgia, Charles. "The Division of Propertius 2." *Materiali e discussioni per l'analisi dei testi classici* 45 (2000): 147–242.

Nethercut, William R. "Notes on the Structure of Propertius Book IV." *American Journal of Philology* 89 (1968): 449–64.

———. "'The Ironic Priest: Propertius' Roman Elegies III, 1–5: Imitations of Horace and Vergil." *American Journal of Philology* 91 (1970): 385–407.

———. "Propertius 3.11." *Transactions of the American Philological Association* 102 (1971): 411–43.

Newlands, Carole. "Mandata memores: Political and Poetic Authority in the *Fasti*." In Hardie 2002, 200–216.

Newman, Kevin. "The Third Book: Defining a Poetic Self." In Guenther 2006, 319–52.

Nugent, S. G. "*Tristia* 2: Ovid and Augustus." In Raaflaub and Tober 1990, 239–57.

O'Neill, Kerill. "The Lovers Gaze and Cynthia's Glance." In Ancona and Greene 2005, 319–52.

Owens, S. G., ed. *Tristium Liber Secundus*. Oxford, 1924.

Parenti, Michael. *The Assassination of Julius Caesar: A People's History of Ancient Rome*. New York, 2003.

Petrie, Jennifer. *Petrarch: The Augustan Poets, the Italian Tradition and the Canzoniere*. Dublin, 1983.

Pincus, Matthew. "Propertius' Gallus and the Erotics of Influence." *Arethusa* 37 (2004): 165–96.

Plutarch. *The Fall of the Republic*. Translated by Rex Warner. Penguin, 1972.

Raauflaub, K.A., and L. J. Samons II. "Opposition to Augustus." in Rauflaub and Tober 1990, 415–54.

Raaflaub, K.A., and Mark Tober, ed. *Between Republic and Empire: Interpretations of Augustus and His Principate*. Berkeley and Los Angeles, 1990.

Revard, Stella. "Donne and Propertius." In *The Eagle and the Dove: Reassessing John Donne*. Edited by Claude J. Summers and Ted-Larry Pedworth. Columbia, 1986. 69–79.

Richardson, Lawrence J. *Propertius, Elegies I–IV*. Norman 1977.

Richlin, Amy. "Julia's Jokes, Galla Placidia and the Roman Use of Women as Political Icons." In *Stereotypes of Women in Power*. Edited by B. Garlick. New York. 65–91.

Rimell, Victoria. *Ovid's Lovers: Desire, Difference and the Poetic Imagination*. Cambridge, 2006.

Skinner, Marilyn, ed. *Blackwell's Companion to Catullus*. Oxford, 2007.

———. "*Ego Mulier:* The Construction of Roman Masculinity." In Hallet and Skinner 1997, 129–50.

Slavitt, David. *Propertius in Love: The Elegies*. Berkeley and Los Angeles, 2002.

Stahl, Hans-Peter. *Propertius: Love and War: Individual and State under Augustus*. Berkeley and Los Angeles, 1985.

Stendhal (Henri-Marie Beyle). *On Love*. Translated by Gilbert and Suzanne Sale. London, 1957.

Sullivan, J. P. *Propertius: A Critical Introduction*. Cambridge, 1976.

Syndikus, Hans-Peter. "The Second Book." In Guenther 2006, 245–318.

Tarrant, Richard. "Ovid and Ancient Literary History." In Hardie 2002, 13–33.

Traina, Giusto. "Lycoris the Mime." In *Roman Women*. Edited by Augusto Fraschetti, translated by Linda Lappin. Chicago, 2001. 82–99.

Vance, Norman, *The Victorians and Ancient Rome*. Oxford, 1999.

Veyne, Paul. *Roman Erotic Elegy: Love Poetry and the West*. Translated by D. Pellauer. Chicago, 1988.

Walcot, Peter. "Plutarch on Sex." *Greece and Rome* 45.2 (1998): 166–87.

Warden, John. "The Dead and the Quick: Structural Correspondences and Thematic

Relationship in Propertius 4.7 and 4.8." *Phoenix* 50 (1996): 118–29.
Welch, Tara S. *The Elegiac Cityscape: Propertius and the Meaning of Roman Monuments*. Columbus, 2005.
West, Rebecca. *St. Augustine*. New York, 1933.
Wheeler, Arthur Leslie. *Catullus and the Traditions of Ancient Poetry*. Berkeley and Los Angeles, 1934.
Williams, Gareth. "Ovid's Exile Poetry, *Tristia, Epistulae ex Ponto* and *Ibis*." In Hardie 2002, 223–45.
Wray, David. *Catullus and the Poetics of Roman Manhood*. Cambridge, 2001.
Wyke, Maria. *The Roman Mistress*. Oxford, 2002.
Zimmermann, Bernhard. "The Reception of Propertius in the Modern Age: Johann Wolfgang von Goethe's *Römischen Elegien* and Ezra Pound's 'Homage to Sextus Propertius.'" In Guenther 2006, 417–28.

INDEX LOCORUM

Apollonius of Rhodes
Argonautica Fragment 94, **34**
Appian
Civil War 5.8, **19**
Aristotle *Nichomachean Ethics* 9.10,
1171a, **49**; 9.10.5, 1171a, **24**
Augustine of Hippo
Confessions 1.13, **36–37**; 1.31, **29**; 6.15,
37–38
Catullus
Poems 64, **46**
Catulus, Q. Lutatius
Epigrams Fr. 1 (ap. Cicero *De Natura
Deorum* 1.79), **7**; Fr. 2 (ap. Gellius,
Noctes Atticae 19.9.10), **8**
Cicero
Philippics 2.44, **18**; 2.46, **18**; 2.76–78, **16**
Dio Cassius
Roman History 53.19.2–6, **128**; 54.15ff.,
128
Euripides
Hippolytus 121–534, **41**; 316, **42**; 363–
440, **42–45**
Homer
Iliad 3.379–417, **40**
Odyssey 5.118–44, **40**
Horace
Satires 1.4.43–44, **67**
Ovid
Amores 3.9, **34**
Tristia 2, 124, **137–45**; 2.12–13, **138**;
2.15–16, **137**; 2.23–24, **138**; 2.27–
28, **139**; 2.329ff., **140**; 2.341–42,
140; 2.354, **141**; 2.361–62, **141**;
2.370, **142**; 2.445–66, **142**; 2.536,
143; 2.540, **143**; 3.7.1–2, **137**;
3.7.43–54, **136**
Pliny the Younger
Letters 5.3.5, **12**
Plutarch
Life of Antony 10.3, **22**
Life of Sulla 2, **12–13**; 35, **14**; 36, **15**
Porcius Licinius
Epigrams Fr. 6 (ap. Gellius, *Noctes Atticae*
19.9.10), **9**
Propertius
Poems 1, **92, 97, 101**; 1.1.1–2, **62–63**;
1.4.62–64, **67**; 1.4.67–68, **67–68**;
1.4.89–102, **68**; 1.4.119–34, **69**;
1.4.135–42, **69–70**; 1.4.147–50, **68**;
1.5.22, **87**; 1.6.25–30, **98**; 1.7.21–26,
100; 1.10.27–30, **99**; 1.11, **98**;
1.12.11, **87**; 1.12.19–20, **70**; 1.14,
110; 1.14.15–16, **110**; 1.14.23–24,

110; 1.19.11, 62; 1.22, 111; 1.22.1–
10, 115–16; 2.1.1–4, 64, 102–3;
2.1.16–17, 102–3; 2.1.25–26, 103;
2.1.35–36, 103; 2.2.1–4, 74–75;
2.2.13–16, 75; 2.2, 74–75; 2.3.19–
22, 80; 2.3.25–32, 77; 2.3.45–46,
78; 2.7.3–6, 108; 2.7.13–14, 6,
108–9; 2.12.20, 87; 2.28.13–14,
75–76; 2.28.29–30, 76; 2.28.49–
50, 76; 2.28.55–56, 77; 2.28B,
75–76; 2.30B, 64 2.30B.31–32, 64;
2.30B.40, 65; 2.34, 104–7; 2.34.22,
104; 2.34.25–26, 105; 2.34.55–60,
105–6; 2.34.61–66, 106; 2.34.93–94,
107; 2A, 92, 101–2, 104; 2B, 92, 95,
101–2, 104, 106–7; 3, 92, 95, 96,
109, 123; 3.3, 108, 123; 3.3.49–50,
108; 3.4.1, 119; 3.4.21–22, 119–20;
3.9.20, 121; 3.9.32–33, 121; 3.9.45–
46, 121; 3.9.56–60, 121; 3.10.8,
107; 3.11.1–2, 120; 3.11.28–30,
120; 3.11.49–50, 120; 3.11.66, 120;
3.13.1–2, 120; 3.13.60, 119; 3.14.4,
119; 3.14.23–27, 119; 3.18.11–12,
117; 3.18.17–20, 117–20; 3.18.32–
34, 118; 3.22, 109–17; 3.22.1–6,
111–12; 3.22.17–18, 112; 3.22.20,
115; 3.22.20–26, 113; 3.22.39–42,
114; 3.23, 98–99; 3.24, 64; 3.24.1–2,
62; 3.24.23, 63; 3.25, 62, 64; 4, 96,
123; 4.1, 59–60, 65–71, 123; 4.1.1–
2, 65; 4.1.37–38, 66; 4.1.55–58, 66;
4.5, 72; 4.7, 72, 79–84; 4.7.1–5,
72–73; 4.7.11–12, 73; 4.7.19–22,
80; 4.7.38–39, 81; 4.7.49–54, 82;
4.7.78, 83; 4.7.85–86, 83; 4.7.93–96,
84; 4.8.27–34, 86; 4.8.47–48, 87;
4.8.52–56, 87–88; 4.8, 72
4.8.70–72, 88; 4.8, 85–89; 4.8.81–82, 88;
4.8.87–88, 89

Sappho
Fragments 35, 34; 36, 34

Sophocles
Fragments 94, 40

Valerius Aedituus
Epigrams fr. 1 (ap. Gellius, *Noctes Atticae*
19.9.10), 8; fr. 2 (ap. Gellius, *Noctes
Atticae* 19.9.10), 8–9

Vergil
Aeneid 4.382–87, 55; 4.393–96, 56;
4.439–40, 56; 4.445–49, 56–57;
Eclogues 2, 50–51; 10, 20, 51–52; 10.70–
74, 52

GENERAL INDEX

Abelard, as passionate lover, 30, 35
Actium, P.'s treatment of, 72, 118
Actium, P., 118
adultery: of Dido and Aeneas, 143; as fashionable, 23, 24; of Jupiter, 64, 74–75, 77; and passionate love, 28. *See also* fidelity; marriage
Aeneas: as adulterer, 143; as analogue for Antony, 27; Augustine as, 38–39; beauty of, 54; as beloved, 54–55; grief of, 56; identity of, 54–55, 56; as lover, 27–29, 54–57; passion of, 57; as symbol of renunciation, 37, 38
Albertine, 29, 47
Alexandrian poetry: as influence on erotic identity, 11; Roman imitations of, 7, 9, 67; social context of, 26
Amores of Ovid, publication of, 129, 133
Ancona, R., 22n
Anna, in the *Aeneid,* 56
Antony, Marc: Aeneas as, 27; Augustan representations of, 19, 72, 120–21; as Curio's "spouse," 18–19; as elegiac lover, 16, 17, 20; as Mad Lover, 15, 27, 28, 114, 120, 122; in P., 19, 72; and the theater, 22
Aphrodite: and Helen, 40; power of, 40, 42–43
Apollo, as savior of P. and Ovid, 69
Arachne, 140, 141
Arden of Feversham, 1
Ariadne: as model for Dido, 45–49; passion of, 46
Aristotle: on marriage, 25; on pederasty, 24, 49; on poetry, 78
Arkins, B., 46n, 49n
Ars Amatoria: as cause of Ovid's exile, 138; in the history of love poetry, 147; publication of, 129, 135–36
art, as imitating and imitated by life, 6–7, 17
astrology, in P., 68–71
audiences: for the *Aeneid,* 54; for Catullus and the Neoterics, 11; for erotic poetry, 9–10; for Ovid, 125, 138, 145; for P., 60–61; for political dissent under Augustus, 125
Augustine of Hippo: as Aeneas, 38–39; as Dido, 36–39; on love, 29; as lover, 37–38; and marriage, 37–38; masculinity of, 38

- 157 -

GENERAL INDEX

Augustus: banishment of Ovid by, 124; compared to Jupiter, 108, 120; control of representation by, 125–26; critics of, 145; and the depiction of Antony, 19, 72, 120–21; as *durus senex*, 64; erotic identity of, 14; and the erotic imperative, 95; and Gallus, 21; ideology of, 39, 61, 135; intentions of, 129; marriage legislation of, 2, 23, 24, 114–15, 132; misfortunes of, 126–27; opposition to, 125–26, 127, 130; Ovid's appeals to, 138–44; and Perusia, 116; plots against, 128, 130; praise and blame of, 125–26; P.'s attitude toward, 59–60, 68, 103, 108; simple lifestyle of, 119; Stendhal's view of, 34; as subject of the *Aeneid*, 39
author, death of, 61, 62

Badian, E., 108
Bailey, Cyril, 1
Bakhtin, M. M., 102
Baldson, J. P. V. D., 4n, 22n, 133n
Bankhead, Tallulah, 2
Barchiesi, A., 125
Bardon, H., 9n
Barnum, P. T., 70
Barthes, R., 1, 9, 27, 58, 62, 63n, 97
Bassus, as foil for P., 100–101
Baudelaire, Charles, 6
beauty, of Cynthia, 73–79
biographical criticism: of Catullus, 46; of P., 58–61, 93; of Vergil, 49–50
bodies, docile, 2, 20. *See also* masculinity
Boucher, J.-P., 104n
Bradley, G., 116n
Bramble, J., 100n
Brown, Julie, 44
Browning, Robert, 24
Butler, Rhett, 62
Butrica, J. L., 92n, 104n
Byron, George Gordon, 46, 146–47

Caesar, C. Julius: catasterism of, 118; and the development of erotic identity, 2–4
Cairns, F., 21n
Callimachus: as model for early elegists, 7; as model for P., 67
Calvus, C. Licinius: and the development of elegy, 3, 11, 20, 48; as influence on Antony, 17; as influence on Ovid, 142; and the Roman social revolution, 5
Calypso, as lover, 40
Camps, W. C., 66n
Carter, J., 127n
Cartledge, P., 109n, 116, 130
Cato the Elder: on love and marriage, 25, 147; as stylistic model for P., 114
Cato the Younger, on love and marriage, 25
Catullus, G. Valerius: biographical criticism of, 46; and the evolution of erotic identity, 3, 10–11, 20–21; as influence on Antony, 17; as influence on Ovid, 142; Catullus, as influence on P., 67; as influence on Vergil, 45–49; and the Roman social revolution, 5; thematic unity of, 47
Catulus, Q. Lutatius, and the development of elegy, 7–8, 15, 20, 26
Cavafy, Constantine, 11
Chaucer, Geoffrey, 148
Chloris, as rival of Cynthia, 81, 83
Cicero, M. Tullius: on Antony, 16, 17–18, 27; and Clodia, 47; as ignorant of erotic fashions, 6, 17; and the neoteric revolution, 3
Clarke, J. R., 5n, 132n
Cleopatra: and Antony, 19, 72, 120–21; Augustan propaganda concerning, 120–21; Dido as, 27; and Julius Caesar, 3; as successor to Fulvia, 22
Clodia Metelli, 17, 23, 47
Clodius, P., 17
Comedy: and elegy, 21–22; and erotic

identity, 11, 18–19
Corinna, 101
Corydon: masculinity of, 50; as model for Dido, 50–51; as transgressive lover, 51
Courtney, E., 9n, 20n
Crowther, N. B., 51n, 100n
crystallization, of passionate love, 32–33, 35, 51, 52; and Aeneas, 57; and Dido, 53; and P., 75
Curio, G. Scribonius, 17; as Antony's "husband," 18–19
Cynthia: compared to Juno, 74, 75; as creation of P., 63; as creator of P.'s identity, 65, 87; and Cytheris, 22; death of, 72–73, 80; as embodiment of elegy, 91, 94; effect of on P., 78–79; as excluded from P.'s life, 59–60; feminist views of, 93; as fictional creation, 78–79; fidelity of, 82–83, 85–86; funeral of, 80; gaze of, 62–63; as ghost, 72–73, 76, 79–84; identity of, 58–59; illness of, 75–76; as inspiration for P., 64; intellectual and artistic talents of, 77; jealousy of, 88–89; meaning of, 93–96; as metaphor for elegy, 93–94; as object of Lynceus' attentions, 103–4; passion of, 89; physical appearance of, 73–79; as poet, 80; as priestess, 88–89; P.'s passion for, 98; P.'s rejection of, 62–65, 110; and P.'s return to elegy, 70–71; punishment of P. by, 88–89; as reader of Vergil, 84; reintroduction of in P.'s poetry, 60, 65–71, 92; as source of P.'s fame, 83, 87; as symbol of poetic freedom, 122–23; tomb of, 83; uniqueness of, 90; as vengeful, 101
Cytheris, 18–19, 20, 21, 94, 99; contrasted with Fulvia, 22

Daedalus, as model for Ovid, 140–41
Davis, P. J., 126n, 127n
de Rougemont, Denis, 28
DeBrohun, J., 71, 89–90n, 116n
Degas, Edgar, 6
Dembowski, Méthilde, 30, 35
desire. *See* love, passionate; lust; passion
Dettenhofer, M. H., 51n, 145n
Dido: adultery of, 143; Augustine's view of, 36–39; centrality of to European cultural history, 39–40; as Cleopatra, 27; and the crystallization of love, 53; erotic identity of, 53; as focus of the *Aeneid*, 54; and Gallus, 52–53; as lover, 27–28, 37, 54–57; as model for Augustine, 38–39; Ovid's view of, 143; passion of, 37, 55; rhetoric used by, 55–56; sources for, 39–53; transgressive desire of, 54; and unrequited love, 50
Dio Cassius, as critic of imperial power, 127, 128–29, 130
disgregation, of P., 109–10; 122–23
Donne, John, 97
Dryden, John, 50
Dufallo, B., 82n
duty, civic: Augustus' views on, 135; and love, 25–26; P.'s avoidance of, 102–3. *See also* leisure

Ennius, as model for P., 67
epic: contrasted with elegy, 27, 100; ideology of, 27; Ovid's rejection of, 140, 142; P.'s rejection of, 95, 102–3, 106, 108, 121
erotic identity: of Aeneas, 57; of Antony, 15–19; in conflict with empire, 13–14; construction of, 28; of Dido, 53; evolution of, 24–25; and gossip, 17; Greek poetic influence on, 10; in the late Republic, 5–7; and loss of self-control, 10–11; and love, 26; and masculinity, 22, 23–24, 25–26; and parties, 12–15; of P., 59, 63–65; Roman definitions of, 2; and social transformation, 3–7; of Sulla, 12–15;

of women, 23–24. *See also* erotic imperative; fashion, erotic; love; Mad Lover; masculinity; slavery, erotic

erotic imperative, 20–21, 44, 93–94; and Augustus, 95; Cynthia as embodiment of, 94; in Ovid, 132; P.'s compliance with, 78, 90, 120–21; P.'s justification of, 103–4, 106–7, 108–9; P.'s rejection of, 91–92, 110. *See also* erotic identity; fashion, erotic; love; Mad Lover; masculinity; slavery, erotic

Euripides, 41–44

Euryalus, 49

Eurydice, 53

Evans, D., 28n

fame: of Cynthia as depending on P., 63, 107; of P. as depending on Cynthia, 83, 87

fantasy, and the crystallization of love, 32

Fantham, E., 61n, 121n

fashion, erotic, 16, 23–24, 27, 30–31, 47, 78, 90–91, 99–100, 122–23, 131–32, 135, 144, 146; Cicero's ignorance of, 6, 17. *See also* erotic identity; erotic imperative; love; Mad Lover; slavery, erotic

fathers: and erotic identity of sons, 11, 18–19, 44–45; and masculinity, 6, 25, 26. *See also* patriarchy; Voice of the Father

feminism, and the depiction of Cynthia, 93

Ferri, R., 95n

fidelity, of Cynthia toward P., 82–83, 84. *See also* adultery

Fischer, R. A., 22n

foil: Dido as for Aeneas, 54; Gallus as for P., 99; Lynceus as for P., 104–7; Ponticus as for P., 100; Tullus as for P., 97–99, 110–12

Forbes, C. A., 145n

formalism, in the reading of P., 60–61

freedom, Ovid's attitude toward, 136, 139

Freud, Sigmund, 28

friendship: in Aristotle and Vergil, 49; of Tullus and P., 111–12

Fulvia (wife of Antony), 16–17; contrasted with Cytheris, 22; and elegy, 24–25

Gaisser, J., 46n

Galinsky, K., 130

Gallus, C. Cornelius: Antony as source for, 17; and the development of elegy, 19–21, 48, 51–53; as foil for P., 99; as Mad Lover, 20, 114, 122; as model for Dido, 51–53; as model for P., 20–21, 91, 94; Ovid on, 142, 143; political career of, 21, 51, 53, 91; in Vergil, 20

Gallus (in P.'s *Monobiblos*), 99–100; identity of, 99; as rival for Cynthia, 99

Garrison, D., 48n

gaze: of Cynthia, 62–63; of P., 62

genre: as central to formalist criticism, 61; constraints imposed by, 90; P.'s change of, 68. *See also* elegy; epic

Gibbon, Edward, 127

Gibson, B., 139n

Gibson, R., 73–74, 78, 138n

gods, beloveds compared to, 8, 10

Goff, B., 42n

Gold, B., 96n

Gonne, Maud, 58

Goody, J., 33

Goold, G. P., 77

gossip, and erotic identity, 17–18

Greece: contrasted with Rome on sexual and social issues, 2, 22, 48, 112–13, 115, 119; mythology of, 112–13, 115; as source of Roman literary developments, 7, 9, 25–26

Greene, E., 61n, 104n

Gregory, P., 5n

Griffin, J., 16

Gruener, A., 10n
Guenther, H. C., 71n
guilt: distinguished from shame, 40, 42; of Phaedra, 42, 44; of P. toward the dead Cynthia, 80–81

Habinek, T., 125n
Harrison, S., 134n
Hartigan, K. V., 43n
Heine, Heinrich, 6
Helen: and Aphrodite, 40, 43; and passion, 40; shame of, 40–41
Heloise, and passionate love, 30, 34
Hemelrijk, E. A., 21n, 80n
Henderson, G., 130n
Heyworth, S. J., 92n, 104n
Hinds, S., 55n, 139n
Hippolytus, 41–44
Hollis, A. S., 138n
Homer: Helen in, 40–41; as model for Vergil, 53; Ovid's view of, 142; Stendhal's view of, 34
homosexuality: in the *Aeneid,* 49; in Catullan poetry, 48; and Gallus, 99; in gossip about Antony, 18–19; in Horace, 48; P. and Ovid's lack of interest in, 48; Plutarch's attitude toward, 15; Roman attitudes toward, 10; in Tibullus, 48. See also pederasty
Horace: misogynistic ranting by, 62; and same-sex love, 48; as satirist, 95
Horos, in P., 68–71
Housman, A. E., 58–59, 93
Humbert, Humbert, 29
Hutchinson, G., 72n, 73n, 89n, 118n

Icarus: as artist, 140–41; as model for Ovid, 140–41, 145
identity, construction of: female, in the late Republic, 23–24; of P., 101–2; Roman, 3–5, 6, 9–11, 26
identity, erotic. *See* erotic identity
ideology, Augustan, 39, 61, 68; Ovid's resistance to, 125–26, 136–37, 139–40; reception of, 125–29
individualism, rise of, 11–12, 24–25, 146. *See also* erotic imperative; erotic identity; masculinity
ingenium, of Ovid, 136, 138, 139, 141, 143, 145

James, S. L., 94n, 110n
Janan, M., 51n, 71n, 90n, 99n, 100n
Jason, as lover, 44–45
jealousy: concerning Juventius, 48–49; of Cynthia, 88–89
Johnson, P., 136n, 145n
Julia (daughter of Augustus): as friend of Ovid, 131–32, 134, 135, 145; banishment of, 129, 133
Julia (granddaughter of Augustus), banishment of, 133
Juno, compared to Cynthia, 74, 75
Jupiter: as adulterer, 64, 74–75, 77; compared to Augustus, 108, 120
Juturna, 113
Juventius: as citizen, 48; as model for Dido, 48–49; as object of jealousy, 48–49

Kafka, Franz, 139
Kallendorf, C., 125n
Keaveney, A., 13n
Kennedy, D., 61n, 93n, 126, 127
Knox, P., 3n
Konstan, D., 11n

La Penna, A., 109, 122
Lacan, Jacques, 28
Langlands, R., 16n, 23n, 24n, 145n
Last, Hugh, 1–2, 21
Le Sueur, J., 47n
Lee, G., 74, 87, 113
leisure: desire for by lovers, 6, 11. *See also* duty; erotic imperative
Lesbia: and Cytheris, 22; as model for Dido, 47; silence of, 47; vagueness of, 47

Lightfoot, J. L., 23n
Livia, simple lifestyle of, 119
love: all-consuming, 29; Aristotle's views on, 49; conjugal, 14–15; dangers of, 39–40; as death wish, 28; definitions and varieties of, 28–36; fashionable, 30–31, 33, 47; and happiness, 36; laws of, 32; lustful, 30, 33, 35, 38; neglect of in scholarship on Rome, 1–2; passionate, 28, 30, 31–33, 35–36; and rational choice, 42–43; scientific theories of, 28–29; Stendhal's definitions of, 30–36; transgressive, 51; unrequited, 49–51, 52–53; vanity, 30–31, 33, 35, 47; as wound, 38. *See also* erotic identity; erotic imperative; fashion, erotic; Mad Lover; lust; passion
lover, elegiac. *See* erotic identity; erotic imperative; Mad Lover
Ludi Saeculares, 109, 129, 138
lust: of Augustine, 37–38; and love, 38; of Phaedra for Hippolytus, 41; of P. for Cynthia, 95. *See also* love; passion
luxury, Roman suspicion of, 119–20. *See also* wealth
Lycoris, 48, 51–52, 94, 99; identity of, 20–21
Lygdamus (P.'s slave), 81, 86–88
Lynceus: as foil for P., 104–7; identity of, 104; as rival for Cynthia, 104–7
Lyne, R. O. A. M., 4n, 92n

MacKay, L. A., 91n
Mad Lover, 5–7, 146–48; Antony as, 15, 27, 28, 114, 120, 122; in country music, 29; Gallus as, 20, 114, 122; and masculinity, 19–20; P. as, 29; Sulla as, 15. *See also* erotic identity; erotic imperative; fashion, erotic; love; slavery, erotic
Maecenas, and P.'s poetic career, 68, 91, 102–4, 107–8, 121–22
Mallarmé, Stéphane, 6

Manuwald, G., 101n
Marcellus: eulogized by P., 117–18; eulogized by Vergil, 130
Marlowe, Christopher, 39, 54
marriage: of Antony and Curio, 18–19; Aristotle on, 25; Augustan legislation concerning, 2, 23, 24, 108–9, 114–15, 118–19; and Augustine, 37–38; and love, 25, 28; parodies of, 18–19; Roman attitudes toward, 14–15, 17, 22, 25; and Sulla's erotic identity, 14–15
Marsyas, in Ovid, 140, 141
masculinity: of Aeneas, 57; of Augustine, 38; and desire, 147; and empire, 11–12; and erotic identity, 22, 23–24, 25–26; and the erotic imperative, 120–21; and erotic surrender, 52; and love, 38; and the Mad Lover, 19–20; and marriage, 22; of P., 65, 95, 105–6, 120–21; and Roman identity, 5–6, 10; and self-control, 147; and unrequited love, 50. *See also* erotic identity; erotic imperative
McDonnell, M., 26n
Medea: as model for Dido, 40, 44–45; passion of, 34, 44–45
Meise, E., 133n
Meleager, 7, 25, 26, 48–49
Metrobius (Sulla's beloved), 13, 15
Millar, F., 116, 128
Miller, P. A., 61n, 96n, 99, 100n
mime: Ovid's view of, 143; and Roman erotic identity, 17
Monica, Saint, 37, 39
Montaigne, M., 124
Murgia, C., 92n

neoteric poetry. *See* Catullus; Calvus; elegy
Nethercut, W. R., 72n, 118n, 121n
Newlands, C., 145n
Newman, K., 63, 113n
Nicopolis (Sulla's beloved), 13

GENERAL INDEX

Nisus and Euryalus, 49
novel, contrasted with elegy, 90
Nugent, S. G., 139n
Nurse, in the *Hippolytus*, 41–42, 44

O'Hara, Frank, 47
O'Neill, K., 63n
Orpheus, 53
otium. See leisure
Ovid: aporia of, 137; audience of, 125, 138; banishment of, 24, 124, 133–34, 141; career of, 90, 133, 134–35; and the creation of the self, 45; crime of, 64; defense of erotic poetry by, 141–43; and the development of elegy, 20, 101, 142; and erotic fashion, 147–48; as friend of Julia, 131–32, 134, 135, 145; *ingenium* of, 138, 139, 141, 143, 145; literary influence of, 147–48; patriotism of, 143; personal life of, 141; as rival of other poets, 134; and postmodern hermeneutics, 125; rejection of epic by, 140; as resisting Augustan ideology, 125–26, 136–37, 139–40; and same-sex love, 48; saved by Apollo, 69; Stendhal's view of, 34–35; as transgressive, 141
Owens, S. G., 140

Parenti, M., 3
parody: of marriage, 18–19; by P., 111, 115
Parthenius, 25, 45–46, 51
passion: of Aeneas, 57; of Ariadne, 46; of Cynthia, 89; of Dido, 55; of Helen, 40; of Medea, 44–45; of Phaedra, 43, 44; of P., 78; and self-control, 43. *See also* love; lust
pastoral, as influence on elegy, 49–53
patriarchy: in the *Aeneid,* 53–54; and Dido, 54; and erotic fashions, 146–47; and female desire, 45. *See also* fathers; Voice of the Father
patriotism: of Ovid, 143; of P., 59, 85, 91, 96, 108–9, 112–14, 116, 120–21, 123
pederasty, as model for heterosexual relations, 24; in Aristotle, 24, 49
Perusia, P.'s treatment of, 115–17
Phaedra: as lover, 41–44; as model for Dido, 40–44; shame and guilt of, 42, 44
Phyllis, in P. 4.8, 86–88
Pincus, M., 100n
pleasure, of reading, 61–62
Pliny, on Augustus, 126–27
Plutarch, as disapproving of Sulla's erotic identity, 12–15
poetry, power of, 138, 139, 141–45
Polyphemus, as model for Corydon, 50–51
Ponticus, as foil for P., 100
Porcius Licinius, 8–9
Portuguese Nun, as passionate lover, 30
Propertius: on Actium, 72, 118; Alexandrianism in, 67; as antiquarian, 59–60, 65–68, 85, 113–14; on Antony, 19; Antony as model for, 17; astrology in, 68–71; attitude toward Augustus, 59, 60, 68, 108; avoidance of civic duty by, 102–3; avoidance of public service by, 98, 101; biographical criticism of, 58–61, 93; change in poetic identity of, 91–92; choice of elegy by, 59, 95; construction of poetic identity of, 101–2; as depending on Cynthia for fame, 83, 87; and the development of elegy, 20; disgregation of, 109–10, 122–23; as enthralled lover, 63–64; and erotic fashion, 147–48; and the erotic imperative, 108–9; and fatherhood, 6, 108–9; financial condition of, 6, 98, 105, 110; formalist readings of, 60–61; gaze of, 62; identity of depending on Cynthia, 93, 94, 96; influence of Gallus on, 20–21; intentions of, 61; literary influence of, 147–48; as

Mad Lover, 29; Marcellus eulogized by, 117–18; on marriage, 108, 119; masculinity of, 65, 95, 105–6, 120; as model for Ovid, 140, 142, 144, 145; parody of Vergil by, 111; as patriotic poet, 59, 65–68, 71–72, 85, 91, 96, 108–9, 112–14, 116, 120–21, 123; and poetic freedom, 95–96; praise of Vergil by, 106; as praise poet, 120–21; punished by Cynthia, 88–89; recent literary criticism of, 61; rejection of epic by, 95, 102–3, 106, 108, 121; return to Cynthia by, 70–71; return to elegy by, 68–71; and same-sex love, 48; as satirist, 118; saved by Apollo, 69; self-confidence of, 101–2; sincerity of, 63, 111; as slave of Cynthia, 70–71; and Stendhal's varieties of love, 33–36; Stoicism in, 117–18; submission to Cynthia by, 88–89; use of ornate style by, 111–12; use of plain style by, 111–12, 114; use of foils by, 97–101; utopian vision of, 64–65

prostitution: of Antony, 19; economics of, 120

Proust, Marcel, 29

public service, P.'s avoidance of, 102–3, 121–22

Purcell, Henry, 54

Raaflaub, K. A., 145n

Richardson, L. J., 84, 91n, 92n

Richlin, A., 131n

rivalry: for Cynthia, 104–6; of Cynthia and Chloris, 81, 83; poetic, 50, 103–4, 106, 134

Romanitas. *See* masculinity; patriotism

Romanticism, 29, 34; and Catullus, 46

Rome: in P.'s poetry, 65–66, 68, 112–13, 115

Romulus and Remus, 66

Samons, L. J., 145n

Sappho, 42, 43; Stendhal's view of, 34

satire, P. as writer of, 118

Shakespeare, William, 19, 50, 79, 147

shame: distinguished from guilt, 40, 42; of Helen, 40–41; of Phaedra, 42

sincerity: of Antony as lover, 17; of P., 63, 111–12

Skinner, M., 46n

slavery, erotic, 10–11, 19, 24, 62–63, 70–71, 93, 95, 120–21. *See also* erotic identity; erotic imperative; fashion, erotic; love; Mad Lover

soldiers, influence of on Roman values, 4–5

Sparta, as erotic utopia, 119

Stahl, H.-P., 111, 115

Stendhal, 39, 45, 46; and Dido, 53; as guide to understanding P., 33–36; on the varieties of love, 29–36; on Vergil, 49–50

Stoicism, in P., 117

Sulla: and the development of erotic identity, 12–15; as lover, 12–15; as poet, 12; and the theater, 22

Sullivan, J. P., 71n

Syndikus, H.-P., 104n

Tacitus, as critic of imperial power, 127

Tarrant, R., 133n

Teia, in P. 4.8, 86–88

Tennyson, Alfred Lord, 29

theater: as source of erotic inspiration, 13; as source of erotic companions, 13, 15, 16, 17, 21–22

Theseus, 46

Tibullus, 99, 101; in the development of elegy, 20; Ovid's view of, 142; and same-sex love, 48; Stendhal's view of, 34–35

Traina, G., 21n

Tristan, as passionate lover, 28

Tullus, as foil for P., 97–99, 110–12, 115

Umbria, P.'s praise of, 67, 115

Valeria (wife of Sulla), 14–15
Valerius Aedituus, 8–9
Vance, N., 46n
Varius Rufus, 134; possible identification with Lynceus, 104
Vergil: biographical criticism of, 49–50; and Cynthia, 84; on Gallus, 20; on Marcellus, 130; as model for P., 113; Ovid on, 143; parodied by P., 111; and passionate love, 34; and the praise of Augustus, 39; praised by P., 106; as rival of Homer, 106; and the sources for Dido, 39–40; Stendhal's view of, 34
Veyne, P., 61n, 93n
Voice of the Father, 24, 112, 133, 145. *See also* fathers; patriarchy
Volumnia. *See* Cytheris

Walcot, P., 14n
Watts, William, 38
wealth: and empire, 119–20; P.'s view of, 6; P.'s lack of, 98; and Roman identity, 4
Welch, T., 72n, 118n
West, R., 37
Wheeler, A. L., 9n
Wilde, Oscar, 11, 124
Williams, G., 137n
women: as audience for elegy, 23–24; erotic identity of, 23–24; social position of, 1–2, 21–24
Wray, D., 46n, 49n
Wyatt, Thomas, 146–47
Wyke, M., 61n, 93n

Yeats, W. B., 58, 122

www.ingramcontent.com/pod-product-compliance
Lightning Source LLC
Chambersburg PA
CBHW020803160426
43192CB00006B/415